Johannes Althusius

Politica

Johannes Althusius

AN ABRIDGED TRANSLATION OF

*Politics Methodically Set Forth and Illustrated with
Sacred and Profane Examples*

━━━━━━━

EDITED AND TRANSLATED, WITH AN INTRODUCTION

by Frederick S. Carney

FOREWORD BY *Daniel J. Elazar*

Liberty Fund
INDIANAPOLIS

This book is published by Liberty Fund, Inc., a foundation established to encourage study of the ideal of a society of free and responsible individuals.

𒂷 𒔼𒀀𒈨

The cuneiform inscription that serves as our logo and as the design motif for our endpapers is the earliest-known written appearance of the word "freedom" (amagi), or "liberty." It is taken from a clay document written about 2300 B.C. in the Sumerian city-state of Lagash.

Liberty Fund, Inc.
8335 Allison Pointe Trail, Suite 300
Indianapolis, Indiana 46250-1684

Frontispiece: Portrait after a painting in the *Grosse Kirche* at Emden, Germany, reproduced from *Politica Methodice Digesta of Johannes Althusius (Althaus)* (Cambridge: Harvard University Press, 1932).

Library of Congress Cataloging-in-Publication Data
Althusius, Johannes, 1557–1638.
    [Politica methodice digesta. English]
    Politica / by Johannes Althusius : an abridged translation of
Politics methodically set forth, and illustrated with sacred and
profane examples : edited and translated, with an introduction, by
Frederick S. Carney : foreword by Daniel Elazar. — A Liberty
classics ed.
      p. cm.
    Translation originally published: Politics. Boston : Beacon Press,
c1964. With new foreword and other changes in accompanying matter.
    Includes bibliographical references and index.
    ISBN 0-86597-114-5 (hardcover : acid-free paper). — ISBN
0-86597-115-3 (pbk. : acid-free paper)
    1. Political science—Early works to 1800.   I. Carney, Frederick
Smith, 1924–   . II. Title.
JC156.A413   1994
321.02—dc20   94-30586

03 02 01 00 95   c   5 4 3 2 1
05 04 03 02 01   p   6 5 4 3 2

Contents

Translator's Introduction

The New Interest in the Political Theory of Althusius

Johannes Althusius has enjoyed the good fortune in recent times of frequent notice in political, theological, sociological, and historical writings. This has been true ever since Otto Gierke in the latter part of the nineteenth century recovered Althusius from two centuries of relative obscurity, and attributed to his *Politica (Politica methodice digesta)* the distinction of making one of the pivotal contributions to Western political thought. He saw in Althusius a seminal thinker who was enabled by an exceptional learning in law, theology, politics, and history to formulate a political theory that served as something of a culmination of medieval social thought and a watershed of modern political ideas. The chief features of this theory, Gierke felt, were to be found in its contractual and natural law principles.

The renewal of interest in Althusius was given further impetus by the labors of Carl Joachim Friedrich, who in 1932 not only republished the largest part of the 1614 edition of the *Politica* in its original language, but also provided for it an introduction that considerably advanced our knowledge of Althusius' life as well as his thought. Friedrich focused attention on the concept of the symbiotic association as the foundation of Althusian theory, and on the Calvinist religion as interpretive of this concept. In so doing, he differed quite noticeably from Gierke in his understanding of Althusius' political theory. Nevertheless, he shared with Gierke a very high estimate of Althusius' importance, even to the extent of considering him to be "the most profound political thinker between Bodin and Hobbes."

In addition to Gierke and Friedrich, the two persons who have done most to establish Althusius' reputation in the contemporary world, there is also a small but growing and impressive group of scholars from various political and religious traditions who have devoted considerable attention to his thought. The names of John Neville Figgis, R. W. and A. J. Carlyle, Pierre Mesnard, Erik Wolf, Ernst Reibstein, Peter Jochen Winters, Heinz Werner Antholz, and others whose works are listed in the Select Bibliography of this translation testify to this. These men have addressed themselves to a range of topics in Althusian scholarship that reflects the wide scope of his thought. Included among such topics have been the constitutionalism of Althusius, the relation in his thought of philosophical norms to political processes, the contributions of Althusius to jurisprudence, his theory of associations, the Calvinist religious elements in his political theory, the role of the Spanish school of social philosophy at Salamanca in the development of his thought, and Althusius' employment of his own political teachings while serving as Syndic of the city of Emden for thirty-four years.

It is a striking feature of Althusian studies, however, that until this translation was made there had not been a published translation of a substantial part of the *Politica* in any vernacular language. Wolf translated a few pages into German from the 1603 edition, and included them in a collection of juridical writings by various authors that he published in 1943. Friedrich circulated in mimeographed form ten pages of selections he put into English from the 1614 edition. And Father Stanley Parry translated, and at times paraphrased, major portions of the 1614 edition for a privately used English typescript in connection with his doctoral studies on Althusius at Yale University. But so far as I am aware, this abridged translation represents the first published attempt in a modern language to present in Althusius' own words the entire basic structure of his political thought, as well as the chief arguments by which he compared and contrasted his own position with that of his contemporaries. The reason why such a translation has not been attempted before may well be because of some unusual problems it presents to the translator. I shall discuss these problems, as well as the justification for abridging the original work, in the final section of this introduction.

It may be helpful in concluding this section to note briefly some of the most important facts of the life of this man whose thought is now acquiring new attention among scholars in a number of disciplines.

Little is known of the early years of Althusius' life, except that he was born in Diedenshausen in Westphalia about 1557. He appeared in 1581 at Cologne, where he apparently studied the writings of Aristotle. It was at Basle, however, that he received his doctorate in both civil and ecclesiastical law in 1586, with a thesis on the subject of intestate inheritance. Surprisingly, he published *Jurisprudentia Romana*, his first book, during the same year. While at Basle he lived for a time in the home of Johann Grynaeus, with whom he studied theology and thereafter maintained a life-long correspondence. Sometime prior to obtaining his doctorate, Althusius also studied at Geneva with Denis Godefroy, the renowned textual scholar of Roman law.

Upon receiving his doctorate, he was called to the Reformed Academy at Herborn as a member of the faculty of law. Herborn Academy, which had been founded only two years earlier (1584) by Count John of Nassau, had become immediately successful and had attracted an international student body. Its first rector was Kasper Olevianus, the co-author with Zachary Ursinus of the Heidelberg Catechism. Althusius, in addition to his professorship in law, became councillor to the count in 1595 and, after some months of theological study at Heidelberg, was made rector of the Academy in 1597. His volume on ethics—entitled *Civilis Conversationis Libri Duo*—was published in 1601. But the greatest achievement of his Herborn years was the publication in 1603 of the *Politica*, a work that received immediate and wide attention.

The *Politica* seems to have been instrumental in securing for Althusius a most attractive offer to become Syndic of Emden in East Friesland. This city had been one of the first in Germany (1526) to embrace the Reformed faith. Ever since John Laski had been invited to Emden in 1542 by Countess Anna to reorganize its religious life, it had become a veritable "Geneva of the North." Its strategic location on the frontiers of both the German Empire and the Netherlands gave it freedom of movement *vis-à-vis* its Lutheran provincial lord and its Catholic emperor. At the same time, its strong Calvinist spirit enabled it to exercise an exceptional influence in key areas of the Netherlands and Germany. Indeed, Emden was often called the "alma mater" of the Dutch Reformed Church, for it was from Emden that some of the early Dutch ministers came, and at Emden that many exiles from the Duke of Alva's persecution later found refuge. Moreover, at the Synod of Emden in 1571 the Reformed churches of East Friesland and the Lower Rhine joined with the Dutch churches to form a union of the largest part of Northern Calvinism. Furthermore, Emden was a leading seaport, in close communication with England, and it served as a haven for a number of English divines during the Catholic reaction under Mary Tudor.

Recently, however, Emden had encountered increasingly serious conflicts with its provincial lord, as well as with various larger and more powerful units of the German Empire and Spanish Kingdom. The City Council was consequently seeking an exceptionally able leader to guide its negotiations and destiny. Johann Alting, a son of Emden's distinguished clergyman Menso Alting and one of a number of students from Emden studying law under Althusius at Herborn, apparently sent copies of the *Politica* home as soon as it was published. The favorable reception by Emdeners of the ideas on government expressed in this volume, coupled with Althusius' growing juristic reputation, led the City Council to invite him to become the Syndic of Emden.

He accepted the offer in 1604, and guided the political destinies of this city without interruption until his death in 1638. During the years of his service in Emden, he published two new and enlarged editions of the *Politica* (1610 and 1614), and also wrote the *Dicaeologica* (1617), an immense work that seeks to construct a single comprehensive juridical system out of Biblical law, Roman law, and various customary laws. In 1617 Althusius was elected elder of the church of Emden, a position he continued to hold until his death twenty-one years later. There is a sense in which his two functions of syndic and elder, coupled with capacities for leadership and hard work, enabled him to coordinate the civil and ecclesiastical jurisdictions of the city, and thus to exercise somewhat the same kind of influence in Emden as Calvin did in Geneva. His correspondence contains frequent condemnations of Arminian theological opinions, and in one letter he especially criticized the *Pietas* of Hugo Grotius on the basis that it would undermine the independent right and liberty of the church by transferring ecclesiastical functions to civil government.

The Basic Structure of His Thought

Althusius consciously organized his *Politica* according to Ramist logic. This is the explanation for the words "methodically set forth" in the title, and for the references occasionally found throughout the text to "the law of method" and "the precepts of logicians." Peter Ramus, a celebrated and highly controversial French logician of the sixteenth century, made use of the two traditional topics of logic: invention and disposition (or judgment). What was largely new with Ramus, however, was the manner in which he employed these two topics. Where invention had previously been understood as the processes for combining predicates with subjects in debatable propositions, under the influence of Ramism it also came to denote the processes for determining what material belongs to subjects as scholarly disciplines. And where disposition had previously referred to methods of arranging propositions into syllogisms or inductions, and these into discourses, with Ramism it also came to refer to the methods of organizing material appropriate to any given discipline. The change that has occurred is one in which logic is used to clarify not only what may be said for or against propositions and combinations or propositions, but also how a field of study may be "logically" organized. An assumption inherent in Ramism is that proper organization of materials is valuable not only for teaching and learning purposes, but also for the discovery and clarification of knowledge.

Ramus' interpretation of invention made use of three laws he adapted from Aristotle's *Posterior Analytics*. (1) The law of justice (*lex justitiae*) indicates that each art or science has its own purpose, that this purpose serves as a principle for determining what is proper to a given art (*suum cuique*), and that everything not proper to it is to be rigorously excluded. Althusius' employment of the Ramist law of justice is introduced initially in the Preface to the first edition, where he says that "it is necessary to keep constantly in view the natural and true goal and form of each art, and to attend most carefully to them, that we not exceed the limits justice lays down for each art and thereby reap another's harvest." The purpose of political science, according to Althusius, is the maintenance of social life among human beings. He therefore proposes to remove certain legal, theological, and ethical material from it by which others in his judgment had confused and compromised its proper operation. He acknowledges, however, that two disciplines may have partly overlapping subject matter, as theology and political science share the Decalogue, and law and political science jointly embrace the doctrine of sovereignty. But he insists that each discipline must limit itself to that aspect of the common material that is essential to its own purpose, and reject what is not. (2) The Ramist law of truth (*lex veritatis*) indicates that an art or science consists of universal and necessary propositions or precepts, and that those that are true only in certain places and times should be sifted out. For Althusius the problem was what to do with such politically relevant, but nevertheless contingent, matters as the varying character and customs of rulers and peoples. "Who can propose general precepts," he asks, "that are necessarily and mutually true about matters so various and unequivalent? The statesman, however, should be well acquainted with these matters." His solution is to retain some of these matters in his *Politica* for expedient reasons, but with advance warning to his readers concerning their quasi-scientific nature. They are especially to be found in the chapters on "Political Prudence in the Administration of the Commonwealth." (3) Ramus' law of wisdom (*lex sapientiae*) indicates that a proposition should be placed with the nearest class of things to which it belongs rather than with matters on a higher or lower level of generality. Although Althusius nowhere explicitly discusses this law, it is evident that he consistently employs it. For example, there are no propositions referring chiefly and generically to the city to be found in his opening discussion of politics in general. They are too restrictive for this level because politics also includes other associations in addition to the city. Nor are they to be located in his discussion of the rural village. They are too extensive for this level because other kinds of local community also qualify as cities. Rather all such propositions will be found in his discussion of the nonuniversal public association that is composed of families and collegia. They belong precisely to this level, as they do to no other. Althusius' use of the Ramist law of wisdom gives to the *Politica* a highly architectonic quality, even though the effect sometimes impresses the reader as somewhat superficial.

The most distinctive feature of the Ramist interpretation of disposition is its emphasis upon method. And this Althusius clearly appropriates. Ramus had written that those who think wisely and methodically "descend from the most general idea to the various divisions thereof, and thence to the particular cases it comprehends" (*Dialectique,* Paris, 1555, p. 4). Althusius opens the *Politica* with a general proposition that indicates the fundamental insight regarding the nature of political science that will be pursued throughout this inquiry, and suggests by implication the limits that will be observed. He then proceeds by dividing and repeatedly subdividing the subject matter, each subdivision in turn opening with a sub-proposition relating to the general proposition and defining the appropriate material therein. He pursues this method with a tiresome regularity throughout the entire volume until the full implications of the opening proposition have been diligently sought out in their application to all forms and activities of political association.

"Politics is the art of associating men for the purpose of establishing, cultivating, and conserving social life among them. Whence it is called 'symbiotics.' " This is the general proposition for the entire volume. It stands at the beginning of Chapter I, and guides and controls everything that follows. By referring to politics as symbiotics (or the art of living together), and to social life as symbiosis (or living together), Althusius means to include all human associations in his study. These he divides into simple and private associations (family and collegium), and mixed and public associations (city, province, and commonwealth). The latter are discussed in both civil and ecclesiastical aspects because provision for both body and soul is deemed essential to public social life. Although the concentration of this volume is upon the commonwealth, Althusius clearly believes that these other associations are the parts out of which, indirectly and directly, the commonwealth is composed, and that they furthermore share common problems of political organization with the commonwealth. Indeed, by first setting forth the principles by which these problems are to be met in the smaller associations, Althusius anticipates the major features of his discussion of the commonwealth except for the addition of the attribute of sovereignty, which is proper to the commonwealth alone.

Symbiotic association involves something more than mere existence together. It indicates a quality of group life characterized by piety and justice without which, Althusius believes, neither individual persons nor society can endure. He repeatedly asserts that piety is required by the first table of the Decalogue and justice by the second, and that the two together are furthermore validated in human experience everywhere. Thus both divine revelation and natural reason are called upon in political science to clarify the true nature of symbiotic association.

Wherever there is symbiosis there is also communication, or the sharing of things, services, and right. (The Latin word *jus* employed in this connection means both right and law.) Although politics is properly involved in each of these three forms of communication, it has one basic concern with them, namely, the effective ordering of all communication. Therefore, politics is not interested in the goods of the tradesman or the skills of the craftsman, except inasmuch as these goods and skills must be socially regulated for the benefit both of the individual and of the association. Thus politics may be distinguished from economics. The communication of right (*jus*), however, is proper to politics in an even more basic manner. For by this kind of communication each association is given its political structure, and achieves that form of self-sufficiency appropriate to it. The right that is communicated is in part common to all associations, in part special to each type of association, and in part particular to each individual association.

Communication requires imperium, or strong rule, to be effective. Althusius has no interest at all in theories about human rights. What does interest him is the extent to which any association fulfills the purposes for which it exists. In this sense, an association has a holy vocation even as a person does. Consequently, Althusius is opposed to tyrannical rule not because it is undemocratic, but because it becomes ineffective in supporting the ends for which persons enter and remain in association with each other. He is opposed, for the same reason, to weak and vacillating rule. His interest in constitutional limitations upon the abuse of power arises from his concern that power be truly and lawfully strong. It is therefore characteristic of his thought that he advocates institutionalized restraints upon rulers in order to maintain effective symbiosis. Such restraints are intended to conserve lawful rule in an association and to correct or remove an erring ruler when necessary, but not to weaken the exercise of rule itself.

Persons enter and remain in association with each other because outside of the mutual communication of things, services, and right they cannot live comfortably and well; indeed, they cannot live at all. Necessity therefore induces association. But the existence of each individual association, as well as the special form it takes, also depends upon the continuing consent of the symbiotes, or members. Althusius is thus led to say that an association is initiated and maintained by a covenant among the symbiotes setting forth their common agreement about the necessary and useful purposes to be served by the association, and the means appropriate to fulfill these purposes. If there is no explicit covenant, then an implicit one is assumed in the continuing consent of those who live together. Symbiotic association thus requires a balance between social necessity and social volition.

When Althusius distinguishes the two types of private association as the natural and the civil, he is setting forth the two poles in this balance. The family, as the natural private association, is considered to be a permanent union of the members "with the same boundaries as life itself." The collegium, as the civil private association, is a more voluntary society "that need not last as long as the lifetime of man," even though "a certain necessity can be said to have brought it into existence." Even within each of these two associations there is some balance between necessity and volition. For the family, however natural, is based upon a tacit or expressed agreement among its members as to the manner of its communication of things, services, and right. The continued existence of the family tends to confirm this agreement. On the other hand the collegium is not completely voluntary. It arises from a natural need, and presumably is not to be disbanded unless alternative means are available to meet this need. This integral relationship between necessity and volition that first finds expression in private associations carries over into public associations, and becomes one of the distinctive characteristics of the entire associational theory of Althusius.

Althusius divides the family into two kinds—conjugal and kinship—and discusses the nature of communication and imperium in each. Although the husband is clearly the ruler of the conjugal family, and the paterfamilias the ruler of the kinship family, Althusius is careful to set forth the conjugal obligations that the husband owes his wife, as well as those the wife owes her husband, and the kinship obligations that both husband and wife as paterfamilias and materfamilias owe their children and domestics.

The collegium (guild or corporation) is an association in which "three or more men of the same trade, training, or profession are united for the purpose of holding in common such things as they jointly profess as duty, way of life, or craft." It is most often an association organized around occupational interests. If it is composed of magistrates and judges, or of persons engaged in agricultural, industrial, or commercial pursuits, it is called a secular collegium. If it is composed of clergymen, philosophers, or teachers, it is called an ecclesiastical collegium. These two kinds of collegium are parallel to the two forms of administration—secular and ecclesiastical—that are to be found in the province and commonwealth. The manner of rule in the collegium follows the general principles that Althusius has set forth for all social authority, except that in the collegium participation by individual colleagues, or members, can be direct rather than, as in public associations, indirect. There is a leader elected by the colleagues to administer the affairs of the collegium. "He exercises coercive power over the colleagues individually, but not over the group itself." For he is bound by the purposes for which the collegium exists, and by the laws defined through its corporate processes.

The public association is derivative from the private association in that families and collegia, not individual persons, are directly constitutive of the city, and indirectly or directly of the province and commonwealth. For without the private association "others would be able neither to arise nor to endure." Furthermore, the public association has jurisdiction over a prescribed territory, which the private association does not. The same general principles of communication and rule, however, apply equally to both private and public associations. Thus Althusius departs from a distinction common in medieval Roman law between public and private. According to this distinction, "private" pertains largely to contractual relations among individuals, or to the internal procedures of groups—whether collegia or cities—that operate by concession but not direct domination of public authority. "Public," on the other hand, refers to administrative agencies and divisions of the empire or, more realistically, of the commonwealth. Althusius affirms, to the contrary, that the foundation of all associations, whether private or public, is symbiotic life. By appealing to symbiosis in this manner, he denies that private and public associations should have essentially different sources of legitimacy and modes of operation from each other. He also seeks by the same stroke to release politics from the hegemony of juridical conceptions of association. Nevertheless, the derivative and territorial characteristics of the public association still remain to distinguish it from the private.

Continuing the Ramist method of dichotomizing, Althusius divides the public association into particular and universal. The particular, in turn, is divided into the city and the province, and the universal is identified as the commonwealth (*respublica*), or realm (*regnum*). The particular association does not possess sovereignty, while the universal does. It should be noted, however, that the city of Venice, because it possesses sovereignty, has the status of a commonwealth. Furthermore, while a city is composed of families and collegia, the province is formed of various kinds of local community ranging from the rural hamlet to the metropolis, and the commonwealth is constituted of provinces and such cities as have the rights and responsibilities of provinces in the assemblies of the realm.

The city, unlike the private association, does not provide the opportunity for direct participation of individuals as such in the process of rule. Here an organized community arises out of smaller associations and finds expression in a senate. At the same time, there is a ruler who exercises authority over individuals and particular associations, but not over the organized community itself. Althusius carefully spells out the relations that ought to prevail between ruler and senate in order that symbiotic needs on the municipal level can be provided for effectively. In brief, the ruler is the chief executive, and presides over the communication of things, services, and right. The senate, on the other hand, determines and defends the fundamental laws of the city, even to the extent if necessary of correcting or removing a ruler who misuses entrusted authority to the detriment of this symbiotic association.

Althusius' discussion of the province contains one of the few basic inconsistencies in the elaboration of his political system. For the ruler of the province is responsible not to the organized community over which this person presides, as is the case in all other associations, but to the supreme magistrate of the commonwealth. The ruler is a prince, duke, count, or other noble who receives this office, whether through heredity or appointment, as a function of the commonwealth, and cannot be removed from this office except in rare instances, and then only by the commonwealth. Thus the symbiotic foundations of rule generally characteristic of Althusius' thought are partly compromised on the provincial level, possibly as a concession by him to the actual practices that prevailed in his time in his native Germany and in most neighboring nations. But, if so, he did not concede very much. For it will be remembered that Althusius is not as interested in the precise arrangements for designating a ruler as he is in the effectiveness of the ruler's administration in conserving and enhancing the communication of things, services, and right. Althusius could accommodate himself without undue difficulty to the notion that a ruler might be designated and maintained in office from outside the provincial community, provided the ruler governs the province well. This is to say that if a province actually meets the purposes for which it exists — if it fulfills its high calling — Althusius can wink at procedural irregularities, even though he may prefer that they do not prevail.

Furthermore, the provincial orders, which collectively compose the organized community of the province, constitute a restraining influence on the misuse of executive power. These orders are both ecclesiastical and secular, and provide for the observance of both tables of the Decalogue in political life. The reason for this is that both revelation and practical experience demonstrate that symbiotic association cannot long endure without public provision for the souls as well as the bodies of men. The ecclesiastical order, which is especially concerned with the cultivation of piety, is conceived by Althusius essentially according to contemporary Calvinist practice. The secular order, which addresses itself primarily to the maintenance of justice, is preferably composed of three estates, namely, the nobility, the burghers, and the agrarians. Sometimes, however, the last two are combined in one estate known as the commons. It is to be noted that these orders and estates are essentially the occupational collegia organized on a provincial level. Representatives of these estates, and in some realms of the ecclesiastical order as well, will meet in convocation where they perform much the same function in the province that the senate does in the city. Their consent is required by the ruler in all major matters confronting the province, such as decisions on war, peace, taxes, and new law.

The commonwealth, as previously noted, differs from the city and province in that it alone possesses sovereignty. This is to say, only the commonwealth recognizes no human person or association as superior to itself. But where in the commonwealth does this sovereignty reside? Jean Bodin, to whom Althusius was highly indebted for so many of the characteristics of his political system, attributed it to the ruler. Althusius disagrees. His position, which follows consistently upon the principles he has already elaborated in smaller associations, is that sovereignty is the symbiotic life of the commonwealth taking form in the *jus regni*, or in the fundamental right or law of the realm. Since the commonwealth is composed not of individual persons but of cities and provinces, it is to them when joined together in communicating things, services, and right that sovereignty belongs. Therefore, it resides in the organized body of the commonwealth, which is to say in the symbiotic processes thereof. This organized body is also known to Althusius as the people (*populus*).

The communication, or communion, that occurs in the commonwealth is, of course, both ecclesiastical and secular. Ecclesiastical communication has to do with the public expression of true religion, with the provision for public schools in which both religion and the liberal arts are taught and handed down to posterity, and with the defense of church and state from religious corruption. In this last matter, however, Althusius pleads for moderation, provided that the essential articles of faith are preserved. He observes that Christ suffered disciples who erred and were weak, and that "no mode of thought has ever come forth as so perfect that the judgment of all learned men would subscribe to it." Secular communication aims at rendering to each his due, which requires public provision for commerce, a monetary system, a common language, the performance of duties on behalf of the realm, the granting of special privileges and titles, the defense of the realm and its goods, and the holding of general councils to make decisions on major matters confronting the commonwealth.

The administrators of the commonwealth, who are the overseers of this communication, are of two kinds: the ephors and the supreme magistrate. The ephors do not ordinarily rule over the commonwealth itself, as does the supreme magistrate, but are held in reserve for emergency situations. They bear the fundamental right and power of the people in these situations. There are five duties expected of them, which they perform as a group rather than as individuals. They constitute, or establish, a supreme magistrate when a vacancy arises in the highest office of the realm. They restrain the supreme magistrate within the limits of the entrusted office. They remove the supreme magistrate who becomes tyrannical. They defend the supreme magistrate from detractors when he is performing this entrusted office properly. And they serve as a trustee for the realm in time of interregnum. Fundamental to this doctrine of the ephors is Althusius' judgment that "great power cannot contain itself within boundaries without some coercion and constraint entrusted to others."

The model that Althusius employs most frequently in his advocacy of ephors is the seven electors of Germany. He also manages to find somewhat comparable officials in other nations. They are usually distinguished rulers of provinces who possess at the same time this general function in the commonwealth. What happens when there are no properly designated ephors to act in the name of the people? Althusius would respond that symbiotic association so greatly requires persons to perform these duties when the need arises in the realm that each body politic should provide them by some process appropriate to its own traditions. We may assume that such persons will be leading citizens of the commonwealth, each with roots deep in some corporate part thereof.

The constituting of the supreme magistrate involves first the election and then, if the electee agrees to the provisions of the election, the inauguration. The election occurs according to the established practice of the land, and may in some instances be little more than the confirmation of an heir determined by customary arrangement. At the inauguration there is a double oath in which the ruler-designate first promises to uphold the fundamental laws of the realm, as well as any special conditions established at the time of the election, and the people through its ephors then promises obedience to the magistrate when he is ruling according to the prescribed laws and conditions.

The actual administration of the commonwealth by the supreme magistrate should be guided, according to Althusius, by political prudence. This part of Althusian political doctrine involves knowledge both of law and of the changing and contingent circumstances to which law is to be applied. The discussion of law at this point is an extended treatment of the relation of the Decalogue to natural law, and of the role of these two together as common law in the formulation of proper law for particular societies. It is important to note that Althusius, a man who was much travelled and well received in orthodox Calvinist circles, maintained a rather warm appreciation for a human's natural knowledge of one's duty to both God and neighbor. The discussion that follows of such contingent factors in political life as the character and customs of rulers and peoples gives Althusius considerable methodological difficulty, largely because he is of the opinion, as I mentioned earlier, that this material does not lend itself to general precepts that can properly claim the name of science. Perhaps this is the reason why this discussion impresses the reader as the weakest and least convincing in the entire volume.

On the other hand some of the most striking features in the volume are found in the chapters on ecclesiastical and secular administration. Here Althusius amplifies the basic structure of his thought that has already taken shape. The analysis of ecclesiastical administration contains the arguments for a religious covenant between the commonwealth and God that Althusius adapts from Junius Brutus. It discusses the respective roles of the supreme magistrate and the clergy in the conduct of the church. And it suggests limits arising both from the nature of faith and from the requirements of symbiosis beyond which the effort to compel observance even of the true religion ought not to go. Of especial interest in the chapters on secular administration is Althusius' discussion of the importance of general councils, or parliaments, to the welfare of the realm, and of the procedures appropriate for calling the orders and estates into council and for conducting the business of the realm therein. The difference in function should be noted between these councils and the body of ephors, even though some overlapping of personnel could ordinarily be expected.

Tyranny, which is the opposite of just and upright administration, must be realistically assessed and its remedies identified if the systematic character of Althusius' political doctrine is to be maintained to the end. He proceeds to this task by acknowledging the distinction, widely employed since Bartolus, between a tyrant by practice (*tyrannus exercitio*) and a tyrant without title (*tyrannus absque titulo*). But he claims that only the former is a true tyrant because the latter, who never rightfully received the office of the supreme magistrate, is only a usurper. The tyrant without title, therefore, deserves none of the respect usually attributed to political superiors, and as a private person who is an enemy of the people may be resisted and even killed by private citizens. But a tyrant who becomes such after having gained legitimate title to the supreme office can be resisted only by public authorities to whom this responsibility has been entrusted, namely, by the ephors. The means, timing, and other relevant matters for effecting a remedy for such tyranny are thereupon discussed by Althusius. It is altogether characteristic of his basically conservative thought that he recommends caution against coming too quickly to the conclusion that a supreme magistrate who fails or errs in some part of his office is necessarily a tyrant, and insists that a public acknowledgment should be made by a properly constituted body before anyone takes action, except in self-defense, against such a ruler.

The final chapter presents the thesis that the best polity is one "that combines qualities of kingship, aristocracy, and democracy." Although the customary distinction between these three types of polity has some validity in that it identifies the most characteristic element in any given case, it is more important, he believes, to focus attention on the processes most likely to achieve both effective rule in the commonwealth and restraint upon the misuse of rule. Thus the controlling principle of these processes remains in the final chapter, as it was in the first, the enhancement of symbiotic association, without which humans cannot live comfortably and well.

His Major Literary Sources

Mention has already been made of the very wide scope of Althusius' erudition. He drew upon an extraordinary number of books from many fields in the composition of his *Politica*, over 150 of which are referred to in this abridged translation. (See Althusius' Literary Sources Referred to in This Translation.) It may be helpful at this point to identify briefly the major categories of writers the reader will encounter in making his way through the *Politica*, as well as to suggest the manner in which Althusius employs some of the writers most important to him.

The first category pertains to those writers who devote considerable attention to the observation of political processes and possibilities in the light of a few general considerations. Aristotle, of course, comes immediately to mind in this regard. Althusius adopts Aristotle's understanding of politics as a practical art or science that is addressed to the problem of ascertaining how human good can be achieved in community. The empirically oriented approach Althusius follows in the *Politica* makes this indebtedness clear, and it is also to be noted that he, like Aristotle, begins with an analysis of the family and moves onward to the commonwealth. The Calvinism of Althusius, however, causes him to differ somewhat from Aristotle on the nature of human good, as well as on the degree of human corruption and the extent to which political institutions may consequently have to make provision for this factor. Another writer in this category is Jean Bodin, the sixteenth-century political, legal, and historical theorist. Of interest to Althusius was Bodin's procedure of surveying history, as well as contemporary experience, for insight into the nature and processes of political community. Even more important, however, was Bodin's doctrine of sovereignty that Althusius took over and systematically developed in the *Politica*, but with the difference already noted concerning the place where it properly resides in the commonwealth. The most frequently cited writer in the *Politica* is Petrus Gregorius, a professor of law at the Jesuit school at Pont-à-Mousson. Althusius was indebted to Gregorius for a myriad of observations about the nature of social organization in just about every area except the ecclesiastical.

The second category includes those writers both Catholic and Calvinist who had an interest in constitutional government, and in the ideological and institutional foundations capable of supporting it. The three main Catholic authors in this group were all Spanish, namely, Fernando Vásquez (an ecclesiastical writer on natural law), Diego Covarruvias (a canonist and bishop whose style of legal writings caused him to be sometimes known as "the Spanish Bartolus"), and Juan de Mariana (a theologian and accomplished humanist who unintentionally got his Jesuit order into serious trouble by the inclusion of a chapter on tyrannicide in his major political text). Equally important to Althusius' constitutionalism were certain Calvinists. The chief ones were the pseudonymous author (Junius Brutus) of the *Defence of Liberty Against Tyrants* (which was perhaps the best written and most widely read of the political tracts that came out of the French Wars of Religion), George Buchanan (a Scot and one of the great humanists of the sixteenth century), and Lambert Daneau (a French Calvinist pastor, theological professor, and political writer). Althusius may be considered the culminating theorist of this group, for he provided their ideas on limiting the power of a ruler with a politically systematic basis they had previously lacked. He did this, of course, by making symbiotic association and its needs the foundation of political doctrine, and by showing what kind of constitutional considerations can be understood to arise therefrom.

A third group upon whom Althusius draws is characterized by a common interest in political prudence, or in what at times finds expression under the topic of practical politics. I have reference here principally to Giovanni Botero (the Italian publicist who made famous the concept "reason of state"), Justus Lipsius (a philologist and professor of history at Leyden and Louvain), Innocent Gentillet (whose *Against Nicholas Machiavell* was written to combat the Medici, or Italian, influence in the French royal court), and Scipio Ammirato (an Italian courtier). The teachings of these authors are frequently reproduced in the section on political prudence, which is not a very satisfactory treatment by Althusius of contingent factors in politics. Botero and Lipsius, however, are also employed by Althusius in other chapters of the volume in keeping with the approach of the first category of writers mentioned above. It is interesting to note that Althusius' occasional references to Niccolò Machiavelli are not to be found in the section on political prudence, as we might expect, but in discussions of the general principles of administration and of the defense of the commonwealth against tyrants. Furthermore, the work of Machiavelli most frequently mentioned by Althusius is not *The Prince*, but the *Discourses*.

The fourth category is that of legal writers. Among the civilians most in evidence are Bartolus (fourteenth century), Paul Castro (fifteenth century), and Andreas Gail (sixteenth century). The *Corpus juris civilis* plays a major role in the *Politica*, not so much as a book of law from which one might deduce political arguments but, together with its better known commentaries, as a seedbed of ideas and concepts that can be built integrally into a political system or used analogically to indicate and illustrate essentially political principles. The Digest and the commentators thereupon are most frequently called forth by Althusius for these purposes, but numerous references may also be found to the Code, Institutes, and Novels. On the other hand, the *Corpus juris canonici* is not directly cited in the *Politica*, although there are important references to a number of canonists, especially to Nicholaus Tudeschi (fifteenth century) and Diego Covarruvias (sixteenth century). In addition, various customary systems of law are mentioned from time to time, often to provide illustrations for Althusius' teaching on the fundamental laws of the realm. In this connection Henry Rosenthal and Peter Heige of contemporary Germany, and Francis Hotman and Charles Dumoulin of contemporary France, are perhaps the most important. Finally, there is the Italian Nicolaus Losaeus, upon whose *De jure universitatum* Althusius draws heavily in the third edition of the *Politica* to describe the internal processes of government appropriate to both collegium and city.

The Calvinist theological writers constitute a fifth category. They serve a number of functions. The Biblical commentaries of Peter Martyr (Vermigli), Francis Junius, and John Piscator are called upon to give meaning to the concepts of piety and justice as interpretive of true symbiosis, and to describe the ancient Jewish polity that Althusius considers to have been the most wisely and perfectly constructed one since the beginning of time. The churchly writings of John Calvin, Jerome Zanchius, Benedict Aretius, and Zachary Ursinus are the major sources for Althusius' exposition of the ecclesiastical order in both the province and the commonwealth. Zanchius' extensive discussion of law in his *De redemptione* contributes more than anything else to Althusius' understanding of the relation of the Decalogue to natural law, and of both to the proper laws of various nations. Then there are special topics on which Althusius finds his theological colleagues to be helpful, such as Peter Martyr's discussion of war.

The sixth category is composed of historians and their writings, especially Carlo Sigonio on ancient Israel and Rome, Emmanuel Meteren on the Netherlands, Jean Sleidan on Germany, Francis Hotman (who was also a legal historian) on France, and Theodore Zwinger on universal history. Their significance to the *Politica* arises especially from the materials they provided for one of the most debatable aspects of Althusius' doctrine, namely, whenever and wherever societies live well they do so by essentially the same political principles, even though identification of these principles may vary and local adaptations of them may occur in practice.

Classical writers are a seventh category. Two of them he employed, I think, in a rather fundamental way in his system. I have already spoken of his use of Aristotle. The other is Cicero, from whom he learned much about the nature of social life and the vocabulary of politics. (Would that Althusius had also permitted his often dull and sometimes barbarous Latin style to be influenced by Cicero!) On the other hand he often uses classical writers, especially Augustine and Seneca, for quotations that may fit his own point but are taken out of context from the original work. And his frequent references to Augustine nowhere reveal that he actually had very little sympathy with Augustine's conception of the state. It is also worth noting that while he occasionally calls upon Plato to support his thesis that harmony is an imperative in social life, he also compares him with Thomas More and criticizes both for the unrealism of their utopian views of society.

The eighth category of writers that plays a major role in the *Politica* is Althusius' select list of opponents in political theory. Included therein is the Catholic layman William Barclay, whose defense of a high monarchical view got him into such trouble with Rome that none less than Bellarmine was required to respond in written disputation to him, and furthermore led him to coin the misleading word "monarch-omach" to describe such persons as George Buchanan, Jean Boucher, and the pseudonymous Junius Brutus. In addition, there was Jean Bodin himself, and Henning Arnisaeus, the latter a physician who wrote in support of Bodin's argument that sovereignty resides in the ruler. Both of these men were correctly seen by Althusius as setting forth positions that his own system would have to be able to answer. The same must also be said for one of the works of Alberico Gentili, the Italian Protestant professor of civil law at Oxford. Some of the most lively parts of the *Politica* occur when Althusius enters the lists against these writers.

It may be of some use to the reader to add another category of a different kind, namely, one composed of writers that Althusius for one reason or another tended to overlook. For example, medieval publicists, as distinguished from medieval legists both civil and canon, find little place in the expression of his political doctrine. There is an occasional mention of Thomas Aquinas' *On Princely Government* and Marsilius of Padua's *Defender of the Peace*, but none of John of Salisbury, Giles of Rome, John of Paris, Augustinus Triumphus, Dante Alighieri, or William of Occam. The one major exception is the German Lupold of Bebenberg, who recurs with some frequency throughout the volume. Another generally disregarded group is English writers, in this instance even extending to legal authors. It is true that Sir Thomas Smith's study of English government is mentioned occasionally, that Sir Thomas More appears on the pages of the *Politica* a couple of times only to be rebuffed for his utopianism, and that the Puritan theologians William Perkins and William Whitaker are included (but not in this abridgment). This is not, however, an adequate sampling of English thought within Althusius' range of interests. The lawyers Henry Bracton and Sir John Fortescue could have spoken quite relevantly and sympathetically to Althusius on a number of points. So could have the theologians John Wyclif and Richard Hooker, although the former for largely differing reasons from the latter. Finally, one must call attention to the fact that prominent Lutherans and Arminians are scarce in the *Politica*. Althusius' opposition to their religious views may have been the reason. But, if so, how does one explain his extensive and generally appreciative use of a number of Catholic writers? Perhaps the answer is better to be attributed to the absence of much interest in systematic political theory in those religious circles prior to 1614. There is some evidence that during this period serious political writing among continental Protestants was largely the work of orthodox and near orthodox Calvinists.

I should observe in closing this section that further material on the relation of Althusius to some of these writers is to be found in the introduction that Friedrich provided his 1932 republication of the *Politica* in its original language.

Some Notes on This Translation

The original Latin text presents a number of problems to the translator. Perhaps the most imposing of them is that a large accumulation of references to other books, of identified and unidentified quotations from them, and even of lengthy condensations of borrowed material has been superimposed upon an otherwise well-ordered and clear general structure. This has been done by inserting everything into the text itself without the use of any footnotes and in a manner that gives the impression of great clutter. The result is a volume of a thousand octavo pages resembling nothing that the reader is likely to encounter in today's literary world unless it be the revival of one of the thousands of legal, historical, or theological texts of the late medieval and early modern period that share this common barbarity. But Althusius' volume, like some of these others, has some very important things to say and, unlike most of them, is essentially systematic in doing so. An abridgment is therefore appropriate. And it is fortunate that the *Politica* lends itself readily to this solution. (It may be helpful to some readers to learn that a German translation of the entire Latin text has been proceeding for several years under the sponsorship of the Johannes Althusius Gesellschaft at the University of Dresden.)

I have attempted in this translation to retain in Althusius' own words the complete basic structure of his political thought as it finds expression in the *Politica*, and furthermore to include the chief arguments by which he clarified his position in relation to those of his contemporaries. The retained material is identified by Roman numerals for chapters and by Arabic numerals for the sections thereof that Althusius employs. The omitted material, except for mere references to other writers, is indicated by elision marks (bracketed elision marks indicate an unacknowledged omission by Althusius in a quotation from another author) and there is a complete collation of the translated material with the chapters and section numbers of the 1614 edition for those who may want to check certain points further.

The elimination of all reference material from this translation would have been very unwise because it contains sources that are important for understanding Althusius' thought. Furthermore, he at times permitted his own arguments to be carried by means of it. Consequently, I have retained references when they either are important to the basic structure of his thought and to his chief arguments with contemporaries, or enable me to fulfill the duty of a responsible translator to present a reasonably accurate reflection of the general types of sources upon which an author draws. When references have been retained, however, they have been reduced as far as possible to footnotes. My footnote explanations are bracketed, to distinguish them from Althusius', which appear without brackets. I have also brought paragraph divisions more into keeping with present usage, indicated major transitions in his thought by the device of leaving blank lines, and in several instances grouped chapters together under an appropriate title. These revisions have been made in the interest of readability. In all instances, however, Althusius' precise order has been followed.

Another problem is that of style. Althusius wrote in a pedantic manner with little grace and much redundancy. Indeed, one of the ways of detecting unacknowledged quotations (still a common practice in his day) is to pay careful attention to occasional improvements in his style. Not all borrowings can be detected in this way, however, because some of his most frequently used sources, especially legal ones, were equally insensitive in such matters. One of Althusius' difficulties is his tendency to employ far more nouns, adjectives, or verbs in sequence than most persons find necessary in similar circumstances to convey their thoughts. I have decided to retain these redundancies for several reasons, but chiefly because often each word in the sequence bears a slightly different meaning from the others, and a translator should avoid condensation, however tempting, as a means of achieving stylistic improvement. Again, Althusius frequently joins clauses that are not of parallel construction, and amalgamates a number of them into a confusing sentence that, if diagrammed, would look like a crab-apple tree. In these instances I have usually broken up the sentences, and changed infinitives to gerunds and gerunds to infinitives to achieve somewhat parallel construction. Still again, I must call attention to his transitions. Some are false and some are missing. But mostly they so abundantly flourish that they are often meaningless.

The next problem confronting the translator is that of rendering key words. In the Latin original of the *Politica* there are combinations of words whose relation to each other is implied in Althusius' thought. I have decided in most instances to render them in such a manner as to retain for the English reader the opportunity of seeing these words in their relationships. For example, "*communicatio*" would ordinarily be translated as "sharing." But if this were done in the *Politica* its relation with "*communio*" would not be evident. Likewise, if "*collega*" is rendered as "member" and "*collegium*" as "corporation," would the reader be likely to see the inherent relation between them? Although the result of such a conservative approach to translation as I have employed may produce moments for the reader when, upon first turning to the *Politica* in English, he feels a slight discomfort with some words he encounters, it is nevertheless hoped that he finally will be aided in his capacity to understand some of the unexplained but fundamental connections in Althusius' thought.

The final problem is one of determining the best means for presenting in this translation the various references Althusius makes to other writings. After considerable thought and experimentation I have decided upon the following procedures. First, quotations from the Bible are translated anew from Althusius' Latin text of the *Politica*, except in a very few instances when the Revised Standard Version is used (and so indicated by the letters R.S.V.). The purpose is to show as clearly as possible the connotations Althusius probably had in mind in using the quotations. For the most part Althusius read the Bible not only as a Calvinist but also as an Aristotelian, and the social connotations he finds in many passages are not often present in modern translations. It is to be noted that his biblical quotations are taken usually from the late sixteenth-century Latin translation by Emmanuel Tremellius and Francis Junius, but occasionally from the Vulgate. Second, quotations from the *Corpus juris civilis* are also newly translated. At the same time, I have changed the method of referring to material in the *Corpus juris civilis* from the old one employed by Althusius and all other scholars of his time to the one in general use today. Thus, for example, the citation 1. *sicut. #si quid. quod cujusque univers. nom.* is rendered as Digest III, 4, 7, 1. And 1. 2 *#hoc etiam. C. de jurejur. propt. calum.* is rendered as Code II, 58,

2, 5. Third, the Decretals of canon law, which are employed by Althusius only occasionally in citing passages from the canonists, are also referred to in this translation by the modern method of citation. Thus *c. cum in cuntis. de his quae fiunt a maj. part.* is listed simply as Decretals III, 11, 1. Fourth, all other references are identified in the footnotes by author, short title, and location of material within the work (when information about the location is available), and in the list of Althusius' literary sources by author, fuller title, and publishing data (except for classical works, which according to customary practice are listed merely by author and title). Fifth, whenever an English translation of a work cited by Althusius has been known to me, I have listed it rather than the Latin title. The reason is simply one of convenience for the English reader. In the list of literary sources, however, I have placed the Latin title and (except for classical works) publishing data in parentheses after the English listing. Sixth, authors' names in most instances are changed from Latin into an appropriate vernacular. In making such changes, I have attempted to follow contemporary use in political, legal, and theological literature. Unfortunately, however, contemporary use is not always consistent. Nor does there seem to be any other unfailing guide. Therefore I must acknowledge a degree of arbitrariness in this endeavor. Seventh, the location of material within works by particular authors is abbreviated as follows. Aristotle's works are cited according to the Bekker notation in order to avoid the confusion inherent in their varying book and chapter arrangement in different editions. A very large group of works is divided first into books (or volumes, tomes, or parts), and then into chapters. For these works a Roman numeral is used to indicate the former, and an Arabic numeral to indicate the latter. Whence II, 3. If there is a further division of the chapter, then another Arabic numeral is used. Whence II, 3, 4. If the work is divided only into chapters, or only into chapters and divisions thereof, then Arabic numerals alone are used. Whence 3, or 3, 4. But if the divisions of a work do not lend themselves to this system of citation, then the following abbreviations are used: ann. (year), apos. (*apotelesma* or response), art. (article), cent. (a hundredth division), chap. (chapter), cons. (*consilium* or counsel), dec. (decision), dial. (dialogue), disc. (discourse), disp. (disputation), exer. (exercise), glos. (gloss), lib. (book), loc. (*locus* or place), num. (number), obs. (observation), p. (page), par. (paragraph), pt. (part), pref. (preface), quest. (question), rub. (rubric), sec. (section), thes. (thesis), theor. (theorem), tit. (title), ult. (the final chapter or other division), vol. (volume).

During the course of my labors on Althusius, which produced first a dissertation and now this translation, the following libraries have been indeed generous in the books and services they have made available: the University of Chicago Library, Bridwell and Fondren Libraries of Southern Methodist University, the Newberry Library of Chicago, the University of Pennsylvania Library, the Princeton University Library, and above all the Harvard Law Library (where George A. Strait has been exceptionally helpful). My study of Althusius has been encouraged by many persons, but I especially want to express appreciation to James Luther Adams of the Harvard Divinity School, who originally stimulated me to make this study; to Gerhardt E. O. Meyer of the University of Chicago, who critically assisted it along the way; to Father Stanley Parry of Notre Dame University, who, by making his unpublished translation of the *Politica* available to me at an earlier stage in my labors, kindly aided it; to Decherd H. Turner, Jr., of Southern Methodist University, who bibliographically nourished it; and to my wife Kim Carney of the University of Texas at Arlington, who rejoices in it.

FREDERICK S. CARNEY
Perkins School of Theology
Southern Methodist University

Althusius' Grand Design for a Federal Commonwealth

The road to modern democracy began with the Protestant Reformation in the sixteenth century, particularly among those exponents of
Reformed Protestantism who developed a theology and politics that set
the Western world back on the road to popular self-government,
emphasizing liberty and equality.[1] While the original founders and
spokesmen for Reformed Protestantism did much political writing,
their writing was often either theological or polemical in character.
Only at the end of the first century of the Reformation did a political
philosopher emerge out of the Reformed tradition to build a systematic
political philosophy out of the Reformed experience by synthesizing
the political experience of the Holy Roman Empire with the political
ideas of the covenant theology of Reformed Protestantism. That man,
Johannes Althusius, presented his political philosophy in a classic work,
Politica Methodice Digesta, first published in 1603, expanded in 1610, and
revised in final form in 1614.

Althusius' *Politica* was the first book to present a comprehensive theory of federal republicanism rooted in a covenantal view of
human society derived from, but not dependent on, a theological
system. It presented a theory of polity-building based on the polity as a
compound political association established by its citizens through their
primary associations on the basis of consent rather than a reified state
imposed by a ruler or an elite.

---

[1] See, for example, Robert Henry Murray, *The Political Consequences of the
Reformation: Studies in Sixteenth-Century Political Thought* (New York: Russell
and Russell, 1960) and Michael Walzer, *The Revolution of the Saints: A Study in
the Origins of Radical Politics* (Cambridge, Massachusetts: Harvard University
Press, 1982).

The first grand federalist design, as Althusius himself was careful to acknowledge, was that of the Bible, most particularly the Hebrew Scriptures or Old Testament.[2] For him, it also was the best—the ideal polity based on right principles. Biblical thought is federal (from the Latin *foedus,* covenant) from first to last—from God's covenant with Noah establishing the biblical equivalent of what philosophers were later to term natural law (Genesis, chapter 9) to the Jews' reaffirmation of the Sinai covenant under the leadership of Ezra and Nehemiah, thereby adopting the Torah as the constitution of their second commonwealth (Ezra, chapter 10; Nehemiah, chapter 8). The covenant motif is central to the biblical world view, the basis of all relationships, the mechanism for defining and allocating authority, and the foundation of the biblical political teaching.

The biblical grand design for humankind is federal in three ways. First, it is based upon a network of covenants beginning with those between God and human beings, which weave the web of human, especially political, relationships in a federal way—through pact, association, and consent. In the sixteenth century, this world view was recreated by the Reformed wing of Protestantism as the federal theology from which Althusius, the Huguenots, the Scottish covenanters, and the English and American Puritans developed political theories and principles of constitutional design.

---

[2] Two of the best available treatments of the federal dimension of the biblical world view are to be found in the works of Althusius and Buber. See, for example, Professor Carney's introduction and Martin Buber's *Kingship of God,* translated by Richard Scheimann (Atlantic Highlands, New Jersey: Humanities Press, 1990). This writer has treated the subject in *Covenant and Polity in Biblical Israel* (New Brunswick, New Jersey: Transaction Press, 1994). See also "Government in Biblical Israel," *Tradition* 13, No. 4–14, no. 1 (Spring–Summer, 1973) 105–24 and "Covenant as the Basis of the Jewish Political Tradition," *Jewish Journal of Sociology XX,* no. 1 (June, 1978) 5–37. The Israel-based Workshop in the Covenant Idea and the Jewish Political Tradition sponsored by the Jerusalem Center for Public Affairs and the Bar-Ilan University Department of Political Studies and its American-based counterpart, the Workshop on Covenant and Politics sponsored by the Center for the Study of Federalism, have been probing that issue among others. The principal work on the Israeli workshop is available in Daniel J. Elazar, ed., *Kinship and Consent: The Jewish Political Tradition and Its Contemporary Uses* (Lanham, Maryland: University Press of America and Center for the Study of Federalism, 1983). The principal work on the American workshop is available in Daniel J. Elazar and John Kincaid, eds., *Covenant, Polity, and Constitutionalism* (Lanham, Maryland: University Press of America and Center for the Study of Federalism, 1983).

Second, the classic biblical commonwealth was a fully articulated federation of tribes instituted and reaffirmed by covenant to function under a common constitution and laws. Any and all constitutional changes in the Israelite polity were introduced through covenanting. Even after the introduction of the monarchy, the federal element was maintained until most of the tribal structures were destroyed by external forces. The biblical vision of the restored commonwealth in the messianic era envisages the reconstitution of the tribal federation. Most of the American Puritans and many Americans of the Revolutionary era, among others, were inspired by the biblical polity to seek federal arrangements for their polities.

Third, the biblical vision for the "end of days"—the messianic era—sees not only a restoration of Israel's tribal system but what is, for all intents and purposes, a world confederation or league of nations, each preserving its own integrity while accepting a common Divine covenant and constitutional order. This order will establish appropriate covenantal relationships for the entire world. The grand designs of Emanuel Kant[3] and Martin Buber[4] draw heavily on that vision.

In some respects, all subsequent federalist grand designs until Pierre-Joseph Proudhoun's[5] in the mid-nineteenth century are derived from or somehow related to that scriptural precedent. This is true even though there were distinctions between Jewish and Christian, Catholic and Protestant, and religious and secular grand designs within the biblical tradition. Althusius' grand design is a comprehensive proposal for developing the ideal polity that will function in harmony with the principal forces in the universe. It is meant to provide a basis for organizing all aspects of the polity and its social order, based on Scriptural law and teachings. Moreover, it is comprehensively federal; that is to say, every aspect of the polity is to be informed by federal principles and arrangements in the manner of the network of biblical covenants. Also, it attempts to be realistic; it is grounded in a realistic understanding of human nature, its limits and possibilities in the manner

---

[3] *The Metaphysical Elements of Justice,* translated by John Ladd (New York: Bobbs-Merrill, 1965). See especially Part II on Public Law (75–141).

[4] Op cit., footnote 2.

[5] *The General Idea of Revolution in the Nineteenth Century,* translated by John Beverly Robinson (London: Freedom Press, 1923).

of what was to become known in the seventeenth century as the "new science of politics."[6]

Althusius' grand design is developed out of a series of building blocks or self-governing cells from the smallest, most intimate connections to the universal commonwealth, each of which is internally organized and linked to the others by some form of consensual relationship. Each is oriented toward some higher degree of human harmony to be attained in the fullness of time. Each grand design in some way combines the political and the redemptive dimension as well in the quest for the good commonwealth, if not the holy one. A federalist grand design is one in which the universe is understood in federalistic terms and the comprehensive polity is constructed accordingly.

Althusius must be considered a figure located at the intersection of the major trends of Western culture in the transition from medieval to modern times. One of the Protestant Christian grand designers, he straddled the Reformation and the opening of the modern epoch. Accordingly, he made an effort to synthesize and somewhat secularize Reformed Protestant thought on the ideal polity and to push it in concrete, practical directions.

In the struggle over the direction of European state-building in the seventeenth century, the Althusian view, which called for the building of states on federal principles—as compound political associations—lost out to the view of Jean Bodin[7] and the statists who called for the establishment of reified centralized states where all powers were lodged in a divinely ordained king at the top of the power pyramid or in a sovereign center. While Althusian thought had its exponents until the latter part of the century, after that it disappeared from the mainstream of political philosophy. It remained for the Americans to invent modern federalism on the basis of individualism and thus reintroduce the idea of the state as a political association rather than a reified entity, an artifact that is assumed to have an existence independent of the people who constitute it.

---

[6] See Daniel J. Elazar, ed., *Federalism as Grand Design: Political Philosophers and the Federal Principle* (Lanham, Maryland: University Press of America and Center for the Study of Federalism, 1987).

[7] *The Six Bookes of a Commonweale,* translated by Richard Knolles (London, 1606). Republished by Kenneth D. McRae (Cambridge, Massachusetts: Harvard University Press, 1962).

In the nineteenth century, one party of German thinkers seeking the unification of Germany on federal principles, epitomized by Otto von Gierke, rediscovered Althusius.[8] There, too, however, Germany's movement toward reified statehood and finally totalitarianism left Althusian ideas out in the cold. They remained peripheral even to students of modern federalism since modern federalism was so strongly connected with the principle of individualism that there was no interest in considering the Althusian effort to deal with the problems of family, occupation, and community along with individual rights in establishing political order. Only recently, as we have come to see the consequences of unrestrained individualism, both philosophically and practically, have political scientists begun to explore problems of liberty in relation to primordial groups—families, particularly, and ethnic communities. Here it was discovered that Althusius had much to offer contemporary society.

Martin Buber was perhaps the first to suggest how Althusian ideas could serve people in the twentieth century. In his *Paths in Utopia,* he based his political works in part on Althusius.[9] Carl Friedrich, the great academic exponent of German liberalism, revived academic interest in Althusius with his publication of the *Politica* in its Latin version with an extensive introduction.[10] More recently, various scholars such as Frederick S. Carney, Patrick Riley, and Thomas Hueglin have explored Althusius' ideas.[11] In his native Germany there has been a renewed interest in Althusian ideas as a foundation for German federal democracy.[12] In

---

[8] Otto von Gierke, *Political Theories of the Middle Ages,* translated with an Introduction by F. W. Maitland (Cambridge, England: The University Press, 1900); reprinted 1988.

[9] Martin Buber, *Paths in Utopia,* translated by R. F. C. Hull (New York: Collier Books, 1988). See also Buber's *Kingship of God* (note 2 above).

[10] Carl J. Friedrich, ed., *Politica Methodice Digesta of Johannes Althusius* (Cambridge, Massachusetts: Harvard University Press, 1932). Friedrich's introduction is a thorough expression of his understanding of Althusius' thought.

[11] Frederick Carney's translation and introduction and Thomas Hueglin, "Johannes Althusius: Medieval Constitutionalist or Modern Federalist?" *Publius* 9, No. 4 (1979): 9–41. For a different perspective on Althusius, see Patrick Riley, "Three Seventeenth-Century German Theorists of Federalism: Althusius, Hugo and Leibniz," *Publius* 6, No. 3 (1976): 7–41.

[12] See, for example, the work of the Althusius Society (Dieter Wyduckel, President), Juristische Fakultät, Technische Universität Dresden, Mommsenstr. 13, 01062 Dresden, Germany.

what was once Yugoslavia, Althusian influence was a powerful counter-weight to communism as the basis for introducing a measure of republican liberty.[13]

There is some dispute among scholars regarding the relationship between Althusius and federalism. Otto von Gierke, the first scholar to try to restore Althusius to his rightful place in the history of political thought, saw him as essentially a medievalist seeking to reconstruct medieval corporatism for a postmedieval and changing time. On the other hand, Carl Friedrich, the first important figure in the twentieth-century Althusian revival, viewed Althusius as being somewhere between medievalism and a precursor of modern federalism.

As a student of federalism in all its forms and a federalist, this writer would suggest that it is necessary to look to Althusius not only in historical perspective as a transitional figure from medieval corporatism to modern federalism, but as a source of ideas and models for a postmodern federalism. Premodern federalism, before the seventeenth century, had a strong tribal or corporatist foundation, one in which individuals were inevitably defined as members of permanent, multi-generational groups and whose rights and obligations derived entirely or principally from group membership. Modern federalism broke away from this model to emphasize polities built strictly or principally on the basis of individuals and their rights, allowing little or no space for recognition or legitimation of intergenerational groups.

A postmodern federalism must reckon with one of the basic principles of postmodern politics, namely that individuals are to be secured in their individual rights, yet groups are also to be recognized as real, legitimate, and requiring an appropriate status. Althusius is the first, and one of the few political philosophers who has attempted to provide for this synthesis. Needless to say, his late-medieval thought cannot be transposed whole into the postmodern epoch in the latter part of the twentieth century. However, in part because he wrote in a period of epochal transition from the late-medieval to the modern epoch, much of his system, its ideas, and even its terminology, may be adaptable to or at least form the basis for a postmodern federalism. This essay does not pretend to be able to make that adaption or synthesis. At most it will suggest some lines of thought

---

[13] Interview with Professor Jovan Djorvec, March 1973.

and investigation that can lead us in that direction. They may be summarized as follows:

1) The foundations of Althusius' political philosophy are covenantal through and through. *Pactum* (covenant) is the only basis for legitimate political organization. More than that, Althusius develops a covenantal-federal basis for his ideas that is comprehensive. Not only is the universal association constructed as a federation of communities, but politics as such is federal through and through, based as it is on union and communication (in the sense of sharing) as expressed in the idea that its members are symbiotes.

Althusius' dual emphasis on federalism as a relationship and on sharing as the basis of federal relationships has turned out to be a basic axiom of federalism. While there can be different forms of a federal relationship and the ideal of sharing can be realized in different ways, federalism remains essentially a relationship and sharing its guiding principle. The polity, then, is a symbiotic association constituted by symbiotes through communication.

Althusius' emphasis on the existence of both natural and civil associations in the private sphere reflects his emphasis on what we would call the natural right of association. The family is a natural association based on two relationships: conjugal and kinship. Since the nuclear family is a conjugal relationship, even it is covenantal. Naturally, the *collegium* or civil association in both its secular and ecclesiastical forms is covenantal.

Mixed and public associations are equally covenantal with the city as a covenantal republic formed of a union of *collegia*, the province a covenantal union of cities, and the commonwealth a covenantal union of provinces (this is so even though Althusius talks of the rights of the province as an arm of the commonwealth and not simply a union of cities). Covenants for Althusius are the ways in which symbiotes can initiate and maintain associations. They are products of both necessity and volition.

2) Althusius deals with the problem of sovereignty, then becoming the critical juridical problem for modern federalism, by vesting it in the people as a whole. On one hand this is what makes the good polity a *res publica* or commonwealth. On the other it also makes it possible to be a *consociatio consociatiorum*, a *universitas* composed of *collegia*, since the people can delegate the exercise of sover-

eign power to different bodies as they please (according to their sovereign will).

The problem of indivisible sovereignty raised by Jean Bodin became the rock upon which premodern confederation foundered.[14] The modern state system was based on the principle of indivisible sovereignty that in an age of increasingly monolithic and energetic states became a *sine qua non* for political existence. Thus the medieval world of states based on shared sovereignty had to give way. It was not until the American founders invented modern federalism that a practical solution to this problem was found enabling the development of modern federation as a form of government. Althusius provided the theoretical basis for dealing with the sovereignty question over 175 years earlier (no doubt unbeknownst to them) and gave it the necessary philosophic grounding.[15]

The revival of interest in Althusius in our time has accompanied the revival of possibilities of confederation. The European Union is the leading example of postmodern confederation; there are now three or four others as well. Although Althusius himself does not develop a theory of confederation per se, his particular kind of federal thinking in which he sees his universal association as constituted by comprehensive organic communities has clearly had something to contribute to an emerging postmodern theory of confederation.[16]

Althusius further understands political sovereignty as the constituent power. This is at once a narrower and more republican definition of sovereignty the plenary character of which is harnessed as the power to constitute government—a power that is vested in the organic body of the commonwealth, i.e., the people. Moreover, once the people act, their sovereignty is located in the *jus regni*, the fundamental right/law of the realm, namely the constitution.

This Althusian concept has important implications for contemporary international law that is grappling with the problem of how to mitigate the effects of the principle of absolute and undivided

---

[14] Op cit., footnote 7.

[15] See Daniel J. Elazar, *The American Constitutional Tradition* (Lincoln: University of Nebraska Press, 1988).

[16] See Daniel J. Elazar, "Europe and the Federal Experience," in *Federalism and the Way to Peace* (Kingston, Ontario, Canada: Institute of Intergovernmental Relations, Queens University, 1994), 53–71.

sovereignty inherited from modern jurisprudence in an increasingly interdependent world. Even where the principle is not challenged, the practical exercise of absolute sovereignty is no longer possible. Moreover, there are an increasing number of situations in which even the principle cannot be applied as it once was. One way out in such cases has been to vest sovereignty in the constitutional document itself, in what Althusius would refer to as the *jus regni*. Vesting sovereignty in a constitutional document is entirely consonant with a covenantal federalism.

3) Althusius serves as a bridge between the biblical foundations of Western civilization and modern political ideas and institutions. As such he translates the biblical political tradition into useful modern forms. In this he must be contrasted with Benedict Spinoza who a few years later in his *Theological Political Tractate*[17] makes the case for a new modern political science by presumably demonstrating that the biblical political tradition applied only to ancient Israel and ceased to be relevant once the Jews lost their state (unless and until the Jewish state was restored). Althusius confronts the same problems of modern politics without jettisoning or denying the biblical foundations. In part this rendered him less useful during the modern epoch when his unbending Calvinist emphasis on the necessary links among religion, state, and society, ran counter to the development of the modern secular state.

The Althusian version of the Calvinist model of the religiously homogeneous polity is not likely to be revived in the postmodern epoch. On the other hand, we are beginning to revive an old understanding that no civil society can exist without some basis in transcendent norms that obligate and bind the citizens and establish the necessary basis for trust and communication. The connection between the Decalogue and *jus* as both law and right, while hardly original to Althusius, may offer possibilities for renewed development in our times. Althusius adopts a conventional understanding of the two tables of the Decalogue of his time, namely that the first table addresses itself to piety and the second to justice, both of which are necessary foundations for civil society.

---

[17] *Tractatus Theologico-Politicus,* 2nd ed., translated by Samuel Shirley (New York: E. J. Brill, 1991).

4) Very important in this connection is Althusius' development of the concept of *jus regni*, which he derives explicitly from the
biblical *mishpat hamelukhah* (law of the kingdom), enunciated in I Samuel 10 and elsewhere, to serve as constitution of the universal association, at one and the same time establishing the constitution as a civil
rather than a religious document, yet one which has its source in or at
least is in harmony with divine and natural law. This is precisely the task
of the *mishpat hamelukhah* that constitutes a civil law separate from the
Torah but in harmony with it.[18] While contemporary political scientists
emphasize the secular character of modern constitutionalism, examination of most contemporary constitutions reveals that they reflect the
same combination of claims, including especially linkage to transcendent law—law that is more often divine than natural, yet containing
human artifacts that are civil in character.[19] While in recent years we
have made considerable advances in developing an understanding of
constitutional design, in doing so we have neglected this linkage and its
implications for right law that Althusius calls to our attention.[20]

5) While Althusius was clearly a product of his times and the
ideal state of his design is one that reflects the class and reference group
structure of seventeenth-century German society, it is significant that
he leaves open the possibility for democracy as we know it, including
female participation in public life and office holding, and a more
classless and egalitarian basis for participation generally. Lacking a
sufficient command of the Latin text to properly explore the issue, this
writer cannot say whether Althusius has an esoteric as well as an
exoteric teaching, but this suggests that there may be a hidden dimension to be explored in the *Politica* and Althusian thought generally. Nor
is the federal aspect insignificant here. Althusius suggests different forms

---

[18] On *mishpat hamelukhah*, see "King, Kingship: The Covenant of Monarchy," in
Encyclopedia Judaica, Vol. 10 (Jerusalem: Keter, 1972), 1019–20; also see Daniel
J. Elazar and Stuart A. Cohen, *The Jewish Polity: Jewish Political Organization from
Biblical Times to the Present* (Bloomington: Indiana University Press, 1985), Part
I, Epoch IV.

[19] See Albert P. Blaustein and Gilbert H. Flanz, *Constitutions of the Countries of the
World* (Dobbs Ferry, New York: Oceana Publications, 1971).

[20] See Vincent Ostrom, *The Political Theory of a Compound Republic: Designing the
American Experiment*, 2nd ed., rev. and enl. (Lincoln: University of Nebraska
Press, 1987); and Daniel J. Elazar and John Kincaid, *Covenant, Polity and
Constitutionalism* (note 2 above).

and extents of participation in the different arenas of government as one possible way to extend participation in public life to groups heretofore disenfranchised in the world that he knew.

A contemporary Althusian politics should address itself to the same possibilities: for example, direct democracy for the most local assemblies; somewhat indirect democracy for county institutions; and republican or representative government for what Althusius would have called provincial and we would call state land, or cantonal, institutions and for the universal association or general government.

6) Althusius recognizes the modern distinction between public and private realms, yet also preserves the connection between them. In this respect, he, like the moderns who were to follow him, breaks with classic notions of all-embracing *polis* to recognize the legitimacy of a sphere of private activity that is constitutional by right, thereby preventing totalitarianism. Yet he recognizes the connection between the simple and private associations of family and *collegium* and the mixed and public associations of city, province, and commonwealth. Indeed, the relationship between private and public spheres and associations is a major concern of his as it increasingly must be to those of us who seek to reckon with the realities of the postmodern epoch in which all of life is more closely interrelated than ever before and everything is tied into everything else in ways that make older forms of separation increasingly more difficult.

One of the advantages of the modern epoch was that it was possible to separate the public and private spheres more sharply because it was a period that fostered increased distance between them. This is no longer the case as the postmodern communications technology requires more Althusian communication; that is to say, as everything impinges upon everything else, more sharing is necessary.

7) Althusius' definition of politics as the effective ordering of communication (of things, services, and rights) offers us a starting point for understanding political phenomena that speaks to contemporary political science. This leads us to the second half of Althusian thought: that dealing with statesmanship, prudence, and administration. It would be possible to say of the second half of Althusian teaching that it is general to all of politics and not specific to federalism, except that this would do violence to the first half of Althusian teaching that sees all politics as federal politics.

We owe Professor Carney a great debt for providing the English-reading public with the opportunity to read Althusius' magnum opus in translation and not to have to rely upon assessments of the Latin text by others. When Althusius wrote the *Politica* in Latin, he undoubtedly did so to reach the widest possible educated audience, using the best tool of his times for doing so. Now Latin is no longer that tool—English is.

To read Althusius is to discover how important his ideas are for our times. Eclipsed for three centuries by the major thrust of the modern epoch toward the homogeneous nation-state built around the individual citizen, standing politically naked before the state machinery, Althusian ideas seem much more in place in the postmodern epoch, with its more modern political networks, its renewed recognition of primordial groups and political associations as part and parcel of contemporary political life, and its federalistic striving for both universalism and particularism, ecumene and community.

DANIEL J. ELAZAR
Temple and
Bar-Ilan Universities

Althusius' Literary Sources Referred to in This Translation

Although Althusius' sources were entirely in Latin, this list whenever possible directs the reader not only to an English translation but also to editions in French and German. In addition, proper names for the most part have been supplied in an appropriate vernacular language.

Many of the items of this list have been personally examined through the graciousness of a number of American libraries; the standard bibliographic catalogues and reference works have been consulted for others; and great care has been taken to make this list as accurate as possible. Nevertheless, the bibliographic confusion and occasional obscurity that surround some of these books make it all too probable that errors will be found. Moreover, it is difficult in certain instances to determine which of several editions of a book should be listed since Althusius never identified which edition he was using. This difficulty burdens the conscience all the more when it is realized that later editions of the same book in the sixteenth and seventeenth centuries were often successively supplemented and even given different internal organization, and that therefore a particular edition, unless personally examined to ascertain whether it answers to Althusius' citations of it, may not be the right one for this list. Presumably a translator of materials of this sort must learn to live with this burden of conscience if he is to avoid a lifetime of labor dedicated largely to minutiae.

This list contains all of Althusius' literary sources referred to in this translation. For a listing of the sources contained in the entire Latin work, see the index in Latin that Carl J. Friedrich provided for his 1932 edition of the *Politica methodice digesta*, an index to which this list is also indebted.

Andrea Alciati (1492–1550). *Commentaria* (Code), in *Omnia opera*. Basle, 1546.

Alexander ab Alexandro (1461–1523). *Genialium dierum libri sex*. With a commentary by André Tiraqueau. Lyon, 1586.

Johannes Althusius (1557?–1638). *Civilis conversationis libri duo*. Edited by Philip Althusius. Hanau, 1601.

————. *Dicaeologicae libri tres*. Frankfurt, 1617. Photographically reproduced 1967.

Scipio Ammirato (1531–1601). *Dissertationes politicae sive discursus in C. Cornelium Tacitum*. Frankfurt, 1612.

Thomas Aquinas (1224?–1274). *On Princely Government*, in *Aquinas: Selected Political Writings*. Edited by A. P. d'Entreves. Oxford, 1948. (*De regimine principum et rusticorum ad regem Cypri libri IV*. Paris, 1509.)

Benedict Aretius (1505–1574). *Problemata theologica continentia praecipuos nostrae religionis locos*. Lausanne, 1573.

Aristotle (384–322 B.C.). *Ethics*.

————. *Politics*.

Henning Arnisaeus (1580–1636). *De jure majestatis libri tres*. Frankfurt, 1610.

Augustine (354–430). *The City of God*.

William Barclay (1546–1608). *The Kingdom and the Regal Power*. Translated by George A. Moore. Chevy Chase, Maryland, 1954. (*De regno et regali potestate adversus Buchananum, Brutum, Boucherium, et reliquos monarchomachos libri sex*. Paris, 1600.)

[Nicolas Barnaud (16th c.)]. *Dialogi ab Philadelpho cosmopolita in Gallorum et caeterarum nationum*. Edinburgh [Geneva], 1574.

Bartolus of Sassoferrato (1314–1357). *Commentarii* (Digest and Code), in *Opera*. Five volumes. Basle, 1588–1589.

————. *Tractatus de tyrannia et tyranno*, in *Consilia, quaestiones, et tractatus*. Basle, 1588. (Ephraim Emerton has translated selected passages from this treatise in his book *Humanism and Tyranny: Studies in the Italian Trecento*. Cambridge, Massachusetts, 1925.)

Giovanni Beccaria. *Refutatio cujusdam libelli sine autore, cui titulus est De jure magistratuum in subditos et officio subditorum in magistratus*. 1590.

Philip Beroald (1452–1504). *De optimo statu*. Paris, 1500.

[Theodore Beza (1519–1605)]. *Concerning the Rights of Rulers Over Their Subjects and the Duty of Subjects Towards Their Rulers*. Translated by Henri-Louis Gonin. Capetown, 1956. (*De jure magistratuum in subditos et officio subditorum erga magistratus.* 1576.) Also available in a modern Latin edition by Klaus Sturm (Neukirchen-Vluyn, 1965); in *Calvinistische Monarch-omachen*, German translation by Hans Klingelhöfer, edited by Jürgen Dennert (Klassiker der Politik, Vol. 8, Cologne and Opladen, 1968); and in another German translation by Werner Klingenheben (Zurich, 1971).

Theodore Beza (1519–1605). *Tractatio de divortiis et repudiis.* Geneva, 1569.

Henry Bocer (16th c.). *De jure pugnae, hoc est belli et duelli tractatus.* Tübingen, 1591.

Jean Bodin (1530–1596). *The Six Bookes of a Commonweale.* Translated by Richard Knolles. London, 1606. Republished, with editorial notes and an introduction, by Kenneth D. McRae. Cambridge, Massachusetts, 1962 (*De republica libri sex.* Lyon, 1586.) Also available in a German translation by Bernd Wimmer, edited by Peter Cornelius Mayer-Tasch (2 vols., Munich, 1981–86).

———. *Method for the Easy Comprehension of History.* Translated by Beatrice Reynolds. New York, 1945. (*Methodus ad facilem historiarum cognitionem.* Paris, 1566.)

Nicholas Boerius (Boyer, 1469–1539). *Decisiones Burdegalenses.* Lyon, 1566.

Jacob Bornitius (Bornitz, late 16th and early 17th c.). *De majestate politica et summo imperio eiusque functionibus.* Leipzig, 1610.

Egidio Bossi (1487–1546). *De principe et ejus privilegiis,* in *Tractatus varii.* Edited by Francis Bossi. Lyon, 1562.

Giovanni Botero (1543 or 1544–1617). *A Treatise Concerning the Causes of the Magnificencie and Greatnes of Cities.* Translated by Robert Peterson. London, 1606. Republished as *The Greatness of Cities,* together with the Waley translation of *The Reason of State.* New Haven, 1956. (*Tractatus . . . de origine urbium, earum excellentia et agendi ratione libris tres.* Ursel, 1602.)

———. *Practical Politics.* Translated by George A. Moore, Chevy Chase, Maryland, 1949. Another translation entitled *The Reason of State* has been made by P. J. and D. P. Waley. Published together with *The Greatness of Cities.* New Haven, 1956. (*Tractatus . . . de illustrium statu et politia.* Ursel, 1602. This work, which had many titles in Latin, is referred to by Althusius sometimes as *De politia constituenda,* and other times as *De politia bene instituenda.*)

Junius Brutus [Philip DuPlessis-Mornay? (1549–1623)]. *Defence of Liberty Against Tyrants.* Translated by William Walker. London, 1689. Republished with historical introduction by Harold J. Laski. London, 1924. Photographically reproduced. London, 1963. (*Vindiciae contra tyrannos.* Edinburgh [Basle?], 1579.) Also available in *Calvinistische Monarchomachen,* German translation by Hans Klingelhöfer, edited by Jürgen Dennert (Klassiker der Politik, Vol. 8, Cologne and Opladen, 1968); and as *Vindiciae, Contra*

Tyrannos, edited and translated into English by George Garnett (Cambridge, England, 1994).

Martin Bucer (1491–1551). *De regno Christi Jesu servatoris nostri libri II*. Basle, 1557.

George Buchanan (1506–1582). *The Rights of the Crown in Scotland*. Translated by Robert MacFarlan. Edinburgh, 1843. (*De jure regni apud Scotos dialogus*. Edinburgh, 1579.)

William Budé (1467–1540). *Commentarii* (Digest and Code), in *Opera*. Three volumes. Basle, 1557.

Franz Burckhard (Burghardus, Andreas Erstenberger, d. 1584). *De Autonomia*. 1586.

Vincent Cabot (1550?–1621). *Variarum juris publici et privati disputationum libri duo*. Orleans, 1598.

Julius Caesar (100–44 B.C.). *The Gallic War*.

John Calvin (1509–1564). "Draft Ecclesiastical Ordinances," in *Calvin: Theological Treatises*. Translated with an introduction by J. K. S. Reid. Philadelphia, 1954. (*Ordinationes ecclesiae Genevensis*. Geneva, 1541.)

———. *Institutes of the Christian Religion*. Edited by John T. McNeill and translated by Ford L. Battles. Philadelphia, 1960. (*Institutio christianae religionis*. Geneva, 1559.)

Philip Camerarius (1537–1624). *Operae horarum subcisivarum sive meditationes historicae*. Frankfurt, 1602.

Cassiodorus (468–ca. 555). *Variarum libri XII*.

Otto Cassman (d. 1607). *Doctrinae et vitae politicae methodicum et breve systema*. Frankfurt, 1603.

Vincent Castellani (d. 1594). *De officio regis liber IV*. Marburg, 1594.

Paul Castro (Castrensis, d. 1441). *Commentaria super codicem, digestum vetus et novum et infortiatum*. Lyon, 1527.

René Choppin (1537–1606). *De domanio Franciae libri tres*. Paris, 1588. (Cited by Althusius as *De domanio regis*.)

Cicero (106–43 B.C.). *Duties*.

———. *Laws*.

———. *The Orator*.

———. *The Republic*.

Hippolytus a Collibus (1561–1612). *Incrementa urbium sive de caussis magnitudinis urbium liber unus*. Hanau, 1600.

———. *Princeps*. Hanua, 1595.

Caspar Contarini (1483–1542). *De magistratibus et republica Venetorum libri V.* Paris, 1543.

Diego Covarruvias y Leyva (1512–1577). *Regulae peccatum, de regulis juris, libri sex.* Salamanca, 1554.

―――――. *Quaestionum practicarum earumque resolutionum amplissimarum liber unus.* 1556.

―――――. *Variarum ex jure pontificio, regio, et caesareo resolutionum libri tres.* Salamanca, 1552.

Aymon Cravetta (1504–1569). *Consiliorum sive responsorum* [*partes VI*]. Frankfurt on the Main, 1611.

Martin Cromerus (Krantz, 1512–1589). *Polonia sive de situ, populis, moribus, majestatibus, et republica regni Polonici libri duo.* Cologne, 1578.

Jacques Cujas (1522–1590). *Commentarii ad tres postremos libros codicis.* Lyon, 1562.

―――――. *Observationum et emendationum libri XVII.* Cologne, 1578.

Lambert Daneau (1530–1596). *Politices christianae libri VII.* Paris [Geneva], 1596.

Tiberius Decianus (1508–1581). *Tractatus criminalis . . . utramque continens censuram.* Venice, 1590.

Charles Dumoulin (Molinaeus, 1500–1566). *Commentarii in consuetudines Parisienses.* Paris, 1576.

Ubbo Emmius (1547–1626). *De agro Frisiae . . . deque urbe Groningae in agro eodem et de jure utriusque.* Groningen, 1605.

―――――. *Historia Nostri Temporis, 1592–1608.* German translation by Eric von Reeken. Frankfurt am Main, 1986.

―――――. *Rerum Frisicarum Historiae Libri 60.* German translation by Eric von Reeken. Frankfurt am Main, 1981–82, 6 vols.

Eusebius of Caesarea (ca. 260–340 ca.) *The Life of Constantine.*

Prospero Farinacci (1554–1613). *Praxis et theoricae criminalis.* Frankfurt, 1610. (*De crimine laesae majestatis*, to which Althusius refers, is Part I of this work.)

Jean Froissart (1337–1410). *Chronicles of England, France, Spain and Adjoining Countries.* Translated by Thomas Johnes. London, 1803–1805. Reprinted with introductory essay by John Lord. New York, 1880. (The Latin editions vary so greatly in the arrangement of Froissart's material and the division of it into chapters that it would be hazardous to cite an edition unless one knew unquestionably that it was the one used by Althusius.)

Andreas Gail (1525–1585). *De pace publica et proscriptis sive bannius imperii liber duo.* Cologne, 1585. (These and the next two items were printed to be bound together in one volume.)

―――. *De pignorationibus liber singularis.* Cologne, 1585.

―――. *Practicarum observationum tam ad processum judiciarum . . . quam causarum decisiones pertinentium libri duo.* Cologne, 1585.

Alberico Gentili (1552–1608). *Tres regales disputationes, id est de potestate regis absoluta.* London, 1605.

―――. *De jure belli libri tres.* Translated by John C. Rolfe. Oxford, 1933. (*De jure belli libri tres.* Hanau, 1598.)

Innocent Gentillet (d. 1595?). *A Discourse upon the meanes of wel governing and maintaining in good peace a kingdome or other principalitie . . . against Nicholas Machiavell.* Translated by Simon Patericke. London, 1602. (*Commentariorum de regno aut quovis principatu recte . . . administrando libri tres . . . adversus Nicolaum Machiavellum.* Ursel, 1599.) Also available in a French edition by C. Edward Rathé (Geneva, 1968).

Jerome Gigas (d. 1560). *Tractatus de crimine laesae majestatis.* Lyon, 1557.

Petrus Gregorius (Pierre Grégoire) (Tholosanus, 1540–1617). *De republica libri XXVI.* Pont-à-Mousson, 1596.

―――. *Syntagma juris universi atque legum pene omnium gentium et rerum publicarum praecipuarum in tres partes digestum.* Lyon, 1582.

Lodovico Guicciardini (1521–1589). *Omnium Belgii sive inferioris Germaniae regionum descriptio.* Amsterdam, 1613.

Peter Heige (1558–1599). *Quaestiones juris tam civiles quam Saxoni.* Leipzig, 1601.

Philip Hoenonius (Hoen, 1576–1649). *Disputationum politicarum liber unus.* Third edition, Herborn, 1615.

Philip Honorius (Giulio Belli, 1550?–1590?). *Thesauri politici libri tres.* Printed both in Italian and in Latin. Frankfurt, 1610.

Francis Hotman (1524–1590). *Disputatio de controversia successionis regiae inter patruum et nepotem, atque in universum de jure successionis regiae in regno Galliae.* Frankfurt, 1585. (Is this the work Althusius refers to as *De antiquo jure regni Gallici?*)

―――. *Francogallia.* English translation [by Robert Viscount Molesworth], London, 1711. (*Franco-gallia.* Frankfurt, 1586.) Also available in a modern Latin edition by Ralph E. Giesey, translation by John H. M. Salmon (Cambridge, 1972); and in *Calvinistische Monarchomachen*, German translation by Hans Klingelhöfer, edited by Jürgen Dennert (Klassiker der Politik, Vol. 8, Cologne and Opladen, 1968). (Chapter citations by Althusius are not applicable to the shorter first edition of [Geneva], 1573, and other editions prior to 1586, when six new chapters were added. Nor, for the same reason, are they applicable to the 1711, 1968, and 1972 editions.)

Franciscus Junius (François DuJon the Elder, 1545–1602). *Commentarius*, in *Opera theologica*. 2 vols. Geneva, 1607.

————. *Ecclesiastici sive de natura et administrationibus ecclesiae Dei.* Frankfurt, 1581.

————. *De politicae Mosis observatione.* Leiden, 1593.

Melchior Junius (1545–1602). *Politicarum quaestionum centum ac tredecim . . . in partes tres distinctarum.* Frankfurt, 1606.

Bartholomaeus Keckermann (1573–1609). *Systema disciplinae politicae.* Hanau, 1607.

Hermann Kirchner (d. 1620). *Respublica.* Marburg, 1609.

Niels Krag (Nicolaus Cragius, 1552?–1602). *De republica Lacedaemoniorum libri IV.* Geneva, 1593.

Conrad Lancellot (16th c.). *Templum omnium judicum, pontificae, caesareae, regiae, inferiorisque potestatis.* 1575.

Justus Lipsius (1547–1606). *Politicorum sive civilis doctrinae libri VI.* Leiden, 1570.

Nicolaus Losaeus (16th c.). *De jure universitatum tractatus.* Turin, 1601.

Lupold of Bebenburg (Egloffstein, 1280?–1363). *De jure regni et imperii tractatus*, in *De jurisdictione, auctoritate, et praeemientia imperiali, ac potestate ecclesiastica, deque juribus regni et imperii variorum authorum, qui ante haec tempora vixerint, scripta: collecta, et redacta in unum.* Edited by Simon Schardius. Basle, 1566.

Niccolò Machiavelli (1469–1527). *Discourses on the First Decade of Titus Livius.* Translated by N. H. Thomson. London, 1883. (*Disputationum de republica quas discursus nuncupavit libri III.* Ursel, 1599.)

Francis Marcus (16th c.). *Decisiones aureae in sacro Delphinatus senatu.* Venice, 1561.

Juan de Mariana (1535–1624). *The King and His Education.* Translated by George A. Moore. Chevy Chase, Maryland, 1948. (*De rege et regis institutione libri tres.* Toledo, 1599.) Also available in a Spanish translation: *La Dignidad Real y La Educatión del Rey* (Madrid, 1981).

Marsilius of Padua (d. 1343). *The Defender of the Peace.* Translated by Alan Gewirth. New York, 1956. (*Defensor pacis.* Frankfurt, 1592.)

Peter Martyr (Vermigli, 1500–1562). *A Commentary on the Book of Judges.* London, 1564. (*In librum judicum . . . commentarii.* Zurich, 1561.)

————. *The Common Places*. Translated by Anthony Marten. London, 1583. (*Loci communes*. London, 1576. Althusius refers to *De bello*, which is IV, 17 of the *Loci communes*, or IV, 16–18 if the chapters on the lawfulness of war for Christians and on the treatment of captives and spoils are added.)

————. *In duos libros Samuelis prophetae . . . commentarii*. Zurich, 1564.

Emmanuel Meteren (1535–1612). *A General History of Netherlands*. Translated by Edward Grimestone. London, 1609. (*Historia Belgiae*. Antwerp, 1600.)

Jacob Middendorf (1538–1611). *Imperatorum, regum, et principum, clarissimorumque vivorum quaestiones theologicae, juridicae, et politicae*. Cologne, 1603.

Sir Thomas More (1480–1535). *Utopia*. English, London, 1551. (Latin, Basle, 1518.)

Joachim Mynsinger (1514–1588). *Singularium observationum imperialis camerae centuriae VI*. Lyon 1608.

Marc Antony Natta (16th c.). *Consilia sive responsa*. Lyon, 1566.

Georg Obrecht (1547–1612). *Tractatus de necessaria defensione*. Strassburg, 1604. (Is this the work Althusius refers to as *De bello?*)

Hieronymus Osorius (1506–1580). *De regis institutione et disciplina libri VIII*. Cologne, 1574.

David Parry (1548–1622). *In dividam ad Romanos S. Pauli apostoli epistolam commentarius*. Heidelberg, 1613.

Francesco Patrizi (1413–1494). *De regno et regis institutione libri IX*. Strassburg, 1594.

Tobias Paurmeister (1553–1608). *De jurisdictione imperii Romani libri duo*. Hanua, 1608.

Lucas de Penna (14th c.). *Super tres libros codicis X videlicet XI et XII*. Paris, 1509.

Marc Antony Peregrinus (1530–1616). *De privilegiis et juribus fisci libri octo*. Venice, 1604.

Arius Pinellus (d. 1601). *De rescindenda venditione elaboratissimi commentarii* (Code IV, 44). Venice, 1570.

Johann Piscator (1546–1625). *Commentarii in omnes libros veteris testamenti*. Third edition. Herborn, 1646.

Plato (B.C. 427?–347). *The Republic*.

Pliny the Younger (61–113). *Panegyric on Trajan*.

Plutarch (46?–120?). "Sayings of Kings and Magistrates," in *Moralia*.

————. "On Monarchy, Democracy, and Oligarchy," in *Moralia*.

Polybius (B.C. 205?–123?). *Histories.*

Friedrich Pruckmann (1562–1630). *Tractatus de regalibus.* Wittenberg, 1592.

Paris de Puteo (Pozzo, d. 1493). *De syndicatu.* Lyon, 1533.

Henrik Rantzau (1526?–1598). *Commentarius bellicus.* Frankfurt, 1595.

Elias Reusner (1555–1612). *Stratagematographia sive thesaurus bellicus.* Frankfurt on the Main, 1609.

Peter Ribadeneira (1527–1611). *Religion and the Virtues of the Christian Prince Against Machiavelli.* Translated and abridged by George A. Moore. Chevy Chase, Maryland, 1949. (*Princeps christianus adversus N. Machiavellum caeterosque hujus temporis politicos.* Mainz, 1603.)

Gregory Richter (1560–1624). *Axiomata politica.* Görlitz, 1604.

William Rose [William Rainolds? (1544?–1594)]. *De justa reipublicae christianae in reges impios et haereticos auctoritate.* Paris, 1590.

Henry Rosenthal (late 16th c.). *Tractatus et synopsis totius juris feudalis.* (Referred to in the footnotes as *De feudis.*) Two volumes. Speyer, 1597 and 1600.

Johann Rosinus (Rossfield, 1551–1626). *Romanarum antiquitatum libri decem ex variis scriptoribus . . . collecti.* Basle, 1583.

Marius Salomonius (early 16th c.). *De principatu libri VII.* Rome, 1544.

Felino Sandeo (1444–1503). *Commentaria in quinque libros decretalium.* Turin, 1522.

Matthew Scholasticus. *De vero et christiano principe libri II.* 1601.

Socrates Scholasticus (5th c.). *Ecclesiastical History.*

Seneca (B.C. 3?–A.D. 65). *Benefits.*

———. *Clemency.*

———. *The Four Virtues.*

———. *Letters.*

Carlo Sigonio (1524–1585). *De antiquo jure Italiae libri tres.* Paris, 1573.

———. *De republica Hebraicorum libri VII.* Bologna, 1582.

Jacob Simanca (d. 1583). *De republica libri IX.* Valladolid, 1565.

Josias Simler (1530–1576). *De republica Helvetiorum libri duo.* Zurich, 1576.

Jean Sleidan (Phillipson, 1506–1556). *De statu religionis et reipublicae, Carolo V Caesare, commentarii.* Strassburg, 1555. Reprinted Osnabrück, 1968.

———. *Historiae Cominaei.* 1574.

Sir Thomas Smith (1513–1577). *De republica Anglorum: the Manner of Government or Policie of the Realm of England.* London 1583. Reprinted with preface by F. W. Maitland. London, 1906. (*De republica et administratione Anglorum.* Translated into Latin. London, 1610?)

Marianus Socinus (1401–1467). *Consilia.* Lyon, 1525.

George Sohn (1552?–1589). *Commentarius* (Psalms).

Matthew Stephani (1576–1646). *Tractatus de jurisdictione . . . tam seculares quam ecclesiastici in imperio Romano.* Frankfurt, 1611.

Henry de Suge (Hostiensis, d. 1271). *Summa aurea super titulis decretalium.* Basle, 1573. Photographically reproduced. Darmstadt, 1962.

Carlo Antonio Tesauro (Thesauro, d. 1586). *Decisiones sacri senatus Pedemontani.* Turin, 1602.

Jacob Thomingius (1518–1576). *Consilia.* Frankfurt, 1608–1609.

André Tiraqueau (1480–1558). *Commentarii de nobilitate et jure primogeniarum.* Lyon, 1573.

Nicolaus Tudeschi (Panormitanus, 1386–1445). *Commentaria . . . in I decretalium librum.* Venice, 1591–1592. (The material actually is in V.)

Baldus de Ubaldis (1327–1400). *Commentarii* (in digestum veterum, infortiatum, digestum novum). Venice, 1572–1576.

Zachary Ursinus (1534–1583). *Dispositiones.*

———. *Exercitationes theologicae,* in *Opera theologica.* Heidelberg, 1612.

Valerius Maximus (1st c.). *Nine Books of Memorable Deeds and Sayings.*

Roland a Valle (16th c.). *Consiliorum sive responsorum liber I–IV.* Venice, 1571–1576.

Fernando Vásquez (1512–1569). *Illustrium controversiarum aliarumque usu frequentium libri tres.* Salamanca, 1559.

Matthew Wesenbeck (1531–1586). *Consilia et responsa.* 1575–1577.

Eberartus a Weyhe (Waremund ab Erenberg, 1553–1633). *Verisimilia de regni subsidiis ac oneribus subditorum.* 1606. Frankfurt, 1624.

Jerome Zanchius (1516–1590). *Tractatus de redemptione,* in *Opera theologica.* 1605.

Ulrich Zasius (1461–1535). *Responsorum juris sive consiliorum liber I–II.* Basle, 1538–1539. *Opera omnia* of 1550–1551 photographically reproduced in 1964–65.

Laelius Zecchus (d. 1610). *De principe et principatus administratione.* Verona, 1601.

Wilhelm Zepper (1550–1607). *De politica ecclesiastica.* Herborn, 1595.

Francis Zoannet (16th c.) *De Romano imperio ac ejus jurisdictione liber in rubricam C. de militari testamento.* Ingolstadt, 1563. (Is this the work Althusius refers to as *De tripartitione defensionis?*)

Theodore Zwinger (1533–1588). *Theatrum vitae humanae.* Basle, 1565.

Politica

A Schema by Johannes Althusius

The subject matter of politics is association

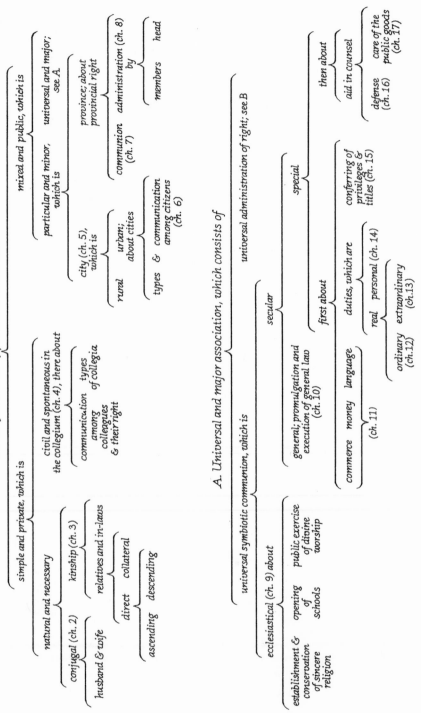

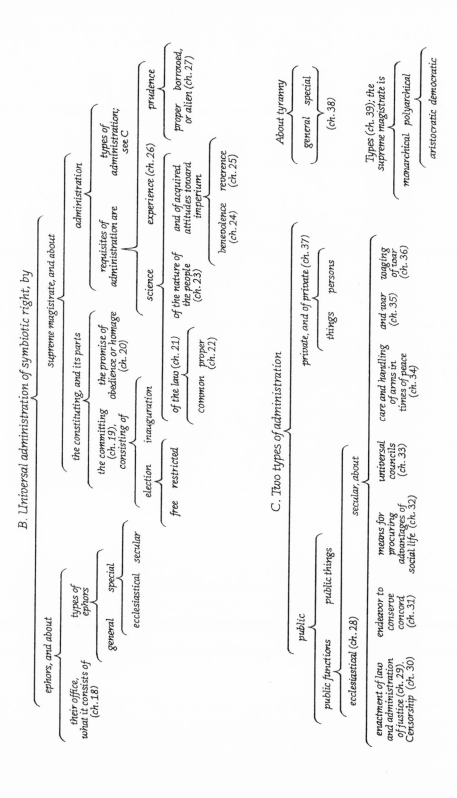

B. Universal administration of symbiotic right, by

- ephors, and about
  - their office, what it consists of (ch. 18)
  - types of ephors
    - general
    - special
      - ecclesiastical
      - secular
- supreme magistrate, and about
  - the constituting, and its parts
    - the committing (ch. 19), consisting of
      - election
        - free
        - restricted
      - inauguration
    - the promise of obedience or homage (ch. 20)
      - of the law (ch. 21)
        - common
        - proper (ch. 22)
  - administration
    - requisites of administration are
      - science
        - of the nature of the people (ch. 23)
      - experience (ch. 26)
        - and of acquired attitudes toward imperium
          - benevolence (ch. 24)
          - reverence (ch. 25)
      - prudence
    - types of administration; see C
      - proper, borrowed, or alien (ch. 27)

About tyranny
- general
- special (ch. 38)

Types (ch. 39); the supreme magistrate is
- monarchical
- polyarchical
  - aristocratic
  - democratic

C. Two types of administration

- public
  - public functions
    - ecclesiastical (ch. 28)
    - secular, about
      - enactment of law and administration of justice (ch. 29). Censorship (ch. 30)
      - endeavor to conserve concord (ch. 31)
      - means for procuring advantages of social life (ch. 32)
      - universal councils (ch. 33)
  - public things
    - care and handling of arms in times of peace (ch. 34)
    - and war (ch. 35)
    - waging of war (ch. 36)
- private, and of private (ch. 37)
  - things
  - persons

Note on the Liberty Fund Edition

For this edition of Professor Carney's translation of Althusius' Politica, *Liberty Fund has used* The Politics of Johannes Althusius, *published by Beacon Press in 1964 and by Eyre & Spottiswoode in 1965. Punctuation and spelling in this new edition have been Americanized. Althusius' original chapter and section numbers have been added, as well as a translation of the outline* (schema) *that appeared in the 1603 and 1614 editions. Professor Dieter Wyduckel of Technische Universität in Dresden, Germany, has appreciably expanded and updated the bibliographies, drawing in part from the bibliography appearing in* Politische Theorie des Johannes Althusius, *edited by Karl-Wilhelm Dahm, Werner Krawietz, and Dieter Wyduckel (Berlin: Duncker & Humblot, 1988). Professor Thomas O. Hueglin of Wilfred Laurier University in Waterloo, Canada, has provided helpful editorial assistance.*

JOHAN. ALTHUSII,
U. J. D.

POLITICA

Methodicè digesta atque exemplis sacris & profanis
illustrata;

Cui in fine adjuncta est

ORATIO PANEGYRICA,

De necessitate, utilitate & antiquitate scholarum.

Editio tertia, duabus prioribus mul-
to auctior.

Herbornæ Nassoviorum. 1614.

Preface to the First Edition (1603)

*Dedicated to the most distinguished and learned man
Martin Neurath, J.U.D., Siegensian advocate and trial
lawyer, my honorable relative and likewise to an excellent
and learned man Jacob Tieffenbach, Cambergian advocate,
my honorable relative*

I HAVE ATTEMPTED, most distinguished and learned men, honorable relatives and friends, to restate in an appropriate order the many political precepts that have been handed down in various writings, and to find out whether a methodical plan of instruction according to the precepts of logicians can be followed in these matters. This plan and goal was conceived and attempted by me that I might possibly offer a torch of intelligence, judgment, and memory to beginning students of political doctrine. And in order to perform this labor with greater effect and success, I have consulted those authors of this science who seem to me to excel others in political experience and practical understanding.

In addition to these writers I have also added some others, even though they do not handle the subject professionally. I have discovered that as each of these other teachers of politics was devoted to this or that discipline and profession, so he also brought from his own profession many elements that are improper and alien to political doctrine. Indeed, now philosophers, then jurists, and still again theologians handle political questions and axioms. I have observed that philosophers have proposed from ethics many moral virtues by which they would like the statesman and prince to be equipped and informed. Jurists have introduced from jurisprudence—a cognate area closely related to politics—many juridical questions about which they have spoken with eminence in legal science and by which they would instruct the statesman. Theologians who have been of this sort have

3

sprinkled teachings on Christian piety and charity throughout; indeed, I should even have said that they have prescribed a certain use of the Decalogue for the instruction of the statesman. I have considered that elements of this sort that are alien and useless in this art ought to be rejected and, by the dictate of justice, returned to the positions they properly hold in other sciences.

I have also noted some things that are missing in the political scientists. For they have omitted certain necessary matters that I think were carelessly overlooked by them; or else they considered these matters to belong to another science. I miss in these writers an appropriate method and order. This is what I especially seek to provide, and for the sake of which I have undertaken this entire labor. For I cannot describe how very beneficial this plan for clear teaching is to students, and even to teachers. Those who are acquainted with these matters, and have learned from experience about them, testify that this method is the fountain and nursery of memory and intelligence, and the moulder of accurate judgment.

The political precepts and examples that I set forth have been selected, for the most part, from these same political authors, and so acknowledged in proper places. And thus you have a summary of the things I reprove in a freely Socratic fashion in so many political thinkers, the things I reject, those I find inadequate, and those I approve. Whether I have done so rightly or not, you and other candid men may judge. Certainly I have attempted to flee from and avoid those things I reprove in others, and to add what I have found missing in them. If I have not completely attained this goal, nevertheless I have tried. And this I consider not reprehensible. Whatever was praiseworthy in any other place or time has been incorporated here. For each contributes in this matter, as in others, what he can. In the construction of the tabernacle in the ancient Jewish church everyone did not contribute the same or equal things. Some brought stones, some wood, some iron, some silver, some gold, some copper, some precious jewels, some cotton cloth, some purple garments, some hides, and some goats' hair. This collection of gifts was dissimilar and very unequal. Yet even the least of these gifts should be praised. For which of them was not needed in the construction of the temple? If in political science something perchance new has been able to come forth by my efforts, however difficult this may be to accomplish in my opinion, this too I consider pleasing and welcome.

Here is the place to say something concerning two difficulties encountered in this enterprise. The first is that I have experienced difficulty in separating juridical matters from this science. For as close as the relationship is of ethics with theology, and of physics with medicine, so close—indeed I should say even closer—is the relationship of politics with jurisprudence. Where the moralist leaves off, there the theologian begins; where the physicist ends, the physician begins; and where the political scientist ceases, the jurist begins. For reasons of homogeneity, we must not leap readily across boundaries and limits, carrying from cognate arts what is only peripheral to our own. Prudence and an acute and penetrating judgment are indeed required to distinguish among similar things in these arts. It is necessary to keep constantly in view the natural and true goal and form of each art, and to attend most carefully to them, that we not exceed the limits justice lays down for each art and thereby reap another's harvest. We should make sure that we render to each science its due (*suum cuique*) and not claim for our own what is alien to it. How many juridical questions taken from the midst of jurisprudence do you find in the political writings of Bodin and Gregorius? What can the beginning student of politics, who is not trained in the science of politics, make of these questions, and how can he pass judgment upon them? I say the same about the theological and philosophical questions that others have added to politics.

How far one may proceed in political science is sufficiently indicated by its purpose. This is, in truth, that association, human society, and social life may be established and conserved for our good by useful, appropriate, and necessary means. Therefore, if there is some precept that does not contribute to this purpose, it should be rejected as heteronomous.

The purpose of jurisprudence is skillfully to derive and infer right (*jus*)[1] from fact (*factum*), and so to judge about the right and merit of fact in human life. Precepts that go astray from this goal, and indicate nothing about the right that arises from fact, are alien and irrelevant in this discipline. However, the facts about which right is affirmed can vary, and are selected from those that are proper to several other arts. For

---

[1] [The Latin word *jus* (pl. *jura*) as here employed by Althusius means both "right" and "law." For further information on this word, *see* page 18, footnote 5.]

this reason, the jurist obtains information, instruction, and knowledge about these facts not from jurisprudence, but from those who are skilled in these other arts. From this information he is then able to judge more correctly about the right and merit of a fact. So it is that many jurists write and teach about rights of sovereignty (*jura majestatis*),[2] even though these rights are so proper to politics that if they were taken away there would be almost nothing left to politics, or too little for it to exist. Now the political scientist properly teaches what are the sources of sovereignty (*capita majestatis*), and inquires and determines what may be essential for the constituting of a commonwealth. The jurist, on the other hand, properly treats of the right (*jus*)[3] that arises at certain times from these sources of sovereignty and the contract entered into between the people and the prince. Both, therefore, discuss rights of sovereignty: the political scientist concerning the fact of them, and the jurist concerning the right of them. If the political scientist were to discourse on the right and merit of these facts that are judged necessary, essential, and homogeneous to social life, he would have overstepped the clear boundaries of his art. If the jurist were to propound political precepts, namely, how an association is to be constituted, and once constituted then conserved, what kind of commonwealth is happier, what form of it is more lasting and subject to fewer perils and changes, and other such things, he would have taught what is professionally alien to him. Nevertheless, all arts in their use and practice are often united, indeed, I should have said always united.

I have assigned the rights of sovereignty and their sources, as I have said, to politics. But I have therein attributed them to the realm, or to the commonwealth and people. I know that in the common opinion of teachers they are to be described as belonging to the prince and supreme magistrate. Bodin clamors that these rights of sovereignty cannot be attributed to the realm or the people because they come to an end and pass away when they are communicated among subjects or the people. He says that these rights are proper and essential to the person of

---

[2] [Although this phrase is consistently translated hereafter as "rights of sovereignty," attention is called to the point that it often conveys the additional meaning of "laws of sovereignty" or sometimes of "powers of sovereignty."]

[3] [law.]

the supreme magistrate or prince to such a degree—and are connected so inseparably with him—that outside of his person they cease to exist, nor can they reside in any other person. I am not troubled by the clamors of Bodin, nor the voices of others who disagree with me, so long as there are reasons that agree with my judgment. Therefore, I maintain the exact opposite, namely, that these rights of sovereignty, as they are called, are proper to the realm to such a degree that they belong to it alone, and that they are the vital spirit, soul, heart, and life by which, when they are sound, the commonwealth lives, and without which the commonwealth crumbles and dies, and is to be considered unworthy of the name.

I concede that the prince or supreme magistrate is the steward, administrator, and overseer of these rights. But I maintain that their ownership and usufruct properly belong to the total realm or people. This is so to the extent that, even if the people should wish to renounce them, it could no more transfer or alienate them to another than could a man who has life give it to another. These rights have been established by the people, or the members of the realm and commonwealth. They have originated through the members, and they cannot exist except in them, nor be conserved except by them. Furthermore, their administration, which has been granted to a prince by a precarium or covenant, is returned on his death to the people, which because of its perpetual succession is called immortal. This administration is then entrusted by the people to another, who can aptly be one or more persons. But the ownership and usufruct of these rights have no other place to reside if they do not remain with the total people. For this reason, they do not by their nature become articles of commerce for one person. And neither the prince nor anyone else can possess them, so much so that if a prince should wish to exercise ownership of them acquired by some title or other, he would thereby cease to be a prince and would become a private citizen and tyrant. This is evident from those matters that I have stated in Chapters VI and following, especially in Chapters XIV, XV, and XIX.[4] The celebrated Covarruvias agrees with me, as do certain others whom I have acknowledged in Chapters XIV and XV.

---

[4] [In the 1614 edition, which has been used in this translation, Chapter VI becomes IX, XIV and XV become XVIII and XIX respectively, and XIX becomes XXIV.]

These problems have been the reasons for my first difficulty. The other difficulty is no less severe, namely, that I have been forced at times to set forth theorems about contingent circumstances that are nevertheless alien to this art. For I have described the character, attitude, customs, and natural disposition of the people, prince, courtiers, and other subjects as they exist in various forms in political life. All these theorems are of this sort. And I realize that they occur in great numbers (ἐπὶ τὸ πλεῖρον), and are developed in relation to contingencies (κατὰ συμβεβηκός). For there are peoples, and one often encounters them, who change their character and customs. There are princes who, because of education, training, the goodness of nature, and the grace of God, do not copy the temper and usage that might and rule customarily bring forth in some persons. There are well-constituted princely courts. There are good and pious courtiers, and there are bad ones. But there are more of the latter than the former, as even David in his time complained in Psalms 52, 53, and 59. The same can be said about the political remedies, advice, and precepts adapted to place, time, and person that I discuss in various places. But who can propose general precepts that are necessarily and mutually true about matters so various and unequivalent? The statesman, however, should be well acquainted with these matters. And political science should not omit matters that the governor of a commonwealth should know, and by which he is shaped and rendered fit for governing.

I have already considerably digressed from my purpose of providing reasons for the labor I have undertaken. It is a pleasure to dedicate to you, most distinguished and learned relatives in the Lord, these political meditations of mine. By this means a testimony may stand forth of our friendship and affinity. If my desire is for very penetrating and fair judges of the things I discuss in this book, I rightly choose the two of you for this responsibility. You excel in erudition, excellent doctrine and precise judgment, not to mention other eminent talents with which God has equipped you. You are involved with the affairs of a commonwealth, and every day handle most of the matters I discuss. You are therefore best able to pass judgment on these matters. You can also influence me more freely and effectively than can others, and are able to recall me to the true way if I have departed from right reason in political precepts and their applications, or in the manner of arranging and ordering them.

May the supremely good and great God grant that while we dwell in this social life by his kindness, we may show ourselves pleasing to him and beneficial to our neighbor. Farewell to you, and to my relatives and friends.

Most devotedly yours,
Johannes Althusius

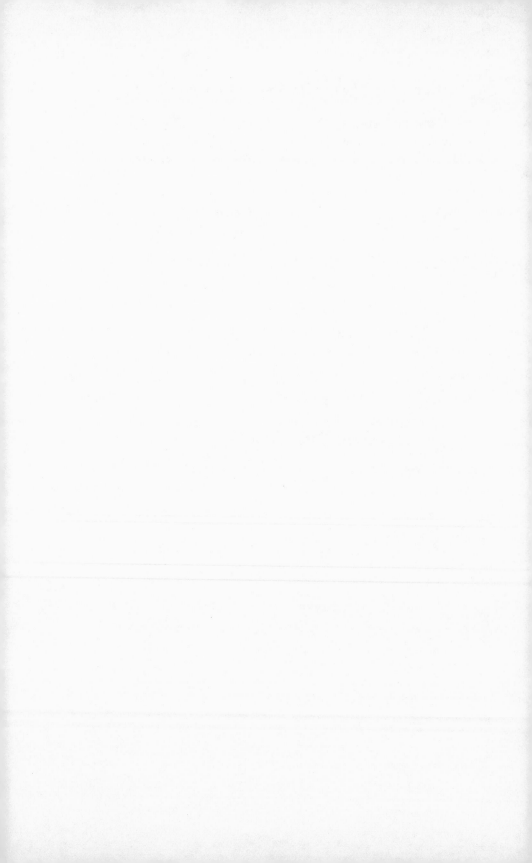

Preface to the Third Edition (1614)

*Dedicated to the illustrious leaders of
the estates of Frisia between the Zuider Zee and the
North Sea most worthy lords*

SINCE I UNDERSTAND, illustrious leaders, that my former political treatise has been read by many persons, and all copies have been sold out, I have brought forth another edition.[1] By re-examining the earlier work, and recalling it to the forge, I have intended to perform a worthwhile service. This has been done during the odd hours permitted me between responsibilities to the Commonwealth.[2]

I call to your attention that these second meditations have developed into a new political work that differs from the earlier treatise in form, method, and many other respects. In this work I have returned all merely theological, juridical, and philosophical elements to their proper places, and have retained only those that seemed to me to be essential and homogeneous to this science and discipline. And I have included among other things herein, all in their proper places, the precepts of the Decalogue and the rights of sovereignty, about which there is a deep silence among some other political scientists. The precepts of the Decalogue are included to the extent that they infuse a vital spirit into the association and symbiotic life that we teach, that they carry a torch before the social life that we seek, and that they prescribe and constitute a way, rule, guiding star, and boundary for human society. If anyone would take them out of politics, he would destroy it;

---

[1] [This preface was prepared originally for the second edition (1610) and retained in the third and later editions.]

[2] [City of Emden.]

indeed, he would destroy all symbiosis and social life among men. For what would human life be without the piety of the first table of the Decalogue, and without the justice of the second? What would a commonwealth be without communion and communication of things useful and necessary to human life? By means of these precepts, charity becomes effective in various good works.

He who takes the rights of sovereignty away from politics destroys the universal association.[3] For what other bond does it have than these alone? They constitute it, and they conserve it. If they are taken away, this body, which is composed of various symbiotic associations, is dissolved and ceases to be what it was. For what would the rector, prince, administrator, and governor of a commonwealth be without the necessary power, without the practice and exercise of sovereignty?

By no means, however, do I appropriate those matters that are proper to theology or jurisprudence. The political scientist is concerned with the fact and sources of sovereignty. The jurist discusses the right that arises from them. The former interprets the fact, and the latter the right and merit of it. Since the jurist receives information, instruction, and knowledge about matters from those arts to which such matters belong, and about the right and merit of fact from his own science, it is not surprising that he receives knowledge of some matters from political science. Therefore insofar as the substance of sovereignty or of the Decalogue is theological, ethical or juridical, and accords with the purpose and form of those arts, so far do those arts claim as proper to themselves what they take for their use from the Decalogue and the rights of sovereignty. And so far also I do not touch the subject matter of the Decalogue or of sovereignty, but rather consider it to be alien and heterogeneous to political science. I claim the Decalogue as proper to political science insofar as it breathes a vital spirit into symbiotic life, and gives form to it and conserves it, in which sense it is essential and homogeneous to political science and heterogeneous to other arts. So I have concluded that where the political scientist ceases, there the jurist begins, just as where the moralist stops the theologian begins, and

---

[3] [*consociatio universalis*: the commonwealth; an association inclusive of all other associations (families, collegia, cities, and provinces) within a determinate large area, and recognizing no superior to itself.]

where the physicist ends the physician begins. No one denies, however, that all arts are united in practice.

I have rightly selected examples for political science from excellent and praiseworthy polities, from the histories of human life, and from past events, and have employed them in that art that ought to be the guide of an upright political life, the moulder of all symbiosis, and the image of good social life. I more frequently use examples from sacred scripture because it has God or pious men as its author, and because I consider that no polity from the beginning of the world has been more wisely and perfectly constructed than the polity of the Jews. We err, I believe, whenever in similar circumstances we depart from it.

Moreover, I have attributed the rights of sovereignty, as they are called, not to the supreme magistrate, but to the commonwealth or universal association. Many jurists and political scientists assign them as proper only to the prince and supreme magistrate to the extent that if these rights are granted and communicated to the people or commonwealth, they thereby perish and are no more. A few others and I hold to the contrary, namely, that they are proper to the symbiotic body of the universal association to such an extent that they give it spirit, soul, and heart. And this body, as I have said, perishes if they are taken away from it. I recognize the prince as the administrator, overseer, and governor of these rights of sovereignty. But the owner and usufructuary of sovereignty is none other than the total people associated in one symbiotic body from many smaller associations. These rights of sovereignty are so proper to this association, in my judgment, that even if it wishes to renounce them, to transfer them to another, and to alienate them, it would by no means be able to do so, any more than a man is able to give the life he enjoys to another. For these rights of sovereignty constitute and conserve the universal association. And as they arise from the people, or the members of the commonwealth or realm, so they are not able to exist except in them, nor to be conserved except by them. Furthermore, their administration, which is granted by the people to a single mortal man—namely, to a prince or supreme magistrate— reverts when he dies or is discharged to the people, which is said to be immortal because its generations perpetually succeed one after the other. This administration of the rights of sovereignty is then entrusted by the people to another. And so it remains with the people through a thousand years, or as many years as the commonwealth endures. I discuss this point extensively in Chapters IX, XVIII, XIX, XXIV, and XXXVIII.

To demonstrate this point I am able to produce the excellent example of your own and the other provinces confederated with you. For in the war you undertook against the very powerful king of Spain you did not consider that the rights of sovereignty adhered so inseparably to him that they did not exist apart from him. Rather, when you took away the use and exercise of them from those who abused them, and recovered what was your own, you declared that these rights belong to the associated multitude and to the people of the individual provinces. You did this with such a courageous spirit, with such wisdom, fidelity, and constancy, that I cannot find other peoples to compare with your example.

And this among other reasons leads me to dedicate these political meditations to you. It even leads me to refer very often in them, when illustrations of political precepts are used, to examples chosen from your cities, constitutions, customs, and deeds, and from other confederated Belgic provinces. I am also moved to do this by the favor, warmth, and disposition that you, together with your confederates, have expressed often towards this Commonwealth that I have served for a number of years, and indeed, even toward me when not many years ago you saw fit to call me—with very fair provisions—to profess the juristic science at your illustrious and much celebrated academy at Franeker. Wherefore I think it only just that I acknowledge and openly proclaim your kindnesses in this preface and dedication, and publicly commend for the imitation of others those virtues through which, by the grace of God, you not only defended and conserved your commonwealth from tyranny and disaster, but also made it even more illustrious. For the success of your admirable deeds, and those of your allies, is so abundant that it overflows into neighboring countries, indeed, into all of Germany and into France. It is even experienced by the nations of the Indies and many other realms plagued by Spanish arms that have been sustained and defended by you and the other provinces united with you. Since the published annals and histories speak of these things to the eternal glory of your name, I choose to pass over them in silence rather than to mention only a small part of them.

May the supremely good and great God grant that while we live in this political life and this symbiosis by his grace, we may make ourselves useful and beneficial to men, and so attain the purpose that has been the concern of this discipline. With this prayer I close this preface.

> With reverent and humble respect and honor for your illustrious splendor
>
> *Johannes Althusius*

I

The General Elements of Politics

P OLITICS IS THE ART OF ASSOCIATING (*consociandi*) men
for the purpose of establishing, cultivating, and conserving social life among them. Whence it is called "symbiotics." The subject matter of politics is therefore association (*consociatio*), in which the symbiotes[1] pledge themselves each to the other, by explicit or tacit agreement, to mutual communication of whatever is useful and necessary for the harmonious exercise of social life. §1 §2

The end of political "symbiotic" man is holy, just, comfortable, and happy symbiosis,[2] a life lacking nothing either necessary or useful. Truly, in living this life no man is self-sufficient (αὐτάρκης), or adequately endowed by nature. For when he is born, destitute of all help, naked and defenseless, as if having lost all his goods in a shipwreck, he is cast forth into the hardships of this life, not able by his own efforts to reach a maternal breast, nor to endure the harshness of his condition, nor to move himself from the place where he was cast forth. By his weeping and tears, he can initiate nothing except the most miserable life, a very certain sign of pressing and immediate misfortune.[3] Bereft of all counsel and aid, for which nevertheless he is then in greatest need, he is unable to help himself without the intervention and assistance of another. Even if he is well nourished in body, he cannot show forth the light of reason. Nor in his adulthood is he able to obtain in and by himself those outward goods he needs for a comfortable and holy life, or §3 §4

---

[1] [*symbiotici*: those who live together.]

[2] [*symbiosis*: living together.]

[3] [This sentence and the previous one are taken without acknowledgment from Juan de Mariana, *The King and His Education*, I, 1.]

17

to provide by his own energies all the requirements of life. The energies and industry of many men are expended to procure and supply these things. Therefore, as long as he remains isolated and does not mingle in the society of men, he cannot live at all comfortably and well while lacking so many necessary and useful things. As an aid and remedy for this state of affairs is offered him in symbiotic life, he is led, and almost impelled, to embrace it if he wants to live comfortably and well, even if he merely wants to live. Therein he is called upon to exercise and perform those virtues that are necessarily inactive except in this symbiosis. And so he begins to think by what means such symbiosis, from which he expects so many useful and enjoyable things, can be instituted, cultivated, and conserved. Concerning these matters we shall, by God's grace, speak in the following pages.

§5   The word "polity" has three principal connotations, as noted by Plutarch.[4] First it indicates the communication of right (*jus*)[5] in the commonwealth, which the Apostle calls citizenship.[6] Then, it signifies the manner of administering and regulating the commonwealth. Finally, it notes the form and constitution of the commonwealth by which all actions of the citizens are guided. Aristotle understands by polity this last meaning.[7]

---

[4] "On Monarchy, Democracy, and Oligarchy," pars. 2 and 3. [Plutarch refers therein to polity as citizenship, as statecraft, and as forms of government.]

[5] [There is no precise English counterpart for the Latin word *jus* (pl. *jura*) as employed by Althusius. Often it means "right" (e.g., *jus coercendi*—right to coerce), sometimes "law" (e.g., *jus naturale*—natural law), and upon occasion even "authority," "responsibility," "power," "legal order," "structure," or "justice." It also functions in many instances as a Janus-headed word eluding the capacity of any single English term to express (e.g., *jura regni*—rights and laws of the realm). Notations in text and footnotes have therefore been made from time to time to assist the reader in observing its complex usage. The general rule employed throughout is to translate *jus* as "right" wherever possible, to indicate by notation all places where *jus* has been translated by some other term, and to insert occasional footnotes that provide variant translations in critical places where the full meaning of *jus* cannot be expressed by a single English word. In keeping with this rule, "right" will henceforth be the most frequent translation (usually without notation) of *jus*. (Unless noted, "law" will always be a translation of *lex*.) The reader should be on guard, however, not to attribute too readily to Althusius' understanding of "right" the connotation of a self-evident system of "public right" or the notion of "unalienable human rights."]

[6] Philippians 3:20.

[7] *Politics*, 1276[b] 17–1277[b] 4; 1293[a] 35–1294[b] 41.

The symbiotes are co-workers who, by the bond of an associ-   §6
ating and uniting agreement, communicate among themselves whatever is appropriate for a comfortable life of soul and body. In other
words, they are participants or partners in a common life.

This mutual communication,[8] or common enterprise, in-   §7
volves (1) things, (2) services, and (3) common rights (*jura*) by which
the numerous and various needs of each and every symbiote are
supplied, the self-sufficiency and mutuality of life and human society
are achieved, and social life is established and conserved. Whence
Cicero said, "a political community is a gathering of men associated by a
consensus as to the right and a sharing of what is useful."[9] By this
communication, advantages and responsibilities are assumed and maintained according to the nature of each particular association. (1) The   §8
communication of things (*res*) is the bringing of useful and necessary
goods to the social life by the symbiotes for the common advantage of
the symbiotes individually and collectively. (2) The community of   §9
services (*operae*) is the contributing by the symbiotes of their labors and
occupations for the sake of social life. (3) The communion of right (*jus*)   §10
is the process by which the symbiotes live and are ruled by just laws in a
common life among themselves.

This communion of right is called the law of association and
symbiosis (*lex consociationis et symbiosis*), or the symbiotic right (*jus
symbioticum*)[10], and consists especially of self-sufficiency (αὐταρκείᾳ),
good order (εὐνομίᾳ), and proper discipline (εὐταξίᾳ). It includes two
aspects, one functioning to direct and govern social life, the other
prescribing a plan and manner for communicating things and services
among the symbiotes.

The law of association in its first aspect is, in turn, either
common or proper. Common law (*lex communis*), which is unchanging,   §11

---

[8] [*communicatio*: a sharing, a making common. Althusius sometimes uses communion (*communio*) and community (κοινωνία) interchangeably with
communication.]

[9] *The Republic*, I, 25.

[10] [the fundamental law of living together; the demand that social life makes upon
human persons both by its nature and by their agreement. This demand has some
elements common to all associations, and others proper to various species of
association (family, collegium, city, province, and commonwealth). In this chapter it is usually called the law of association (*lex consociationis*), but in later chapters
symbiotic right (*jus symbioticum*) is the more common expression.]

indicates that in every association and type of symbiosis some persons are rulers (heads, overseers, prefects) or superiors, others are subjects or inferiors. For all government is held together by imperium and subjection; in fact, the human race started straightway from the beginning with imperium and subjection. God made Adam master and monarch of his wife, and of all creatures born or descendant from her.[11] Therefore all power and government is said to be from God.[12] And nothing, as Cicero affirms, "is as suited to the natural law (*jus naturae*)[13] and its requirements as imperium, without which neither household nor city nor nation nor the entire race of men can endure, nor the whole nature of things nor the world itself."[14] If the consensus and will of rulers and subjects is the same, how happy and blessed is their life! "Be subject to one another in fear of the Lord."[15]

§12

§13   The ruler, prefect, or chief directs and governs the functions of the social life for the utility of the subjects individually and collectively. He exercises his authority by administering, planning, appointing, teaching, forbidding, requiring, and diverting. Whence the ruler is called rector, director, governor, curator, and administrator. Petrus Gregorius says that just as the soul presides over the other members in the human body, directs and governs them according to the proper functions assigned to each member, and foresees and procures whatever useful and necessary things are due each member—some useful privately and at the same time to all or to the entire body, others useful publicly for the conservation of social life—so also it is necessary in civil society that one person rule the rest for the welfare and utility of both individuals and the whole group.[16] Therefore, as Augustine says, to rule, to govern, to preside is nothing other than to serve and care for the utility of others, as parents rule their children, and a man his wife.[17] Or,

---

[11] Genesis 1:26 f.; 3:16; Ecclesiasticus 17.

[12] Romans 13.

[13] [Althusius employs *jus naturae* (or *naturale*) interchangeably with *lex naturae* (or *naturalis*). Both expressions are henceforth translated as "natural law."]

[14] *Laws*, III, 1.

[15] Ephesians 5:21.

[16] *De republica*, I, 1, 18 f. [I, 1, 8 and 10 in the 1609 edition].

[17] *The City of God*, XIX, 15 [XIX, 14 in the Modern Library edition]. *See also* Seneca, *Letters*, num. 91 [num. 90 in the Loeb edition]; Marius Salomonius, *De principatu*, II; Giovanni Botero, *The Greatness of Cities*, I, 1.

as Thomas Aquinas says, "to govern is to lead what is governed to its appropriate end."[18] And so it pertains to the office of a governor not only to preserve something unharmed, but also to lead it to its end.[19] The rector and moderator so endeavors and proceeds that he leads the people by method, order, and discipline to that end in which all things are properly considered.

Government by superiors considers both the soul and the body of inferiors: the soul that it may be formed and imbued with doctrine and knowledge of things useful and necessary in human life, the body that it may be provided with nourishment and whatever else it needs. The first responsibility pertains to education, the second to sustentation and protection. Education centers on the instruction of inferiors in the true knowledge and worship of God, and in prescribed duties that ought to be performed towards one's neighbor; education also pertains to the correction of evil customs and errors. By the former, inferiors are imbued with a healthy knowledge of holy, just, and useful things; by the latter, they are held firm in duty. The responsibility for sustentation of the body is the process by which inferiors are carefully and diligently guided by superiors in matters pertaining to this life, and by which advantages for them are sought and disadvantages to them are avoided.[20] Protection is the legitimate defense against injuries and violence, the process by which the security of inferiors is maintained by superiors against any misfortune, violence, or injury directed against persons, reputations, or properties, and if already sustained, then avenged and compensated by lawful means.

§14

§15

§16

§17

The inferior, or subject, is one who carries on the business of the social life according to the will of his chief, or prefect, and arranges his life and actions submissively, provided his chief does not rule impiously or unjustly.

§18

Proper laws (*leges propriae*)[21] are those enactments by which

§19

---

[18] *On Princely Government*, I, 13 and 14.

[19] Or, as Hieronymus Osorius says, to rule is to direct toward the right end. *De regis institutione*, I.

[20] "Whoever presides, let him preside with care." Romans 12:8. "If anyone does not take responsibility for his own, and especially those of his own household, he has denied the faith, and is worse than an infidel." I Timothy 5:8.

[21] [as contrasted with common law (*lex communis*), discussed in the last four paragraphs.]

particular associations are ruled. They differ in each specie of association according as the nature of each requires.

§20   The laws by which the communication of things, occupations, services, and actions is accomplished[22] are those that distribute and assign advantages and responsibilities among the symbiotes according to

§21   the nature and necessities of each association. At times the communication regulated by these laws is more extensive, at other times more restricted, according as the nature of each association is seen to require, or as may be agreed upon and established among the members.

§22   ON THE BASIS OF THE FOREGOING considerations, I agree with Plutarch that a commonwealth is best and happiest when magistrates and citizens bring everything together for its welfare and advantage, and neither neglect nor despise anyone who can be helpful to the commonwealth.[23] The Apostle indeed advises us to seek and promote advantages for our neighbor, even to the point that we willingly give up our own right, by which we guard against misfortune, to obtain a great advantage for the other person.[24] For "we have not been born to ourselves, inasmuch as

§23   our country claims a share in our birth, and our friends a share."[25] The entire second table of the Decalogue pertains to this: "you shall love your neighbor as yourself"; "whatever you wish to be done to you do also to others," and conversely, "whatever you do not wish to be done to you do not do to others"; "live honorably, injure no one, and render to each his due."[26] Of what use to anyone is a hidden treasure, or a wise man who denies his services to the commonwealth?

§24   In light of these several truths, the question of which life is to be preferred can be answered. Is it the contemplative or the active? Is it the theoretical and philosophical life or the practical and political life? Clearly, man by nature is a gregarious animal born for cultivating society with other men, not by nature living alone as wild beasts do, nor

§25   wandering about as birds. And so misanthropic and stateless hermits, living without fixed hearth or home, are useful neither to themselves

---

[22] [the second aspect of the law of association.]

[23] "Sayings of Kings and Magistrates," [1st par.]

[24] Philippians 2:4–6; I Corinthians 10:24; 12:25 f.; Galatians 1:3, 5; 5:14; Romans 12:18, 20; 13:8, 10.

[25] Cicero, *Duties*, I, 7.

[26] Matthew 22:39; 7:12. [Shabbath 31ª; Digest I, 1, 10, 1.]

nor to others, and separated from others are surely miserable. For how can they promote the advantage of their neighbor unless they find their way into human society?[27] How can they perform works of love when they live outside human fellowship? How can the church be built and the remaining duties of the first table of the Decalogue be performed? Whence Keckermann rightly says that politics leads the final end of all other disciplines to the highest point, and thus builds public from private happiness.[28]

For this reason God willed to train and teach men not by angels, but by men.[29] For the same reason God distributed his gifts unevenly among men. He did not give all things to one person, but some to one and some to others, so that you have need for my gifts, and I for yours. And so was born, as it were, the need for communicating necessary and useful things, which communication was not possible except in social and political life. God therefore willed that each need the service and aid of others in order that friendship would bind all together, and no one would consider another to be valueless. For if each did not need the aid of others, what would society be? What would reverence and order be? What would reason and humanity be? Everyone therefore needs the experience and contributions of others, and no one lives to himself alone.

Thus the needs of body and soul, and the seeds of virtue implanted in our souls, drew dispersed men together into one place. These causes have built villages, established cities, founded academic institutions, and united by civil unity and society a diversity of farmers, craftsmen, laborers, builders, soldiers, merchants, learned and unlearned men and so many members of the same body. Consequently, while some persons provided for others, and some received from others what they themselves lacked, all came together into a certain public body that we call the commonwealth, and by mutual aid devoted themselves to the general good and welfare of this body. And that this was the true origin first of villages, and then of larger commonwealths embracing wide areas, is taught by the most ancient records of history and confirmed by daily experience. Opposed to this judgment is the life

§26

§27

§28

---

[27] *See* Ecclesiastes 4:5–8 and the *Commentarius* thereon of Franciscus Junius, in which are indicated the benefits of social life.

[28] Bartholomaeus Keckermann, *Systema disciplinae politicae.*

[29] John Calvin, *Institutes of the Christian Religion*, IV, 3, 1.

and teaching of recluses, monks, and hermits, who defend their error and heresy by an erroneous appeal to Luke 1:80; 10:41; Hebrews 11:38; I Kings 19:8. But scripture places this kind of life among its maledictions. Deuteronomy 28:64, 65; Psalms 107 and 144; Code X, 32, 26. Note also that a wandering and vagabond life was imposed upon Cain in punishment for his fratricide. Genesis 4:14. Contrary examples of pious men embracing active political life are to be found throughout sacred scripture.

§29   From what has been said, we further conclude that the efficient cause of political association is consent and agreement among the communicating citizens. The formal cause is indeed the association brought about by contributing and communicating one with the other, in which political men institute, cultivate, maintain, and conserve the fellowship of human life through decisions about those things useful

§30   and necessary to this social life. The final cause of politics is the enjoyment of a comfortable, useful, and happy life, and of the common welfare—that we may live with piety and honor a peaceful and quiet life, that while true piety toward God and justice among the citizens may prevail at home, defense against the enemy from abroad may be maintained, and that concord and peace may always and everywhere thrive. The final cause is also the conservation of a human society that aims at a life in which you can worship God quietly and without error.

§31   The material of politics is the aggregate of precepts for communicating those things, services, and right that we bring together, each fairly and properly according to his ability, for symbiosis and the common advantage of the social life.

§32   Moreover, Aristotle teaches that man by his nature is brought to this social life and mutual sharing.[30] For man is a more political animal than the bee or any other gregarious creature, and therefore by nature far more of a social animal than bees, ants, cranes, and such kind as feed and defend themselves in flocks. Since God himself endowed each being with a natural capacity to maintain itself and to resist whatever is contrary to it, so far as necessary to its welfare, and since dispersed men are not able to exercise this capacity, the instinct for living together and

§33   establishing civil society was given to them. Thus brought together and united, some men could aid others, many together could provide the

---

[30] *Politics*, 1252ᵃ 24–1253ᵃ 38.

necessities of life more easily than each alone, and all could live more safely from attack by wild beasts and enemies. It follows that no man is able to live well and happily to himself. Necessity therefore induces association; and the want of things necessary for life, which are acquired and communicated by the help and aid of one's associates, conserves it. For this reason it is evident that the commonwealth, or civil society, exists by nature, and that man is by nature a civil animal who strives eagerly for association. If, however, anyone wishes not to live in society, or needs nothing because of his own abundance, he is not considered a part of the commonwealth. He is therefore either a beast or a god, as Aristotle asserts.[31]

Furthermore the continuous governing and obedience in social life mentioned earlier are also agreeable to nature. For, as Petrus Gregorius adds, "to rule, to direct, to be subjected, to be ruled, to be governed" are natural actions proceeding from the law of nations (*jus gentium*). "Anything else would be considered no less monstrous than a body without a head, or a head without members of the body lawfully and suitably arranged, or even lacking them altogether. For it is especially useful to the individual member who cannot meet his own needs to be aided and upheld by another. The better member is said to be the one who meets his own needs, and is also able to help others. The greater the good he communicates with others, the better and more outstanding the member is. Then, this world has so great and so admirable a diversity [. . .] that unless it be held together by some order of subordination, and regulated by fixed laws of subjection and order, it would be destroyed in a short time by its own confusion. Nor can the diverse parts of it endure if each part seeks to perform its own function indifferently and heedlessly by itself. Power set over against equal power would bring all things to an end by continuous and irreconcilable discord, and would involve in its ruin things that do not belong to it, and that it does not know how to govern."[32] As long as each

§34

§35

---

[31] *Politics*, 1253ᵃ 31.

[32] Petrus Gregorius, *De republica*, XIX; I, 1, 7 and 16 f.; I, 3, 12 f. [In the 1609 edition the precise quotation is found in VI, 1, 1 f., although the other passages indicated by Althusius are also generally relevant to the discussion. Note, however, that Gregorius says that "to rule, to direct, to be subjected, to be ruled, to be governed are agreeable to the natural law (*jus naturae*), and are consistent with the divine law (*jus divinum*), the human law of nations (*jus gentium*), and civil law (*jus civile*). Anything else" etc.

part decides to live according to its own will, it may disregard the rule of discipline.[33] Finally, the conservation and duration of all things consist in

§36   this concord of order and subjection. "Just as from lyres of diverse tones, if properly tuned, a sweet sound and pleasant harmony arise when low, medium, and high notes are united, so also the social unity of rulers and subjects in the state produces a sweet and pleasant harmony out of the rich, the poor, the workers, the farmers, and other kinds of persons. If agreement is thus achieved in society, a praiseworthy, happy, most

§37   durable, and almost divine concord is produced. [. . .] But if all were truly equal, and each wished to rule others according to his own will, discord would easily arise, and by discord the dissolution of society. There would be no standard of virtue or merit, and it follows that equality itself would be the greatest inequality," as Petrus Gregorius rightly asserts.[34] Hence, when this harmony of rulers and subjects ceases, and there are no longer servants and leaders, such a situation is considered to be among the signs of divine wrath.

§38   I add to this that it is inborn to the more powerful and prudent to dominate and rule weaker men, just as it is also considered inborn for inferiors to submit. So in man the soul dominates the body, and the mind the appetites. So the male, because the more outstanding, rules

§39   the female, who as the weaker obeys. Thus, the pride and high spirits of man should be restrained by sure reins of reason, law, and imperium less he throw himself precipitously into ruin.

Also to be noted is that Althusius will have nothing to do, here or elsewhere, with Gregorius' often repeated division of the corporeal world into four elements (earth, water, air, and fire), and therefore omits them from the quotation rather than attributing the diversity of the world to them, as Gregorius does. Although these four elements recur throughout his *De republica*, Gregorius's best discussion of them is found in his legal work, *Syntagma juris universi*, I, 1–9.

Finally, the sentence immediately after this quotation is in large part borrowed, following Gregorius, from Cassiodorus, *Variarum*, 16.]

[33] The absence of a ruler is held to be the root of evils in Judges 17:6 and 21:25. The same is considered to be a punishment in Isaiah 3. [These Biblical passages are also cited in Gregorius, *De republica*, VI, 1, 3.]

[34] *Ibid.*, VI, 1, 5. [Gregorius acknowledges no source for his comparison of social with musical harmony, but the same comparison in almost identical words is found in Cicero, *The Republic*, II, 42, and Augustine, *The City of God*, II, 21. Earlier Plato had compared the harmony of the inward person with musical harmony in *The Republic*, IV, 443. In the sixteenth century Francis Hotman also employed this comparison, attributing it to Plato by way of Cicero. *See* his *Franco-gallia* (1573), 10 or (1586), 12.]

II-III

The Family

II   THUS FAR WE HAVE DISCUSSED the general elements of politics. We turn now to types of association or of symbiotic life. Every association is either simple and private,[1] or mixed and public.[2]   *§1*

      The simple and private association is a society and symbiosis initiated by a special covenant (*pactum*) among the members for the purpose of bringing together and holding in common a particular interest (*quid peculiare*). This is done according to their agreement and way of life, that is, according to what is necessary and useful for organized private symbiotic life. Such an association can rightly be called primary, and all others derivative from it. For without this primary association others are able neither to arise nor to endure.   *§2*

      The efficient causes of this simple and private association and symbiosis are individual men covenanting among themselves to communicate whatever is necessary and useful for organizing and living in private life. Whence arises the particular and private union and society among the covenanters, whose bond (*vinculum*) is trust granted and accepted in their communication of mutual aid, counsel, and right (*jus*).[3] And such an association, because it is smaller than a public and universal one, also requires less extended communication, support, and assistance.   *§3*

      The members of the private association are individuals harmoniously united under one head and spirit, as members of the same   *§4*

---

[1] [family and collegium.]

[2] [city, province, and commonwealth.]

[3] [just structure or order.]

27

body. For, as Petrus Gregorius says, "just as there is one end for the sake of which nature made the thumb, another the hand or foot, still another the whole man; so there is one end to which nature directs the individual man, another the family, and another the city and realm. But that end is most to be esteemed for which nature made the whole man. Accordingly, it is not to be thought that since there is a definite end for each type of assemblage there is none for the whole, nor that since there is order in the parts of human life there is only confusion in the more inclusive kind of life, nor lastly that since the parts are united among themselves by reason of their intending one end the whole itself is disunited."[4]

§5   The particular interest that is communicated among the symbiotes by a special covenant of this kind, and through which they are united as by a certain bond, consists in symbiotic right (*jus symbioticum*),[5] together with structure and good order for communicating it

§6   with consensus, mutual service, and common advantage. Symbiotic right is what the private symbiote fulfills on behalf of his fellow symbiote in the private association, which varies according to the

§12   nature of the association. . . . Because of this symbiotic right, the private association often performs as one person, and is acknowledged to be one person. . . .

§13   There are two types of simple and private association. The first

§14   is natural, and the second is civil.[6] The private and natural symbiotic association is one in which married persons, blood relatives, and in-laws, in response to a natural affection and necessity, agree to a definite communication among themselves. Whence this individual, natural, necessary, economic, and domestic society is said to be contracted permanently among these symbiotic allies of life, with the same boundaries as life itself. Therefore it is rightly called the most intense society, friendship, relationship, and union, the seedbed of every other symbiotic association. Whence these symbiotic allies are called relatives, kinsmen, and friends.

§15   This simple and private natural association is nourished, fostered, and conserved by private functions and occupations through

---

[4] *De republica*, V, 5, 13.

[5] [See page 19, footnote 10.]

[6] [the family and the collegium respectively.]

which these associated symbiotes communicate each to the other every aid and assistance needed in this symbiosis. They do this according to the judgment of the chief and the laws (*leges*) of good order and proper discipline prescribed by him for inferior symbiotes. These functions are §16 either agricultural, industrial, or commercial. . . .[7] Moreover, there are §37 two kinds of private and natural domestic association. The first is conjugal (*conjugalis*), and the second is kinship (*propinqua*).[8] The conju- §38 gal association and symbiosis is one in which the husband and wife, who are bound each to the other, communicate the advantages and responsibilities of married life. . . .[9] The director and governor of the common §40 affairs pertaining to this association is the husband. The wife and family are obedient, and do what is commanded.

The advantages and responsibilities are either proper to one of §41 the spouses, or common to both. Proper advantages and responsibilities §42 are either those the husband communicates to his wife, or those the wife communicates to her husband. The husband communicates to his wife his name, family, reputation, station in life, and economic condition. . . .[10] He also provides her with guidance, legal protection, and defense §43 against violence and injury. . . . Finally, he supplies her with all other §44 necessities, such as management, solicitude, food, and clothing. . . .

The wife extends to her husband obedience, subjection, trust, §45 compliance, services, support, aid, honor, reverence, modesty, and re-

---

[7] [Here follows a lengthy discussion of the functions of farmers, craftsmen, and merchants. Althusius considers farmers to be hardworking, temperate, and not given to faction, while craftsmen are argumentative, intemperate, and prone to faction. Merchants, on the other hand, are not discussed in these terms. Instead, their functions of exporting agricultural and industrial surpluses, and importing what is not found locally, are presented merely in terms of the standards of conduct they ought to observe. Moreover, merchants are acknowledged to be "the feet of the body politic" inasmuch as they provide contact with the outside world.]

[8] Concerning the former *see* Genesis 3 and 4; concerning the latter *see* Genesis 10.

[9] [Here follows an extended quotation from Cicero that discusses the reproduction instinct between husband and wife as giving birth to children, who in turn go forth to establish new connections, and concludes that "such propagation and offspring are the origin of commonwealths." *Duties, I, 17.]*

[10] [Althusius drew heavily upon Biblical materials in support of his discussion of the communication of advantages and responsibilities between husband and wife. These paragraphs refer to eighty-two passages in the Old Testament, and sixty-nine in the New Testament.]

spect. She brings forth children for him, and nurses and trains them. She joins and consoles him in misery and calamity. She accommodates herself to his customs, and without his counsel and consent she does nothing. And thus she renders to her husband an agreeable and peaceful life. . . .

§46   There are also common advantages and responsibilities that are provided and communicated by both spouses, such as kindness, use of the body for avoiding harlotry and for procreating children, mutual habitation except when absence may be necessary, intimate and familiar companionship, mutual love, fidelity, patience, mutual service, communication of all goods and right (*jus*), . . . management of the family, administration of household duties, education of children in the true religion, protection against and liberation from perils, and mourning of the dead. . . .

§1   **III**   THE KINSHIP ASSOCIATION is one in which relatives and in-laws are united for the purpose of communicating advantages

§2   and responsibilities. This association arises from at least three persons, but it can be conserved by fewer. Frequently it consists of a much larger

§16   number. . . . He is called the leader (*princeps*) of the family, or of any clan of people, who is placed over such a family or clan, and who has the right to coerce (*jus coercendi*) the persons of his family individually and collectively. . . .

§18   The rights communicated among the persons who are united in this natural association are called rights of blood (*jura sanguinis*). They consist partly in advantages, partly in responsibilities, and in the bringing together and sustaining these advantages mutually among the kins-

§20   men. . . . Such advantages are, first, the affection, love, and goodwill of

§21   the blood relative and kinsman. From this affection arises the solicitude by which the individual is concerned for the welfare and advantages of

§23   his kinsman, and labors for them no less than for his own. . . . Second among the advantages of the family and kinsmen I refer to the communion in all the rights and privileges belonging to the family and

§24   relationship. And to this point I refer the enjoyment of the clan or

§27   family name, and of its insignia. . . . Third among the common rights of the family and relationship I refer to the provision for support in case

§28   of necessity or want. Fourth, a privilege granted to one of the kinsmen is extended by right of relationship to his family, wife, children, and even brother. . . .

The responsibilities of the family and relationship are services   §34
and works that the member owes to his kinsman, such as forethought,
care, and defense of the family and of the members of the household.
. . . The leadership in meeting these responsibilities rests upon the   §35
paterfamilias as master and head of his family. . . . Upon the older   §36
members of the family rests the duty of correcting and reprehending
their younger kinsmen for mistakes of youthful indiscretion and hot-
headedness. . . .

These advantages and responsibilities are intensified as the   §37
degree of relationship among the kinsmen increases. Therefore they are
greater between parents and children. For parents should educate their
children, instruct them in the true knowledge of God, govern and
defend them, even lay up treasures for them, make them participants in
everything they themselves have, including their family and station in
life, provide suitable marriages for them at the right time, and upon
departing from life make them their heirs and provide optimally for
them. . . .[11]

CERTAIN POLITICAL WRITERS eliminate, wrongly in my judgment, the   §42
doctrine of the conjugal and kinship private association from the field of
politics and assign it to economics. Now these associations are the
seedbed of all private and public associational life. The knowledge of
other associations is therefore incomplete and defective without this
doctrine of conjugal and kinship associations, and cannot be rightly
understood without it. I concede that the skill of attending to household goods, of supplying, increasing, and conserving the goods of the
family, is entirely economic, and as such is correctly eliminated from
politics. But altogether different from this is association among spouses
and kinsmen, which is entirely political and general, and which communicates things, services, rights, and aid for living the domestic and
economic life piously, justly, and beneficially. Economic management,
however, concerns merely household goods—how much and by what

---

[11] [Here follows a discussion of members of the household. Servants, children,
and others who dwell under one roof are expected to obey the imperium of the
paterfamilias, and of his ally the materfamilias, in all things pertaining to this
social life. In turn, he has clearly defined responsibilities to them, including the
sharing with them of the rights of religion and the providing for their
maintenance.]

means they may be furnished, augmented, and conserved. By such management the skill is made available for cultivating fields, tending herds, ploughing, sowing, reaping, planting, pruning, and doing all kinds of agricultural work. But by politics alone arises the wisdom for governing and administering the family. It is politics that teaches what the spouses, paterfamilias, materfamilias, servants, and attendants may contribute and communicate among themselves—and what the kins-men among themselves—in order that private and domestic social life may be piously and justly fulfilled.

So therefore economics and politics differ greatly as to subject and end. The subject of the former is the goods of the family; its end is the acquisition of whatever is necessary for food and clothing. The subject of the latter, namely politics, is pious and just symbiosis; its end is the governing and preserving of association and symbiotic life.

Furthermore, certain persons wrongly assert that every symbiotic association is public, and none private. Now this axiom stands firm and fixed: all symbiotic association and life is essentially, authentically, and generically political. But not every symbiotic association is public. There are certain associations that are private, such as conjugal and kinship families, and collegia. And these are the seedbeds of the public association. Whence it follows that the private association is rightly attributed to politics.

IV

The Collegium

THIS COMPLETES THE DISCUSSION of the natural associ- §1
ation. We turn now to the civil association, which is a
body organized by assembled persons according to their own pleasure
and will to serve a common utility and necessity in human life. That is
to say, they agree among themselves by common consent on a manner
of ruling and obeying for the utility both of the whole body and of its
individuals.[1]

This society by its nature is transitory and can be discontinued. §2
It need not last as long as the lifetime of a man, but can be disbanded
honorably and in good faith by the mutual agreement of those who
have come together, however much it may have been necessary and
useful for social life on another occasion. For this reason it is called a §3
spontaneous and merely voluntary society, granted that a certain necessity can be said to have brought it into existence. For in the early times of
the world, when the human race was increasing and, though one family,
yet dispersing itself—since all persons could no longer be expected to
live together in one place and family—necessity drove diverse and
separate dwellings, hamlets, and villages to stand together, and at length
to erect towns and cities in different places. Accordingly, "when the
head of the family goes out of his house, in which he exercises domestic
imperium, and joins the heads of other families to pursue business
matters, he then loses the name of head and master of the family, and
becomes an ally and citizen. In a sense, he leaves the family in order that

---

[1] [A parallel, though briefer, discussion by Althusius of the collegium is found in
a chapter entitled "Men United By Their Own Consent" in his major work on
jurisprudence, *Dicaeologica*, I, 8.]

he may enter the city and attend therein to public instead of domestic concerns."[2]

§4   This is therefore a civil association. In it three or more men of the same trade, training, or profession are united for the purpose of holding in common such things they jointly profess as duty, way of life, or craft. Such an association is called a collegium,[3] or as it were, a gathering, society, federation, sodality, synagogue, convention, or synod. It is said to be a private association by contrast with the public

§5   association.[4] The persons who unite in order to constitute a collegium are called colleagues, associates, or even brothers. A minimum of three persons is required to organize a collegium, because among two persons there is no third person to overcome dissension. This is so even though two persons may be called colleagues so far as the power and equality of office is concerned. Fewer than three, however, are able to conserve a collegium.[5]

§6   Whoever among the colleagues is superior and set over the others is called the leader of the collegium, the rector or director of the common property and functions. He is elected by common consent of the colleagues, and is provided with administrative power over property and functions pertaining to the collegium. For this reason he exercises coercive power over the colleagues individually, but not over the group

§7   itself. Therefore the president of a collegium is superior to the individual colleague but inferior to the united colleagues, or to the collegium over which he presides and whose pleasure he must serve. . . .

§8   We will consider first the communication of the colleagues, and their symbiotic right (*jus symbioticum*) in this private and civil association, then the various types of the collegium. Communication among the colleagues is the activity by which an individual helps his colleague, and so upholds the plan of social life set forth in covenanted agreements. These covenants and laws (*pacta et leges*) of the colleagues

---

[2] Jean Bodin, *The Commonweale,* I, 6.

[3] [*collegium* (pl. *collegia*): guild; corporation; voluntary association.]

[4] Examples of this association can be seen in Acts 6:2 f.; 12:12; 13:15, 27; 15:21; 28:23, 30 f.; Matthew 4; 6:2; 10:24; 13; Exodus 29:42; Numbers 10:10.

[5] [The discussion of the collegium in this chapter is heavily supported by references to Roman law, especially to the following three titles: Digest III, 4 ("Quod cuiuscumque universitatis"); Digest XLVII, 22 ("De collegiis"); and Code X, 32 ("De decurionibus").]

are described in their corporate books, which we call *Zunftbücher.* Such communication pertains to (1) things, (2) services, (3) right, and (4) mutual benevolence.

The communication of things centers in mutual contributions *§9* of the colleagues to the collegium, and in acquisitions from other sources made according to its law. These things include the building of the collegium in which the colleagues meet and deliberate on their corporate business, as well as the money, income, drinking cups, seals, coffers, books, corporate records, and other things useful and necessary to the collegium assessed from the individual members or given from some other source to the collegium. The common purpose requires *§10* that all colleagues be considered participants within a common legal structure, not as separate individuals but as one body. So it is that what the collegium owes is not owed by the individuals separately, and what is owed to the collegium is not owed to the individuals separately.[6] . . .

The communication of services is determined by mutual *§12* agreement among the colleagues. The communication of skilled services consists, for the most part, in promoting the duties, business, and advantages of a craft, profession, or vocation, and in averting disadvantages. This is done according to the manner that has been tacitly or explicitly agreed upon by the colleagues. In this connection, the colle- *§13* gium bestows its approval on apprentices who have passed an appointed examination in the art, craft, or trade that the collegium professes.

Some services are more or less uniform and equally performed among the colleagues. Others, however, are dissimilar and unequal in character, and are the responsibility not of all colleagues, but either of some among them or of the one who serves as leader of the collegium. Among the latter services are the right and responsibility of calling the *§14* colleagues into session,[7] of proposing the things that are to be deliberated upon, of conducting the voting, of opening letters to the collegium from outside sources, of maintaining the seal, coffer, privileges, and other goods of the collegium, and of adjourning its meetings. There may be further services required by the nature and order of the functions and activities for which the collegium was organized. If so, they

---

[6] Digest III, 4, 7, 1.

[7] Bodin assigns this right to the older or more distinguished part of the collegium. [*The Commonweale*, III, 7.]

are either distributed on a changing and rotating basis among the colleagues, or assigned to the common procurator or syndic of the collegium by the common consent of the colleagues.

§15   The colleagues are recorded in the register of the collegium according to the law and convention they have agreed upon. But if there is no such law or convention, "the status of each is to be observed so that they may be recorded in that order in which each of them has enjoyed the highest distinction. [. . .] In rendering opinions, also, the same order is to be respected that is observed in recording their names in the register."[8]

§16   The communication of right among the colleagues is achieved when they live, are ruled, and are obligated in their collegium by the same right and laws (*jus et leges*), and are even punished for proper cause according to them, provided this is done without infringing upon the magistrate or usurping an alien jurisdiction. The problem of when a collegium or community (*universitas*)[9] is able to establish its own statutes is discussed by Losaeus.[10] Certainly the colleagues may establish statutes obligating them in whatever pertains to the administration of their goods, to their craft and profession, and to their private business. Their jurisdiction, however, must not infringe on the public jurisdiction, nor extend to those matters that are rightfully prohibited.

§17   The common right (*jus commune*)[11] of the collegium or the colleagues, which is customarily described in the corporate books, is

---

[8] Digest L, 3, 1. [The omission in this quotation provides further directions for the recording of rank.]

[9] [Althusius employs the word *universitas* here (following one of the uses of Losaeus) as an alternative to *collegium*, which differs from his use of it in the next chapter as a public and territorial association.]

[10] Nicolaus Losaeus, *De jure universitatum*, III, 15. *See also* Francis Marcus, *Decisiones aureae*, I, dec. 802.

[11] [fundamental law or constitution of an association. This use of *jus commune* differs from that employed by Althusius in Chapters XXI–XXII, where it means the unchanging moral law binding upon all persons and associations, and is there compared with proper law (*jus proprium*), or the specific application of common law (*jus commune*) established in a particular association in accord with its circumstances. There Althusius follows the Digest, which says that "all peoples who are ruled by laws (*leges*) and customs use partly their own law (*jus proprium*), and partly the common law (*jus commune*) of all men" (I, 1, 9). Here, however, Althusius considers common right or law (*jus commune*) to be the foundational right or law (*jus proprium*) of a particular association.]

either received from and maintained by the common consent of the colleagues, or is conceded and granted to them by special privilege of the superior magistrate.

A majority of all assembled colleagues binds the minority by its vote in those matters common to all colleagues, or pertaining jointly and wholly to the colleagues as a united group, but not in matters separately affecting individual colleagues outside the corporate fellowship. So in those matters that are to be done necessarily by the collegium, a majority is certainly sufficient, provided that in making decisions two-thirds of the collegium is present. The reason is that what is common to everyone is not my private concern alone. . . . However, in matters common to all one by one, or pertaining to colleagues as individuals, a majority does not prevail. In this case, "what touches all ought also to be approved by all."[12] Even one person is able to object. The reason is that in this case what is common to everyone is also my private concern. In these things that are merely voluntary nothing ought to be done unless all consent, not separately and at different times, but corporately and unanimously. . . .[13]

§18

§20

The colleagues, on the basis of this right (*jus*)[14] that is accepted by their common consent, can be fined whenever they commit anything against the laws (*leges*) of the collegium. Whence it comes about that one of the colleagues may exercise coercion over individuals, but not over the group itself. These fines are paid into the common chest or treasury of the collegium.

§22

Mutual benevolence is that affection and love of individuals toward their colleagues because of which they harmoniously will and "nill" on behalf of the common utility. This benevolence is nourished, sustained, and conserved by public banquets, entertainments, and love feasts.

§23

---

[12] Code V, 59, 5, 2.

[13] [This discussion of the internal procedures of the collegium, which is altogether missing in the much briefer first edition (1603) of the *Politica,* has drawn especially upon the following writers: Bartolus, *Commentarii* (Digest I, 8, 6, 1; III, 4, 3, and 4); Andreas Gail *De pignorationibus,* I, obs. 20, num. 2 ff.; *Practicarum observationum,* II, obs. 56, num. 6; Nicolaus Losaeus, *De jure universitatum,* I, 3, 77 f. and 84; Jean Bodin, *The Commonweale,* III, 7; Paul Castro, *Commentaria* (Digest III, 4, 3, and 4); Nicolaus Tudeschi, *Commentaria* (Decretals III, 11, 1); and Francis Marcus, *Decisiones aureae,* I, dec. 1036 and 1335.]

[14] [law.]

§24   The types of collegia vary according to the circumstance of persons, crafts and functions. Today there are collegia of bakers, tailors, builders, merchants, coiners of money, as well as philosophers, theologians, government officials, and others that every city needs for the proper functioning of its social life. Some of these collegia are ecclesiastical and sacred, instituted for the sake of divine things; others are secular and profane, instituted for the sake of human things. The first are collegia of theologians and philosophers. The second are collegia of magistrates and judges, and of various craftsmen, merchants, and rural folk. The collegia of magistrates are of particular importance because by their public power (*jus potestatis*) they set bounds for each and every other collegium. . . .[15]

§30   At the present time in many places the people of a provincial city, realm, or polity, by reason of their occupation or kind and diversity of organized life, customarily distributed in three orders, estates, or larger general collegia (*generalia majora collegia*). The first is of clergymen, the second of nobility, and the third of the people or plebs, including scholars, farmers, merchants, and craftsmen. Such general collegia and bodies contain within them smaller special collegia (*specialia minora collegia*). Such are the particularly important collegia of judges and magistrates, the collegia of ministers of the church, and the collegia of various workers and merchants necessary and useful in social life, which we will discuss later. . . .[16]

---

[15] [Here follows a lengthy discussion of the collegia and tribes in ancient Rome, Israel, and Egypt that is indebted to Alexander ab Alexandro, *Genialium dierum;* Theodore Zwinger, *Theatrum vitae humane;* Johann Rosinus, *Romanarum antiquitatum;* Petrus Gregorius, *De republica;* and Carlo Sigonio, *De antiquo jure Italiae* and *De republica Hebraicorum.*]

[16] [*See* especially Chapters V, VIII, XVIII.]

V–VI

The City

V   **W**ITH THIS DISCUSSION of the civil and private asso-   *§1*
ciation, we turn now to the public association.
For human society develops from private to public association by the
definite steps and progressions of small societies. The public association
exists when many private associations are linked together for the purpose of establishing an inclusive political order (*politeuma*). It can be
called a community (*universitas*),[1] an associated body, or the pre-eminent
political association. It is permitted and approved by the law of nations   *§2*
(*jus gentium*). It is not considered dead as long as one person is left. Nor   *§3*
is it altered by the change of individual persons, for it is perpetuated by
the substitution of others. Men assembled without symbiotic right (*jus*   *§4*
symbioticum) are a crowd, gathering, multitude, assemblage, throng, or
people. The larger this association, and the more types of association
contained within it, the more need it has of resources and aids to
maintain self-sufficiency as much in soul as in body and life, and the
greater does it require good order, proper discipline, and communication of things and services.

     Political order in general is the right and power of communi-   *§5*
cating and participating in useful and necessary matters that are brought
to the life of the organized body by its associated members. It can be
called the public symbiotic right. This public symbiotic association is   *§6*
either particular or universal. The particular association is encompassed

---

[1] [an association embracing all other associations within a given geographical
area; a public as distinguished from a private association. It is here used as a
generic name inclusive of commonwealth, province, and city. This is an
occasional use for Althusius. Its more customary use is described in footnote 2
below.]

by fixed and definite localities within which its rights are communi-
§7   cated. In turn, it is either a community (*universitas*)[2] or a province.

§8   The community is an association formed by fixed laws and
composed of many families and collegia living in the same place. It is
elsewhere called a city (*civitas*) in the broadest sense, or a body of many
and diverse associations. Nicolaus Losaeus defines it as "a coming
together under one special name of many bodies each distinct from the
§9   other."[3] It is called a representational person[4] and represents men
collectively, not individually. Strictly speaking, however, the community is not known by the designation of person, but it takes the place of a
person when legitimately convoked and congregated.[5]

§10   The members of a community are private and diverse associations of families and collegia, not the individual members of private
associations. These persons, by their coming together, now become not
spouses, kinsmen, and colleagues, but citizens of the same community.
Thus passing from the private symbiotic relationship, they unite in the
§11   one body of a community. Differing from citizens, however, are foreigners, outsiders, aliens, and strangers whose duty it is to mind their
own business, make no strange inquiries, not even to be curious in a
foreign commonwealth, but to adapt themselves, as far as good conscience permits, to the customs of the place and city where they live in
order that they may not be a scandal to others.[6] . . .

§22   The superior is the prefect of the community appointed by the
consent of the citizens. He directs the business of the community, and
governs on behalf of its welfare and advantage, exercising authority (*jus*)
§23   over the individuals but not over the citizens collectively. An oath of
fidelity to certain articles in which the functions of this office are

---

[2] [a local community embracing all private associations within a municipal area;
a city in its fullest associated expression, as distinguished from a province (the
other kind of particular public association) and a commonwealth (the universal
public association).]

[3] *De jure universitatum*, I, 1, 2. [It is noteworthy that this book by Losaeus, which
was published in 1601 at Turin, was not mentioned by Althusius in the first
edition (1603) of the *Politica*, but is referred to in the third edition (1614) sixty-
two times in the chapters on the collegium and the city alone, and occasionally
thereafter throughout the reminder of the work.]

[4] [*persona repraesentata*: literally, a person having come to represent.]

[5] Digest, XLVI, 1, 22.

[6] [Here follows an extended discussion of types of full and limited citizenship.]

contained stands as a surety to the appointing community. From the individual citizens, in turn, is required an oath of fidelity and obedience setting forth in certain articles the functions of the office of a good citizen.

§24   Such a superior is either one or more persons who have received the prescribed power of governing by the consent of the community. . . . And so these general administrators of the community §25 are appointed by the city out of its general and free power, and can even be removed from office by the city. They are therefore temporal, while the community or city may be continuous and almost immortal.

§26   The inferiors or subjects are all the remaining citizens individually and collectively who are subjects of the community, or of those who represent it, but not of individuals as such.

§27   Even though the individual persons of a community may be changed by the withdrawal or death of some superiors and inferiors, the community itself remains. It is held to be immortal because of the continued substitution and succession of men in place of those withdrawing.[7] Whence it appears that the community is different from the individual persons of a community, although it is often considered to be a representational and fictional person.[8]

§28   Furthermore, this community is either rural or urban. A rural community is composed of those who cultivate the fields and exercise §29 rural functions. Such a community is either a hamlet, a village, or a town. §30 A hamlet (*vicus*) is a settlement of a few houses situated around a small §34 open place. . . . The superior of the hamlet is a leader who is elected by consent of the hamlet dwellers (*vicini*) and has the right of admonishing them, of calling them together, and of conducting their common business. The remaining hamlet dwellers are subjects. A village (*pagus*) §35 consists of two or more hamlets without fortifications or surrounding wall. The superior of the village is called the leader of the village dwellers §36 (*pagani*), or the administrator and syndic of the village. . . . A town §38 (*oppidum*) is a larger village girded and fortified by a ditch, stockade, or wall. . . . If very large, it is called a city according to Losaeus.[9] The §39

---

[7]Baldus de Ubaldis, *Commentarii* (Digest III, 4, 7, 2); Paul Castro, *Commentaria* (Digest III, 4, 7, 2).

[8]Bartolus, *Commentarii* (Digest XLVI, 1, 22); Andreas Gail, *De pace publica*, I, 5; Nicolaus Losaeus, *De jure universitatum*, I, 1, 41 and 42; Code, II, 58, 2, 5.

[9]*De jure universitatum*, I, 2, 45.

prefect of the town is the administrator and leader of the town dwellers (*oppidani*), and has the right of calling them together and proposing matters to them. In common consultation with them, he also has the power of collecting their votes, of issuing and executing public decrees, of dismissing the council, and of directing and administering the common affairs of the community.

§40
§41   An urban community is composed of those who practice industrial functions and pursuits while living an urban life. It is a large number of hamlets and villages associated by a special legal order (*jus*) for the advancement of the citizens, and guarded and fortified against
§48   external violence by a common moat, fortress, and wall. . . .[10] A community of citizens dwelling in the same urban area (*urbs*), and content with the same communication and government (*jus imperii*)[11] is called a city (*civitas*) or, as it were, a unity of citizens. And they are citizens of this community or city who are partners in it, as distinguished from foreigners and aliens who do not enjoy the same standing within the city's legal order (*jus civitatis*).[12]

§49   The prefect or superior of the city is the administrator and leader of the citizens, having authority and power over individuals by general mandate of the organized community, but not over the group.
§50   In many places he is said to be the consul. Associated with him are counselors and senators who give advice for the welfare of the city and constitute a senatorial collegium. The citizens are individually and
§51   collectively expected to observe his legitimate decrees. . . . The prefect of the city is called the president or leader (*princeps*) of the senate. Sometimes the prefect is one person, other times—in proportion to the size of the city and the extent of its business—two, three, or four persons, who continue to perform the office throughout changes in personnel. They are also called administrators of the commonwealth.
§52   The senatorial collegium, composed of the president and senators, binds itself by oath at the beginning of its administration to the prescribed articles of administration, and collectively fulfills the func-

---

[10] [Suburbs beyond the wall, as well as open fields for cultivation within the wall, are considered by Althusius to be a part of an urban community. Thus Althusius seems to have in mind a city that includes all the inhabitants of the surrounding district under its jurisdiction and protection.]

[11] [structure and power of rule.]

[12] [do not exercise the rights and responsibilities of citizens.]

tions of the entrusted office. The office of the leader of the senate, or the §53
consul, consists in the power of calling the senate into session; the power
of referring and proposing business to it; the right of seeking and
gathering the judgments of individual senators; the power of caring for
the seal and keys of the city, of opening letters sent to the senate, of
receiving petitions, of responding in the name of the collegium; and
lastly the power of carrying out the conclusions of the senate, and of
dismissing it.

The senate is a collegium of wise and honest select men to §54
whom is entrusted the care and administration of the affairs of the city.[13]
This collegium, when legitimately convoked, represents the entire §55
people and the whole city. It does not, however, have as much power, §56
authority, and jurisdiction as the community, unless it is given such by
law (*lex*) or covenant. . . .[14] In the absence of the consul or rector, this §58
office falls to the senior senator, or to the person designated from the
senate by the rector for this purpose. But, if all senators are assembled
without being formally called into session, the community is nevertheless considered legitimately convoked.

Senators are those who have the right of delivering judgments §59
in the senate concerning the things that have been proposed by the
leader for their consideration. They are also called decurions or counselors of the city. Their names are inscribed in the register, and they
enjoy certain privileges. Such senators are elected by the senatorial §60
collegium, or by specified electors designated by the community. In
some cities, to be sure, senators and consuls are elected in duplicate
number in order that the prince or count of the province can choose
and confirm certain ones among them. In other cities, however, the
complete election is in the power of the collegium of the community or
its guilds (*collegia artificum*), or in the power of specified persons designated by individual collegia of the city for this function. The senators

---

[13] *See* the Digest I, 2, 2, 9, which says that because the people was able to convene
in so great a crowd of men only with extreme difficulty, and therefore was not able
to rule, "necessity itself brought the care of the commonwealth to the senate."

[14] [This passage is obviously derived from Losaeus, who wrote that "the council
of the city does not have by common law (*jus commune*) the same power,
authority, and jurisdiction as the total people, custom." *De jure universitatum*, I,
3, 48. Althusius notes that Bartolus disagrees with this position. He apparently
has in mind the opinion of Bartolus that the council of the city does have the
same power as the total people. *Commentarii* (Code IV, 32, 5).]

who constitute the collegium of senators, the consistory, or the council of counselors, which we usually call the senate, are greater or fewer in number in proportion to the size of the city and the extent of the business.

§61   These senators are either ordinary or extraordinary. Ordinary senators are those who, at agreed and appointed times, consider and decide all business matters that have arisen and come before the commonwealth. Extraordinary senators are those who, summoned for difficult problems of the commonwealth, assist the ordinary senators by their counsel and have the power of deciding with them. These extraordinary senators, who are variously named in different places, are identified for the most part by their number, such as the one hundred men, the fifty, the forty, the thirty, the twenty, the four men, and so forth.

Sometimes in the gravest matters the votes of the individual collegia of the community or city are employed, or of the individual clans or groups into which the city is divided. They are then called together by the senatorial collegium.

§62   The form and method of making decisions in the consistory or senatorial collegium is by the judgment and vote of a majority of the senators, either of all senatorial colleagues without exception, or with at least two-thirds of the colleagues of the entire collegium being present. These votes, which are sought and collected in matters that are of concern to the senate, must be taken at the same time and in the accustomed place. After the proposition has been set forth by the consul or president, the individual senators make known their votes concerning the thing proposed in that order in which they are consulted, provided that the liberty and opportunity of dissenting are provided.

§64   . . . After the votes of the individual senators have been given, the consul or leader of the senate counts the affirmative votes, as well as the negative votes if there are any, and decides by them. If the gravity of the matter so demands, however, and the majority is thought to have decided incorrectly, he may order the majority to examine and ponder the votes of the dissenting minority, and to discuss the matter anew. After further discussion and examination, he again collects the judgments of individuals, and decides on the basis of the considered votes of the majority. The dissenting minority is required to submit itself to this decision, so that the decision of the majority is declared and held as the judgment of the whole senate or consistory, and binds the entire community. For a consensus, when produced at the same time and place, is sufficient in those matters that pertain to persons as a group, or that are done by the many as by everyone and the group. On the other hand, a consensus of the majority is not sufficient in those matters that are done by the many as individuals. In these matters the will of the individuals is required, and it may even be separately declared at different times and places. What touches individuals ought to be approved by individuals. . . .[15]

VI   A CITY MAY BE either free, municipal, mixed, or metropolitan.   §1

A free city is so called because it recognizes as its immediate   §2
superior the supreme magistrate,[16] and is free from the rule of other princes, dukes, and counts. It is called an imperial city in the German polity, where it has been assessed contributions or special services for the realm because of the right of participation and suffrage it enjoys in the councils of the empire and its listing as a member of the empire. And no one doubts that these cities have the rights of princes within their boundaries.

The municipal or provincial city is one that is subject to a   §3
territorial lord. It recognizes a superior other than the supreme magistrate.

A mixed city is so called because it recognizes partly the   §4
emperor and partly a duke or count as its superior, and enjoys both imperial and provincial privileges. There are some cities in which dukes   §5
or counts have usurped rights, even though the territory does not actually belong to them. These cities recognize them in certain respects through fixed pacts and conditions, and evidence their liberties in others. Such are Goslar, Magdeburg, Cologne, Aachen, Erfurt, and several others.

A metropolis is so called because it is the mother of other cities   §6
that it brings forth as colonies, or because it is pre-eminent among them and is recognized by them as a mother by whom they are ruled and defended as children. The metropolis is therefore a large and populous city. Other cities and towns of the realm follow its example because of its

---

[15] [Here follows a discussion of the causes of the founding and growth of cities that is largely dependent upon Giovanni Botero, *The Geatness of Cities*, and Hippolytus a Collibus, *Incrementa urbium*.]

[16] [the emperor.]

size, population, rank, houses of religion and justice, and temples of piety and law (*jus*), by means of which it displays the light of religion and justice to the other cities of the realm and presents itself in an elevated place to be seen by all. It also cultivates men distinguished in piety, doctrine, and life that others are able to consult in cases of doubt and perplexity. . . .[17]

§15   Communication among citizens of the same community for the purpose of self-sufficiency and symbiosis pertains to things, services, right, and mutual concord. Whence arises this political order, or the symbiotic right (*jus symbioticum*) of the city, which is called the legal

§16   order of the city (*jus civitatis*). And as man is said to be a microcosm, so also is a city or small commonwealth, for the common business of a city is conducted and managed in almost the same manner as that of a realm or province.[18]

We will speak first about this communication, and then about

§17   the administration of it. The communication of things among the members and citizens of the same community, town, or village is so carried out that the things communicated by the common consent and covenant of each and all are set aside for the various uses of the community. This is done according to the manner, order, and proce-dure that was agreed upon and established among the members and citizens. And such communication of things is rightly called the sinews of the city. . . .[19]

---

[17] [Examples of the metropolis cited by Althusius are Nineveh, Babylon, Rome, Paris, Ghent, Prague, and London.]

[18] Plato says that since no one of us is self-sufficient, but instead needs many things, the city came into being. So we take partners, fellow communicators, and helpers for our benefit, and thereby make a gathering that is called a city. For since men need many things that no isolated person is able to provide for himself, a number of them come together in one place that they may bring mutual support in life to each other. *The Republic*, II, 369.

[19] [Here follows a discussion of the types of things communicated in the community. They may be things held in common for the use of individuals, such as fields and forests for pasture and firewood, fishing places, rivers, roads, baths, temples, schools, market places, and courts of justice. Or they may be private things owned and operated by the community, such as granaries, armories, metal mines, breweries, civic archives, and tax collections.

A distinction is also made, following Roman law, between sacred and holy things. Those things are sacred that are dedicated to divine worship, such as temples, tithes, and ecclesiastical revenues. Holy things, on the other hand, are

The communication of services among the citizens of the *§28* same community is the performing of functions necessary and useful to symbiosis and mutual intercourse. These are performed by one citizen for another who needs and desires them in order that love may become effectual through the observance of charity. . . . The communication *§29* of such services is especially accomplished in the execution and administration of (1) public duties and (2) private occupations necessary and useful to social life and symbiosis, the direction of which belongs to the senatorial collegium.

The administrators of public duties are those who expedite the public functions of the commonwealth or city, both political and ecclesiastical. The political functions of the city concern the use of this *§30* life, its self-sufficiency, and, in brief, whatever is contained in the second table of the Decalogue. These functions are administered by judges, senators, counselors, syndics, censors, treasurers, directors of public works, curators of public roads, ports, buildings, and other such things of the community, as well as superintendents of granaries, prefects of the city, the security guard, and so forth. Ecclesiastical functions, which oversee the communion of the saints, the building of the church, holy worship, and the knowledge of God, are the responsibility of ministers of the church, school teachers and headmasters, deacons, and so forth. There are, however, certain common services *§31* and functions of the church that are incumbent as much upon inferiors as upon superiors, such as concern and solicitude for the worship of God and promotion of the welfare of the church. . . .

Occupations are private functions inclining principally to the *§32* utility of those who perform them, and consequently to the public utility of the city or of all the citizens collectively. Such are the various industrial, agricultural, and commercial occupations that I have discussed above.[20] In order that these occupations may offer mutual services to each other for their common advantage, it is necessary that they be brought together. For thus the farmer needs the carpenter, builder, miller, shoemaker, tailor, and others. And they need the aid and communication of the farmer.

---

the walls, gates, fortifications, and so forth, of the city. *See* the *Institutes* II, 1, 7–10.]

[20] [*See* page 29, footnote 7.]

§33   Mutual services are also offered by the citizens in the construction, extension, and repair of the public works, such as walls, ramparts, ditches, and gates to the city or urban community, as well as temples, theaters, courts, courtyards, roads, bridges, public water systems, water §34   mills, and other public works. Citizens likewise contribute their services in guarding and defending the city or urban community, in paying expenses undertaken in the name of the community, and in sustaining its public ministers.

§35   There are other services that are devoted more to private benefit than to the public utility and advantage of the community. These are performed more because of the charity and benevolence of the citizen than because the covenant of the community requires them. Examples occur when a citizen gives material help or counsel according to his ability to his fellow citizen, or promotes the advantage of his fellow citizen while removing, whenever he is able, disadvantages and perils. . . .

§39   The rights (*jura*)[21] of the city, its privileges, statutes, and benefits, which make a city great and celebrated, are also communicated by the citizens. They are shared with the people in the suburbs, outposts, and surrounding villages, but not with travellers and foreign-§40   ers. For citizens enjoy the same laws (*leges*), the same religion, and the same language, speech, judgment under the law, discipline, customs, money, measures, weights, and so forth. They enjoy these not in such §41   manner that each is like himself alone, but that all are like each other. I also include the autonomy of the city, its privileges, right of territory, and other public rights that accompany jurisdiction and imperium. Even a city recognizing a superior can have these rights by its own authority (*jus*), and in other things be subject to its superior magistrate by fixed covenants. And even more certainly these rights pertain to a §42   free city recognizing none except the emperor as its superior. These cities, however, cannot have the personal rights of princes, nor exercise §43   jurisdiction beyond their territories.[22] But municipal tribunals of justice, similar to those the Jewish polity had, belong to this communi-

---

[21] [laws.]

[22] Matthew Stephani, *De jurisdictione,* II, pt. 1, chap. 7; II, pt. 1, chap. 1. In former times, however, in the Jewish and other polities, cities were understood to have had their own autonomy, polity, and king. Genesis 14; 19.

cation.[23] I also include the right and power (*jus et potestas*) of dwelling in the city, of setting up residences and households, or transferring one's family and possessions thereto, of having a workshop in the same place, of being received into the collegium or sodality of one's vocation and profession, and of engaging in commercial activity. I ascribe to this communication the power of using and enjoying all rights, advantages, and benefits that the whole city has established for all citizens, and approved by common consent.

Every city is able to establish statutes concerning those things that pertain to the administration of its own matters, that belong to its trade and profession, and that relate to the private functions of the community. . . . Also pertaining to this communication are the right of *§44* the vote (*jus suffragii*) in the common business and actions of managing and administering the community, and the form and manner by which the city is ruled and governed according to laws it approves and a magistrate that it constitutes with the consent of the citizens. When, on *§45* the contrary, these common rights of the community are alienated, the community ceases to exist. . . .

Enthusiasm for concord is the means of conserving friendship, *§46* equity, justice, peace, and honor among the citizens, and of overcoming strife, if it arises among the citizens, as soon as possible. In brief, whatever cultivates love among the citizens and conserves the common good is to be nurtured, and the causes of discord among citizens and neighbors are to be guarded against, following the examples of Abraham and Isaac.[24] "Behold how good and delightful it is for brothers to dwell in unity."[25] And thus we see that the Lord in this manner has enjoined blessing and life continuously in the world.

Concord is fostered and protected by fairness (*aequabilitas*) *§47* when right, liberty, and honor are extended to each citizen according to the order and distinction of his worth and status. For it behooves the citizen to live by fair and suitable right with his neighbor, displaying neither arrogance nor servility, and thus to will whatever is tranquil and honest in the city. Contrary to this fairness is equality (*aequalitas*), by which individual citizens are levelled among themselves in all those

---

[23] II Chronicles 19; Ruth 4; Deuteronomy 10; 16:18.
[24] Genesis 13; 26.
[25] Psalm 133:1.

things I have discussed. From this arises the most certain disorder and disturbance of matters.

§48   THE ADMINISTRATION AND DIRECTION of the communication of these rights in the community is entrusted, with the consent of the citizens, to the senatorial collegium. In the municipal cities the head or superior of the province, or his substitute serving in his name, presides over §49   the senatorial collegium. . . . In free cities, however, the leader of the senate or the consul, who has royal privileges in connection with the territory, presides.

§50   Things done by the senatorial collegium are considered done §51   by the whole community that the collegium represents. Under the control of this senatorial collegium is, therefore, the power of managing and executing the business of the community and so of knowing and judging all that pertains to the community. This includes the right of holding investigations, the administration of public matters both civil and ecclesiastical, the responsibility for and assignment of public duties and offices, the planning, collection, care, and expenditure of public revenues, the right of publishing laws pertaining to good order and self-sufficiency, the care of public properties, the punishment of law breakers, the censorship of customs, the management of the urban community, and other such things.

§52   Therefore, what the count is in the province, the prince or duke in the duchy, or the king in the kingdom, so this senatorial collegium is, for the most part, in the city. . . .

VII–VIII

The Province

VII W<small>E HAVE COMPLETED</small> the discussion of the commu- *§1*
nity. We turn now to the province,[1] which con-
tains within its territory many villages, towns, outposts, and cities
united under the communion and administration of one right (*jus*).[2] It
is also called a region, district, diocese, or community. I identify the *§2*
territory of a province as whatever is encompassed by the limits or
boundaries within which its rights (*jura*)[3] are exercised. . . . Two mat- *§3*
ters are to be discussed. The first is the communion of provincial right,
and the second is the administration of it. These two matters contain the
entire political doctrine of the province.

The communion of right is the process whereby everything
that nourishes and conserves a pious and just life among the provincial
symbiotes is procured by individuals and province alike for the need and
use of the province. This is done through the offering and communication of functions and goods. . . .

The functions of the provincial symbiotes are either holy or *§4*
civil. Holy functions concern those that are necessary for living and
cultivating a pious life in the provincial association and symbiosis. A *§5*
pious life requires a correct understanding of God and a sincere worship
of him. A correct understanding of God is obtained from sacred *§6*
scripture and from articles of faith. "This is eternal life, that they know

---

[1] [This discussion of the province as a distinct type of association is missing in the
first edition of 1603. In that edition there are only four types of association
(family, collegium, city, and commonwealth), and the province is considered for
the most part to be an administrative unit of the commonwealth.]

[2] [legal order.]

[3] [laws.]

51

thee the only true God, and Jesus Christ whom thou hast sent."[4] A correct worship of God is derived from those rules and examples of the divine word that declare and illustrate love toward God and charity toward men.

§7   True and correct worship of God is either private or public. Private and internal worship consists of the expression of confidence, adoration, and thankfulness, the first precept of the Decalogue. Private and external worship consists of rites and actions that revere God, the second precept, or of words that do the same, the third precept. Public worship of God consists of holy observance of the Sabbath by corporate public celebration, the fourth precept.

§8   Civil functions are those that maintain a just life in the provincial association and symbiosis. Whence they include everything that pertains to the exercise of social life. The symbiote is expected to perform those duties of love by which he renders to each his due, and does not do to his fellow symbiote what he does not wish done to himself.[5] Rather he loves him as himself, and abstains from evil.

§9   The duties of justice to the neighbor are either special or general. Special duties are those that bind superiors and inferiors together, so that the symbiote truly attributes honor and eminence by word and deed to whomever they are due, and abstains from all mean §10 opinion of such persons, the fifth precept of the Decalogue. General duties are those every symbiote is obligated to perform toward every other symbiote. They consist of defending and preserving from all injury the lives of one's neighbor and oneself, the sixth precept; of guarding by thought, word, and deed one's own chastity and that of the fellow symbiote, without any lewdness or fornication, the seventh precept; of defending and preserving the resources and goods of the fellow symbiote, and of not stealing, injuring, or reducing them, the eighth precept; of defending and preserving one's own reputation and that of one's neighbor, and of not neglecting them in any manner, the ninth precept; and of avoiding a concupiscent disposition toward those things that belong to our neighbor, and of seeking instead satisfaction and pleasure in those things that are ours and tend to the glory of God, the tenth precept.

---

[4] John 17:3.

[5] [*Institutes* I, 1, 3: Digest I, 1, 10, 1; Matthew 7:12; Luke 6:31.]

The practice of provincial political justice is twofold. First, individual symbiotes manifest and communicate the duties of love reciprocally among themselves, according to special means, person, place, and other circumstances. Second, the provincials as a group and as individual inhabitants of the province uphold and communicate the duties of both tables of the Decalogue for the sake of the welfare of the provincial association. The former are the private and special practice among the provincials, and the latter are the public and general practice.   §11

These latter general duties are performed by the common consent of the provincial symbiotes. They are (1) the executive functions and occupations necessary and useful to the provincial association; (2) the distribution of punishments and rewards by which discipline is preserved in the province; (3) the provision for provincial security; (4) the mutual defense of the provincials against force and violence, the avoidance of inconveniences, and the provision for support, help, and counsel; (5) the collection and distribution of monies for public needs and uses of the province; (6) the support of commercial activity; (7) the use of the same language and money; and (8) the care of public goods of the province. . . .[6]   §12

VIII   The administration of provincial right is the process by which the employment and practice of provincial right, both general and special, is appropriately directed to the welfare of the province. Whence this right relates entirely to good ordering and arranging, and has in mind a structure of proper practice and discipline. The administration of this right involves two parts. One part pertains to the members of the province, and the other to its head or president.   §1

---

[6] [Here follows a long discussion of executive functions and occupations, after which there is a brief restatement of the seven other general public duties. Especially noteworthy is the observation that "the female sex does not bar one from office when the function is suitable to the sex." Althusius acknowledges, however, that the following writers disagree with him: Petrus Gregorius, *De republica*, VII, 11; Lambert Daneau, *Politices christianae,* VI, 3; Melchior Junius, *Politicarum quaestionum,* I, quest. 13; Justus Lipsius, *Politicorum sive civilis doctrinae,* II, 3; Jean Bodin, *The Commonweale,* VI, 5.

Also to be noted is his suggestion that the best persons for high office in the province are to be found among the middle class, "for these persons do not aspire after what is alien, nor are they envious of the goods of others."]

§2   The members of the province are its orders and estates, as they are called, or larger collegia.[7] The provincials have been distributed in these orders and estates according to the class and diversity of life they have organized in keeping with their profession, vocation, and activity. Therefore, when ecclesiastical and civil functions of the province are under consideration, each estate or order can center its attention upon the operation of the provincial right and business among men of its own class, provided it does not usurp and exercise the ordinary jurisdiction. In Germany they are called *die Stende der Landschaft.*

§3   The reason for these estates is that they are necessary and useful to the province, as Jethro, the father-in-law of Moses, declares.[8] For no one can be sufficient and equal to the task of administering such various, diverse, and extensive public business of a province unless in part of the burden he avails himself of skilled, wise, and brave persons from each class of men. . . . Indeed, by this arrangement certain traces of liberty are retained by the provincials, for each and all see themselves admitted to the administration of public matters. Whence love, benevolence, and common concern are fostered among the provincials when all know that a precise care is exercised for individuals and groups in each class of life, and that their requests for the procurement of necessary and useful things for social life, and for the avoidance of inconvenience and harm, will be heard, and remedies will be sought, even to the extent of aid against those who are more powerful or who disturb the public peace.

§4   The provincial order or estate may be either sacred and ecclesiastical, or secular and civil. In Germany they are known as *der Geistliche*

---

[7] [*majora collegia:* as distinguished from *minora collegia. See* page 38.]

[8] Exodus 18:17–25. ["Moses' father-in-law said to him, 'What you are doing is not good. You and the people with you will wear yourselves out, for the thing is too heavy for you; you are not able to perform it alone. Listen now to my voice; I will give you counsel, and God be with you! . . . Choose able men from all the people, such as fear God, men who are trustworthy and who hate a bribe; and place such men over the people as rulers of thousands, of hundreds, of fifties, and of tens. And let them judge the people at all times; every great matter they shall bring to you, but any small matter they shall decide themselves; so it will be easier for you, and they will bear the burden with you. If you do this, and God so commands you, then you will be able to endure, and all this people also will go to their place in peace!'" R.S.V.] *See also* Deuteronomy 1:13–18; II Chronicles 19; Numbers 11.

und Weltliche Stand.[9] These orders, together with the provincial head,   §5
represent the entire province. All weightier matters are guided by their
counsel, and the welfare of the commonwealth is entrusted to them.
They admonish the head of the province when he errs, correct the
abuse of his power, and punish his seducers and base flatterers.

A collegium of pious, learned, and most weighty men from   §6
the collegia of provincial clergymen, elected and commissioned by
common consent, represents the sacred and ecclesiastical order.[10] Entrusted to this collegium is the examination and care of doctrine, of
public reverence and divine worship, of schools, of ecclesiastical goods,
and of the poor. Indeed, the care of all ecclesiastical business and of the
holy life in the entire province is entrusted to it in order that all the saints
may unite for a common ministry, and constitute one mystical body.
. . . Whence these ecclesiastical colleagues are called bishops, inspectors, rectors, and leaders of provincial ecclesiastical matters. . . .

The care of religion and divine worship obligates these in-   §7
spectors to inquire and discover whether the doctrine of God and of
our salvation is rightly and publicly taught in the entire province and
the parts thereof, and whether God is truly, sincerely, freely, and
publicly worshipped according to his Word by everyone in the entire
province. At opportune times, they are obligated to remove corruptions, idolatries, superstitions, atheisms, heresies, and seeds of schism,
that nothing in any way detrimental to pure religion may be undertaken, and that the life of the church and the functions of religion may
be administered well.

Because the ecclesiastical order of the province cannot prop-   §8
erly discharge and fulfill this office entrusted to it throughout the
province without the aid and ministry of others, its first responsibility is
therefore to divide the province into districts and to require that each
district have a well-constituted presbytery. . . . A district is a union of   §9
many neighboring villages, towns, and cities of the same province for

---

[9] Also *see* II Chronicles 19:5–11, where Jehoshaphat appointed some prefects for
civil matters and others for ecclesiastical matters.

[10] [The ensuing discussion of the ecclesiastical order draws especially upon John
Calvin, *Institutes of the Christian Religion,* and "Draft Ecclesiastical Ordinances";
Franciscus Junius, *Commentarii* and *Ecclesiastici;* Wilhelm Zepper, *De politica
ecclesiastica;* Benedict Aretius, *Problemata theologica;* Jerome Zanchius, *De redemptione;* and Novel CXXIII.]

§10   the purpose of maintaining the public expression of divine worship. It is a communion separated from others in spiritual matters. The presbytery is a collegium of pious and weighty men elected by the district. It is entrusted by the district church with the care and administration of ecclesiastical things and functions. It represents the district, and presides over it in the communion of spiritual and temporal things necessary for building up and conserving the church. It administers and provides these things in the Lord without usurping lordship for the clergy. . . .[11]

§12   The presbytery, or ecclesiastical senate, contains two kinds of men. The first are pastors or ministers of the word to whose labors in preaching and teaching are entrusted the ministry of reconciliation. The second are presbyters and deacons to whom is assigned the administration of ecclesiastical things—that is, the administration of things other than the word and sacraments—for holding the saints together, for the work of the ministry, and for building up the body of Christ. In other places, however, all those serving the church in general are called

§13   presbyters. Pastors and ministers of the Word are chiefly concerned with those things that pertain to bringing forth and sustaining faith in Christ, that is, to administering the Word, prayers, and sacraments in

§14   the body of the faithful. Upon the presbyters rests especially the care of those things that have been instituted for arousing repentance in the brethren and for conserving discipline. Therefore, together with bishops, who are properly called presbyters, they preside over the censorship of morals. Their office is also to observe that ministers perform their duties, and to disclose errors, schisms, scandals, and public necessities to the ministers for the purpose of producing prayers and repentance.

§15   Deacons are superintendents who dispense alms on behalf of the church, and carry out its responsibility to the poor. They especially handle those things that pertain to charity, and bear the responsibility for ecclesiastical goods.

§16   Collectively, the ministers, presbyters, and deacons, or the entire collegium and presbytery, care for and manage the things that pertain to the communion of the saints throughout the entire district. These things are (1) the defense and promotion of the truth of the

---

[11] [Althusius says that the Apostle Paul called the presbytery a senate, that Christ called it a church "because it represents the whole church," that the Jews in the Old Testament named it a synagogue, and that in his own times it was often called a consistory.]

heavenly doctrine; (2) the calling of ministers of the Word; (3) the censorship of morals; (4) schools for children and youth; (5) the integrity of rituals and ceremonies in the church of God; (6) structure and good order; (7) the manner and time of holding meetings; (8) the prayers, exhortations, and sacraments of the church; (9) the evidence of reformation, as well as the punishment that brings about, cultivates, and preserves holiness and peace; and (10) the diaconate and the administration of alms. Concerning these things of the church, the ministers, presbyters and deacons come together, deliberate, and decide among themselves in their own meeting. For the exercise and discharge of this task, the presbytery receives from God the power of the keys by which the kingdom of heaven opens and closes. . . .

Three steps are to be considered in the election of the minister; nomination, approval, and confirmation. The presbytery nominates a person to be a minister whom orthodox pastors of the church have examined, both for sound and orthodox doctrine and for adequate erudition in the sacred writings, and have judged fit and qualified for teaching the people. Their judgment is based on a twofold examination that involves, first, questions and responses and, then, a public discourse by the candidate. *§18* *§19*

The approval of the minister belongs to the membership of the church. Before the candidate is approved, it investigates and examines his life. "Let them first be investigated" according to the qualities and gifts the Apostle Paul recommends for such a ministry, "and then let them serve."[12] When these steps have been completed, the presbytery presents the candidate to the appointed magistrate. If the magistrate rejects the candidate for just reasons, the presbytery proceeds with a new election. If he approves, a proclamation is made at public worship on the Lord's Day in which all are admonished that, if they know anything against the life or doctrine of the candidate, they disclose it within a prescribed time to someone in the magistracy or presbytery. Those who remain silent and do not contradict this call to the ministry are understood to be consenting to the things that come to pass. If a church by a majority vote objects, the presbytery then proceeds to a new election. *§20* *§21*

The confirmation of the one who has been called, examined in doctrine and life, and approved for the ministry is carried out in the

---

[12] I Timothy 3:10; Titus 1:5–9.

following manner. On the Lord's Day the one who has been called is brought before the entire church after public worship. The church acknowledges his calling and ministry, and in its presence he is reminded of the parts of his office. Then prayers are publicly offered for him by the church. Confirmation in former times was concluded by the external sign of the imposition of hands, and is so considered today in certain places. Calvin demonstrates that the primitive church elected its clerical ministers, and brought those who were to be confirmed to the magistrate, who ordered the acts of the presbytery to be established and made firm by his own authority.[13] In some churches the minister thus confirmed afterwards takes an oath to the magistrate that he will faithfully and diligently perform the office laid upon him.

§22   The church of Geneva and other reformed churches observe this form for the calling of a minister. The same form is to be followed in calling presbyters and deacons, except that they are not publicly brought before the church, nor examined by it.[14]

§23   In the censorship of morals and discipline that pertains to the presbyterial collegium, individual presbyters inquire about the doctrine, morals, and character of the individual members of the church. All are guardians or protectors of the laws of Christ to others and do everything with a spirit of gentleness and charity that they judge to be proper for the correction of individuals and the good of the entire church. By this means the lives of individuals may respond to the Christian profession, and scandals may be prevented or removed. Thus the name of God is not injuriously heard among others because of the wicked lives of Christians. To the contrary, upon hearing our pious and upright conversation they

§24   may praise and glorify God. This ecclesiastical censorship and discipline entrusted to the presbytery is called the power of the keys. . . .

The visitation of the parish and its churches relates to this censorship. Persons commissioned by the magistrate from the presbytery visit individual churches of the province at fixed times and, holding an inquiry, examine whether the pastor of the church employs any new kind of teaching contrary to the orthodox doctrine, whether he teaches in an edifying manner, whether he performs his office correctly, and

---

[13] *Institutes of the Christian Religion,* IV, 3, 15; IV, 4, 12–14.
[14] For the formula of the oath, *see* John Calvin, "Draft Ecclesiastical Ordinances."

whether he lives an honest life. Upon returning from their visitation, those so commissioned report to the magistrate everything that needs correction and demands a remedy from him. . . .

§27 The ministers of the church preside alternately over this collegium or presbytery for sacred prayers, good counsels, and salutary admonitions.[15] Those who preside propose matters to the collegium, request, collect, and announce decisions of their fellow ministers and presbyterial colleagues, inquire and respond in the name of the collegium, govern every action by its authority, and carry out what is decreed by common counsel, no less than occurs in secular collegia.[16] Whence those who so guide are called governors.

§28 Decisions are reached in the deliberations of the presbytery not by the judgments of the majority, but by those judgments that agree with the Word of God. Therefore, votes are not so much counted as weighed and examined with the Word of God as a touchstone and norm. . . .

§31 It is evident from selected passages of scripture that the care and administration of ecclesiastical things and functions belong not to the secular magistrate, but to the collegium of these presbyters. . . .[17] §32 To this administration even the magistrate is subject with respect to warnings, censures, and other things necessary for the welfare of the soul.[18] Therefore, the guidance of the ministerium, and obedience to it, are commended to each and every person. Sacred and secular duties are distinct, and ought not to be confused. For each demands the whole man.

§33 Many districts of an extensive and populous city, or of a province, together with their presbyteries, constitute a diocese with its

---

[15] "We beseech you, brethren, to respect those who labor among you and preside over you in the Lord and admonish you, and to esteem them very highly in love because of their work." I Thessalonians 5:12 f.

[16] Calvin illustrates this by examples from the primitive church. *Institutes of the Christian Religion,* IV, 4, 2.

[17] Acts 18:14–16; Deuteronomy 17:8–13; 21:5; 30:9; John 18:36; Ephesians 1; 5; I Corinthians 12; 15; II Chronicles 19:5–7; 26:7; Exodus 29:1, 44; 30:7; Matthew 9:13; Micah 1; Jeremiah 1; Novel CXXIII. [Althusius several times includes this Roman law novel ("De diversis capitibus ecclesiasticis") in listings of scriptural passages.]

[18] II Samuel 12; 24; I Kings 13; 16; 21; II Kings 1; 20:19; 21; II Chronicles 16; 20; Ezekiel 3; Luke 10:16; I Thessalonians 5:12; Hebrews 13:17.

assembly of many churches. The more serious controversies and questions concerning doctrine and church matters that cannot be decided

§34   by a presbytery are referred to this assembly for decision. The one who presides over a diocese is called a bishop or inspector. The other ministers of the same diocese hold him responsible for the faithful performance of his office. The inspector of more than one diocese is

§35   called a co-bishop. Some of these dioceses are larger, some smaller, depending upon the size of the province and the density of population. The presiding officers and co-bishops of many dioceses constitute the collegium of the ecclesiastical order, as we have said, over which he who presides is called an archbishop or general superintendent of the prov-

§36   ince. An assembly from all districts of the province constitutes a provincial synod.

§37   The ecclesiastical order of the province will observe, investigate, and examine all dioceses therein, and all districts of every diocese, that they do their duty. This will be accomplished by means of organized visitations three, four, or more times each year, or as often as

§38   needed. In these visitations the ecclesiastical order will institute an inquiry and examination, first, concerning the doctrine and life of the presbyters and, then, concerning anything else that may require correction. And it will request the aid of the magistrate, whose duty it will call forth in these matters and who will have deputies for this purpose, that remedies may be sought for those circumstances needing correction, and that nothing may be lacking for the true worship of God nor remain as an impediment thereto. . . .

§40   THE SECULAR ORDER OF THE PROVINCE is assigned, with the consent of the provincial members, the responsibility for the body, food, clothing, and other things that pertain to this life. It observes whether there is any need for remedy, aid, or amendment in political matters relating to the second table of the Decalogue. It does this in order that advantages to the province may be provided, and disadvantages to the provincial members avoided. In Germany it is called *der Weltliche Stand*.

This secular and political order is twofold. It includes the nobility (*ordo nobilitatis*) and the commons (*ordo plebeius*), the latter of which embraces the inhabitants both of cities and of country villages. Whence there are three secular estates: the nobility (*status nobilitatis*), the burghers (*status civitatum*), and the agrarians (*status agrariorum*). In Germany they are called *der Ritterstand, der Stättestand, und der Hausmans-oder Baurenstand.* Some provinces do not recognize the third order of agrarians.[19] Most Belgian provinces—Holland, Zeeland, West Friesland, North Brabant, and Groningen—have two estates or orders, the nobility and the burghers. Nor do they recognize the ecclesiastical order. But I would consider the diversity of affairs to require the experience in their duties of agrarians, so that this order should be recognized.

The order of the nobility is constituted principally for defense,   *§41* for repelling and driving force and violence away from the province. Whence in Germany it is called *der Wehrstand.* . . . The order of   *§45* burghers and agrarians is constituted principally for the adequate procurement of those things necessary and useful to civil life in the province. Whence in Germany it is called *der Nehrstand.* . . . And their   *§47* occupations are of three kinds. First are merchants and businessmen, then farmers and herders, and finally craftsmen and mechanics. . . .

As the ecclesiastical order of the province will bring forth   *§48* pious, learned, wise, and good men, so the political and secular order of the nobility will be concerned to bring forth for the province strong, militant, and brave men who are ready with arms and counsel, and are experienced in military matters. So also the order of burghers and agrarians—the commons—will strive to produce and bring forth for the fatherland merchants, farmers, and workmen who are skilled, industrious and distinguished. By the service, labor, and industry of these orders, self-sufficiency can be obtained in association and symbiosis. . . .

The prefect of these sacred and secular provincial orders is the   *§50* superior to whom is entrusted the administration of the province and of provincial matters. He receives his trust from the realm under which the province exists, and of which it is a member. He may be called a dynast, eparch, satrap, governor, president, rector, or moderator of the province. . . . Today in many places in Europe such prefects are called counts, and are designated by the name of the province entrusted to them, or of the principal fortress or metropolis of the province. Such are the counts of Nassau, Friesland, Schwartzenberg, Hanover, Mansfield, Oldenburg,

---

[19] [In this instance, and in several instances henceforth, Althusius uses the term "order" when, according to the above distinction, he intends the connotation of "estate."]

and many others. In difficult matters involving the entire province, namely, of war, peace, imposition of taxes, publication of general law and decrees, and other such things, the prefect can do nothing without the consent and agreement of the provincial orders. . . .

§51   Whenever two or more provinces are entrusted to the administration of one person, he is usually called a duke, prince, marquis, or landgrave. . . . Sometimes such an administration or prefecture is entrusted to a metropolis of the province. This is the case with Nuremberg, Strassburg, Antwerp, Danzig, Groningen, Bremen, Ulm, Augsburg, Aachen, Lübeck, Frankfurt, and many other cities. Today any city that has a distinct and separate rule and territory is said to be a province.

§52   The reason for establishing this head is necessity and utility to the province. For the public business of the various and differing orders of the province cannot be administered and governed conveniently and beneficially, let alone consistently and for any length of time, by many persons, much less by all, because of discord, dissension, and difference of opinions. Therefore, it is necessary that some director and governor be established who can hold the others, both orders and individuals, to their duties. "Where there is no governor the people perishes."[20] And the subjects are "as sheep without a pastor."[21] Whence the Apostle Paul says that the magistrate is ordained for the good and advantage of his subjects. . . .[22]

§53   Even though these heads, prefects, and rectors of provinces recognize the supreme magistrate of the realm as their superior, from whom their administration and power are conceded, nevertheless they have rights of sovereignty in their territory, and stand in the place of the supreme prince. They prevail as much in their territory as does the emperor or supreme magistrate in the realm, except for superiority, pre-eminence, and certain other things specifically reserved to the supreme magistrate who does the constituting. Such is the common judgment of jurists.[23] The head of the province therefore has the right of superiority and regal privileges in his territory, but without prejudice to the

[20] Proverbs 11:14.

[21] Numbers 27:17.

[22] Romans 13:1–7.

[23] Joachim Mynsinger, *Centuriae,* cent. 6, obs. 99; Diego Covarruvias, *Practicarum quaestionium,* 4, 1 f.; Marc Antony Peregrinus, *De jure fisci,* I, tit. 3, num. 75 f.; Henry Rosenthal, *De feudis,* I, 5, 11 ff.; Ulrich Zasius, *Responsorum,* I,

universal jurisdiction that the supreme prince has. This supreme and universal jurisdiction is itself the form and substantial essence of the sovereignty of the king, which the king by himself cannot abdicate. The rights of universal superiority and pre-eminence are indeed to be reserved in such a concession to the one who grants the concession. Thus the duke or head of a province differs in power and authority from his constituter.[24] For the constituter is greater than the one constituted, and has general power in all provinces and in the whole realm. The one constituted, on the other hand, is less than the constituter, and has special power limited by the constituter to the province. He holds his position in the place of and by the favor of his constituter, and if he becomes consumed by his own power, he can be deprived of his position by his constituter. . . .

  The duty of the provincial head is, first, to exercise diligent watch and care over sacred and secular provincial affairs, and to provide that they be lifted up and directed to the glory of God and to the welfare of the entire province and the members thereof. . . . His duty, secondly, is rightly to administer justice to individual persons, with the power and the right of inflicting penalties of life, body, goods, and reputation, and of rewarding those who do good. . . . His duty, thirdly, is to inquire concerning those things that need correction or support, to understand the state of his province, and to hear the complaints of orders and individual subjects. When these things are known to him, he announces a provincial convocation to the orders of the province, and proposes to this convocation matters to be deliberated and reflected upon that he considers to be of concern to the province. Especially does he do this when assessments or taxes are to be imposed on subjects. After these matters have been decided, either unanimously or by majority vote of the orders, he confirms the decisions, gives authority and the force of binding law to them, commands their execution, and then dismisses the convocation. . . .

  Each order of the province has one vote, although very frequently there may be many delegates representing each order and serving

§54

§55

§56

§61

§63

§64

§65

§66

---

cons. 1; Roland a Valle, *Consiliorum,* I, cons. 29, num. 26; Matthew Wesenbeck, *Consilia,* cons. 40, num. 44; cons. 27, num. 28; Andreas Gail, *De pace publica,* I, 6, 19; *Practicarum observationum,* II, obs. 57, 7 f.

[24] Henry Rosenthal adds that an emperor cannot constitute an equal to himself. *De feudis,* I, 5, 10.

as agents thereof according to the mandate and commission of their principals, to whom they must render an account of the things they have done upon returning home. Therefore, each order constitutes a member order of the provincial collegium in which questions proposed by the head are examined and decided.[25] In deliberations each order examines a proposed question separately in its own chamber, and its deputies agree among themselves concerning their decision. When the allotted time has expired and all orders of the province are assembled together in a common chamber, they communicate with each other the decision they

§67 have made. The head of the province, and his accompanying officials and advisers in the provincial convocation, should not impede or impinge upon free decisions. They are not above the orders, and do not dominate them in the convocation. After requesting and hearing the decisions of all orders, the head adds his own also, and brings any dissenting orders into harmony with the others, if this can be done.[26]

§68   The power of deciding those things that have been proposed by the head of the province is not in the control of any particular order, or of orders individually, but of all orders together. This power belongs to all orders collectively, not to individual orders, and in a collegium that meets together as a whole, not in separate collegia of individual orders. For this reason, one order without another cannot decide upon those things that pertain to all as a whole, as we have already said concerning decisions and decrees of colleagues and senators[27] and as we

§69 will later discuss more fully.[28] But if one order does not come to the announced convocation, it loses the right of deliberating and deciding upon the proposed questions; and the things that are decided by those present, and confirmed by the head of the province, are directed to be carried out with reference to it, no less than if it were present and

§70 consented to them.[29] When, however, there are differing votes, opin-

---

[25] Examples in the provinces of Holland, Zeeland, and Friesland are to be found in Emmanuel Meteren, *A General History of the Netherlands,* XIV and XX; and Ubbo Emmius, *De jure et agro Groningae. See also* Josias Simler, *De republica Helvetiorum.*

[26] For a discussion of whether the head can obstruct a decree if he alone dissents, *see* Chapter XXXIII.

[27] Chapters IV and V [on the collegium and the city].

[28] Chapter XXXIII [on councils of the realm].

[29] Bodin says, however, that in matters of great weight and moment it is not enough for all to be called, but two-thirds must be present at the session, even if not all agree. *The Commonweale,* III, 7.

ions, and judgments of the colleagues or orders present, the decision may be made according to the judgments of the more numerous or larger part in the things that concern all orders together, but not in those that concern them separately. . . .[30]

Today heads of provinces in German policy are of two kinds. §88
Some are subject to the emperor or caesar immediately, others mediately. . . . The first kind of head is required to render an account of his §91
administration directly to the emperor or supreme magistrate of the empire. If under the appearance of duty, he is cruelly misusing his power over subjects, or is practicing tyranny, the emperor can remove him and deprive him of his conceded jurisdiction.[31] The second kind of head is required to render an account of his administration to his prince, by whom he is judged and punished if he is treating his provincial subjects tyrannically or cruelly. Wherefore, if the head of such a province does §92
not protect his subjects in time of need, or refuses to support them, they can submit themselves to another.[32]

---

[30] [Here follows a lengthy discussion of orders and estates, also called tribes, in ancient Israel and Rome. Althusius draws especially upon the historian Carlo Sigonio's *De republica Hebraicorum* and *De antiquo jure Italiae*.]

[31] For further information, see Fernando Vásquez, *Illustrium controversiarum,* I, 8, 17 f.; Joachim Mynsinger, *Centuriae,* cent. 5, obs. 8; Nicolas Boerius, *Decisiones,* dec. 304; Andreas Gail, *Practicarum observationum,* I, obs. 17.

[32] [Althusius refers to the following jurists in support of this position: Jerome Gigas, *De crimine laesae majestatis,* I, quest. 56; Jacob Thomingius, *Consilia,* cons. 13, num. 43 f.; Felino Sandeo, *Commentaria* (Decretals II, 26, 12); Tiberius Decianus, *Tractatus criminalis,* VII, 49, 27 f.; Matthew Wesenbeck, *Consilia,* cons. 48, num. 23; Andrea Alciati. *Commentarii* (Code I, 2, 5); Joachim Mynsinger, *Centuriae,* cent. 6, obs. 2; Alberico Gentili, *De jure belli,* I, 23; Marianus Socinus, *Consilia,* cons. 39; Paul Castro, *Commentaria* (Digest I, 1, 5).]

IX

Political Sovereignty and Ecclesiastical Communication

Now that we have discussed particular and minor public associations, we turn to the universal[1] and major public association. In this association many cities and provinces obligate themselves to hold, organize, use, and defend, through their common energies and expenditures, the right of the realm (*jus regni*)[2] in

§2 the mutual communication of things and services. For without these supports, and the right of communication, a pious and just life cannot be established, fostered, and preserved in universal social life.

§3 Whence this mixed society, constituted partly from private, natural, necessary, and voluntary societies, partly from public societies, is called a universal association. It is a polity in the fullest sense, an imperium, realm, commonwealth, and people united in one body by the agreement of many symbiotic associations and particular bodies, and brought together under one right. For families, cities, and provinces existed by nature prior to realms, and gave birth to them.

Many writers distinguish between a realm (*regnum*) and a commonwealth (*respublica*), relating the former to a monarchical king and the latter to polyarchical optimates.[3] But in my judgment this distinction is

§4 not a good one. For ownership of a realm belongs to the people, and administration of it to the king. Thus Cicero, as cited by Augustine, says "a commonwealth is the weal of the people, although it may be well and

---

[1] [*universalis:* inclusive of all other associations within a given large area, and recognizing no superior to itself; sovereign in its own territory.]

[2] [fundamental law of the realm.]

[3] [*optimates:* the chief men of the realm; those who hold the more powerful offices. In some realms optimates are not merely nobles, but also leading burghers or their representatives.]

justly ruled either by a king, by a few optimates, or by the whole people."[4] Indeed, any polity whatever, including a city, can be called a commonwealth, such as the Athenian, Spartan, Hebrew, and Roman commonwealths, of which many have not been without their kings. . . .

We will discuss, first, the members of a realm and, then, its §5 right. The members of a realm, or of this universal symbiotic association, are not, I say, individual men, families, or collegia, as in a private or a particular public association. Instead, members are many cities, provinces, and regions agreeing among themselves on a single body constituted by mutual union and communication. Individual persons from these group members are called natives, inhabitants of the realm, and sons and daughters of the realm. They are to be distinguished from foreigners and strangers, who have no claim upon the right or the realm. It can be said that individual citizens, families, and collegia are not members of a realm just as boards, nails, and pegs are not considered parts of a ship, nor rocks, beams, and cement parts of a house. On the other hand, cities, urban communities, and provinces are members of a realm, just as prow, stern, and keel are members of a ship, and roof, walls, and floor are essential parts of a house. . . .

The bond of this body and association is consensus, together §7 with trust extended and accepted among the members of the commonwealth. The bond is, in other words, a tacit or expressed promise to communicate things, mutual services, aid, counsel and the same common laws (*jura*) to the extent that the utility and necessity of universal social life in a realm shall require. Even the reluctant are compelled to comply with this communication. However, this does not prevent separate provinces of the same realm from using different special laws. Plato rightly said that this trust is the foundation of human society, while lack of trust is its plague, and that trust is the bond of concord among the different members of a commonwealth. For the promise of so many different men and orders has as its purpose that the diverse actions of the individual parts be referred to the utility and communion of one commonwealth, and that inferiors be held together with superiors by a certain fairness in the law (*jus*). . . .

---

[4]Cicero, *The Republic,* III, 27; Augustine, *The City of God,* II, 21. A more accurate reference in Cicero for this notation is in I, 26 of the same work. The precise quotation used by Althusius, however, is found in the Augustine reference.]

§9   The more populous the association, the safer and more fortunate it is. Therefore the depopulation of a city and realm is understood
to be among the more severe punishments. It is useful and necessary to
have an abundance of citizens both in time of war and in time of peace.
In time of war a large number can better restrain and hold out against
external force. A small number is more easily and quickly diminished
and ruined by a baneful misfortune. . . . In time of peace a large
number of people augments the public treasury by their taxes, tolls,
fines, business, commerce, and goods. . . .

§10   On the other hand, a commonwealth or region overflowing
with an excess of people is not free from disadvantages, and is exposed
to many corruptions. For by such an excess of men all things are more
easily consumed and exhausted, a great scarcity of things develops, and
poverty occurs. Nor can so many be ruled easily and well. Nor can
concord, good order, and proper discipline be preserved as easily
among many persons. They overflow with sycophants, with wealth
and corruption, until wealth is preferred among them to virtue, bribes
to justice, timidity to courage, and evil to good. Just as iron by its nature
produces rust by which it is gradually corroded, and just as ripe fruit
produces worms by which it is gradually consumed, so also large,
populous, and mighty imperia[5] manifest many corruptions by which
they are gradually worn down. Experience testifies that might leads to
over-confidence, over-confidence to folly, folly to contempt, contempt to the weakening of authority, and so to the loss of imperium.
Might also leads to wealth, wealth to the pursuit of sensual pleasures,
and so to everything corrupt. When the might of a commonwealth
grows, fortitude and virtue decline. Thus the Roman imperium was in
its highest state of authority and dignity under Augustus. Under
Tiberius, however, the pursuit of sensual pleasures began, and virtue
was stifled by lust. Under Caligula, Claudius, and Nero virtue was
utterly destroyed. For a while, first under Vespasian and then under
Trajan and Anthony Pius, virtue again came forth, and with it came

---

[5] [*imperium* (pl. *imperia*): sometimes empire, sometimes rule, and sometimes both
empire and rule. In the universal public association, it very often means empire,
as it does here. However, in smaller associations, both private and public, the
word means merely rule. Throughout this translation the word has usually been
rendered "imperium" in order to convey Althusius' understanding of the
centrality and continuity of the principle of rule in all associations.]

imperial grandeur. However, soon afterwards under Domitian, who followed Vespasian and Titus, and under Commodus, who followed Trajan and Anthony Pius, virtue once more gave way, and with it the imperial glory.

From these considerations one may conclude that a common- §11
wealth of medium size is best and steadiest. Such a commonwealth can resist external force, and is not dominated by the corruptions I have discussed. It also labors less under misguided affections, commotions, avarice, and ambition. As it is forced to be suspicious of the might of its neighbors, so it also is forced to be more cautious. The Roman commonwealth is an example. When it was of medium size, it was free from many corruptions. When it grew to a great size, however, with greater might and a larger population, as in the time of Marius, Sulla, Pompey, and Julius Caesar, it abounded with corruptions so much that it was thrown into great calamities. But the Venetian commonwealth, because it remains of medium size and vigorously resists wilful corrup- tions by the severity of its laws, has endured for the longest time, as one was also able to say of the city of Sparta.

SUCH ARE THE MEMBERS of the realm. Its right is the means by which §12
the members, in order to establish good order and the supplying of provisions throughout the territory of the realm, are associated and bound to each other as one people in one body and under one head.[6] This right of the realm (*jus regni*) is also called the right of sovereignty §13
(*jus majestatis*).[7] It is, in other words, the right of a major state or power as contrasted with the right that is attributed to a city or a province. . . .

What we call this right of the realm has as its purpose good §15
order, proper discipline, and the supplying of provisions in the universal association. Towards these purposes it directs the actions of each and all of its members, and prescribes appropriate duties for them. Therefore, the universal power of ruling (*potestas imperandi universalis*) is called that

---

[6] "Then Samuel proclaimed the right of the realm (*jus regni*) among the people, and wrote it in a certain book." I Samuel 10:25.

[7] [In the equivalent chapter (VI) of the edition of 1603, Althusius limited the right of sovereignty to the power of administration, which he placed under the fundamental right or law of the realm. Here, of course, it is identified with this right or law. Sovereignty henceforth pertains to the people and their constitu- tion, not merely to the chief administrator and his actions.]

which recognizes no ally, nor any superior or equal to itself. And this supreme right of universal jurisdiction is the form and substantial essence of sovereignty (*majestas*) or, as we have called it, of a major state. When this right is taken away, sovereignty perishes. . . .

§16   The people, or the associated members of the realm, have the power (*potestas*) of establishing this right of the realm and of binding themselves to it. So Vásquez demonstrates from Bartolus and other authorities.[8] And in this power of disposing, prescribing, ordaining, administering, and constituting everything necessary and useful for the universal association is contained the bond, soul, and vital spirit of the realm, and its autonomy, greatness, size, and authority. Without this §17   power no realm or universal symbiotic life can exist. Therefore, as long as this right thrives in the realm and rules the political body, so long does the realm live and prosper. But if this right is taken away, the entire symbiotic life perishes, or becomes a band of robbers and a gang of evil men, or disintegrates into many different realms or provinces.

§18   This right of the realm, or right of sovereignty, does not belong to individual members, but to all members joined together and to the entire associated body of the realm. For as universal association can be constituted not by one member, but by all the members together, so the right is said to be the property not of individual members, but of the members jointly. Therefore, "what is owed to the whole (*universitas*) is not owed to individuals, and what the whole owes individuals do not owe."[9] Whence it follows that the use and ownership of this right belong neither to one person nor to individual members, but to the members of the realm jointly. By their common consent, they are able to establish and set in order matters pertaining to it. And what they have once set in order is to be maintained and followed, unless something else pleases the common will.[10] For as the whole body is related to the individual citizens, and can rule, restrain, and direct each member, so the people rules each citizen.[11]

---

[8] Fernando Vásquez, *Illustrium controversiarum,* I, 47; Bartolus, *Commentarii* (Digest I, 1, 9; I, 4, 1; I, 1, 5; XII, 6, 64); Conrad Lancellot, *Templum omnium judicum,* I, 2; Paul Castro, *Commentaria* (Digest I, 1, 5).

[9] Digest III, 4, 7, 1.

[10] *See* Francis Hotman, *De antiquo jure regni Gallici,* I, 19 and 23; Fernando Vásquez, *Illustrium controversiarum,* I, 47.

[11] However, Vásquez wrongly rejects this comparison.

This power of the realm (*potestas regni*), or of the associated   *§19*
bodies, is always one power and never many, just as one soul and not
many rules in the physical body. The administrators of this power can be
many, so that individuals can each take on a share of the function of
governing, but not the plenitude of power. And these individuals are
not themselves in control of the supreme power. Instead they all jointly
acknowledge such a power in the consent and concord of the associated
bodies. Whence jurists have declared the rights of sovereignty and of the
realm (*jura majestatis et regni*) to be indivisible, incommunicable, and
interconnected, so that whoever holds one holds them all.[12] Otherwise
two superior entities would be established in one imperium. But a
superior entity can have no equal or greater superior. And imperium
and obedience cannot be mingled. These rights can, however, be
lawfully delegated, so that in their administration someone other than
their owner may perform the duties of a supreme magistrate.

Bodin disagrees with our judgment by which supreme power   *§20*
is attributed to the realm or universal association. He says that the right
of sovereignty, which we have called the right of the realm, is a supreme
and perpetual power limited neither by law (*lex*) nor by time.[13] I
recognize neither of these two attributes of the right of sovereignty, in
the sense Bodin intends them, as genuine. For this right of sovereignty is
not the supreme power; neither is it perpetual or above law. It is not   *§21*
supreme because all human power acknowledges divine and natural law
(*lex divina et naturalis*) as superior. Note the argument of Romans 13: the
minister of God is for your good. If he is the minister of God, he can do
nothing contrary to the commandment given by his Lord.[14] Indeed, an
absolute and supreme power standing above all laws is called tyrannical.
Bartolus says, "great is Caesar, but greater is the truth."[15] Augustine says,
"when justice is taken away, what are realms except great bands of
robbers?"[16] On this point, however, not even Bodin disagrees with us.

---

[12] Roland a Valle, *Consiliorum,* I, cons. 1, num. 138; Marc Antony Natta,
Consilia, cons. 636 and 640; Charles Dumoulin, *Consuetudines Parisienses,* tit. 1,
art, 8 glos, 4, num. 16 f.; Diego Covarruvias, *Practicarum quaestionium,* 4.

[13] *The Commonweale,* I, 8. Jacob Bornitius further develops his idea of sovereignty in *De majestate politica,* I.

[14] *See also* Deuteronomy 17:18–20; Joshua 1:7 f.; Psalm 119.

[15] *Commentarii* (Digest IV, 4, 38).

[16] *The City of God,* IV, 4.

For he does not release the power he calls supreme from the imperium of divine and natural law (*jus divinum et naturale*).[17]

Our question, therefore, concerns civil law and right (*civilis lex et jus*). Should he who is said to have supreme power subordinate his imperium and high office to civil law as well? Bodin says no, and many others agree with him. In the judgment of these men there is supreme power above civil law and not limited by it. This is a judgment I would not hold. To liberate power from civil law is to release it to a certain degree from the bonds of natural and divine law (*lex naturalis et divina*). For there is no civil law, nor can there be any, in which something of natural and divine immutable equity has not been mixed. If it departs entirely from the judgment of natural and divine law (*jus naturale et divinum*), it is not to be called law (*lex*). It is entirely unworthy of this name, and can obligate no one against natural and divine equity. Therefore, if a general civil law enacted by a prince is fair and just, who can free him from the obligations of this very law? On the contrary, it should be the judgment of the supreme legislator that whatever we wish men to do to us, we should do those things to them.[18] But insofar as this civil law departs in certain respects from natural equity, I will grant that he who has supreme power, and does not recognize any superior except God, together with natural equity and justice, is not bound by this law, especially in applying punishment to himself.[19]

§22   If law (*lex*), and freedom from law by a supreme power, are accepted in this sense, I concede to the judgment of Bodin, Petrus Gregorius, Cujas, Doneau, Duaren, and other jurists. But by no means can this supreme power be attributed to a king or optimates, as Bodin most ardently endeavors to defend. Rather it is to be attributed rightfully only to the body of a universal association, namely, to a commonwealth or realm, and as belonging to it. From this body, after God, every legitimate power flows to those we call kings or optimates. Therefore, the king, prince, and optimates recognize this associated body as their superior, by which they are constituted,

---

[17] [Althusius seems to make no distinction between *lex divina et naturalis* and *jus divinum et naturale*.]

[18] Matthew 7:12; Luke 6:31.

[19] Jacob Bornitius, however, would indiscriminately subordinate the prince to civil law to the extent that such law can be analogically accommodated to him. *De majestate politica*, I, 10.

removed, exiled, and deprived of authority. . . . For however great is   §23
the power that is conceded to another, it is always less than the power
of the one who makes the concession, and in it the pre-eminence and
superiority of the conceder is understood to be reserved. Whence it is
shown that the king does not have a supreme and perpetual power
above the law, and consequently neither are the rights of sovereignty
his own property, although he may have the administration and
exercise of them by concession from the associated body. And only so
far are the rights of sovereignty ceded and handed over to another that
they never become his own property.

Bodin defends the opposite position by distinguishing be-   §24
tween the sovereignty of the realm and of the ruler.[20] But if sovereignty
is therefore twofold, of the realm and of the king, as Bodin says, I ask
which is greater and superior to the other? It cannot be denied that the
greater is that which constitutes the other and is immortal in its
foundation, and that this is the people. Nor can it be denied that the
lesser is that which appears as one person, and dies with him. The king
represents the people not the people the king, as we explain later.[21] And
greater is the power and strength of many than of one. Whence the
supreme monarch is required to give an account of his administration, is
not permitted for his own pleasure to alienate or diminish the provinces,
cities, or towns of his realm, and can even be deposed. . . .

We must now define this supreme power. We attribute it by   §25
right of sovereignty to the associated political body, which claims it for
itself alone. In our judgment, it is derived from the purpose and scope of
the universal association, namely, from the utility and necessity of
human social life. According to this position, therefore, the nature and
character of imperium and power will be that they regard and care for
the genuine utility and advantage of subjects. Vásquez demonstrates this
when he says that there is no power for evil, but only for good, none
for doing harm or for ruling in the interest of pleasure or self-
aggrandizement, but only for considering and supporting the genuine
utility of subjects.[22] Whence Augustine says that to rule is nothing other
than to serve the utility of others, as parents rule their children, and a

---

[20] *The Commonweale,* I, 7 and 8.
[21] Chapters XVIII and XIX.
[22] *Illustrium controversiarum,* I, 26 and 45.

§27   man his wife.[23] . . . Universal power is called pre-eminent, primary, and supreme not because it is above law or absolute, but in respect to particular and special subordinate power that depends upon it, arises and flows from it, returns in time to it, and is furthermore bound to definite places. Such is the power that is given to universal administrators, and to special heads of provinces as their deputies, delegates, administrators, procurators, and ministers. All have only the use and exercise of power for the benefit of others, not the ownership of it.

§28   THIS RIGHT OF THE REALM (*jus regni*) is twofold. It pertains both to the welfare of the soul and to the care of the body. Religion, by recognizing and worshiping God, seeks the welfare of the soul. The care of this life seeks the welfare of the body. Prayers are to be poured forth "for kings and all who are in high positions, that under them we may lead a peaceful and quiet life in all piety and respectfulness."[24] We are trained "to renounce all impiety and worldly desires, and to live temperately, justly, and piously in the present world."[25] We should live temperately toward ourselves, justly toward our neighbor, and piously toward God. Piety is to be understood according to the first table of the Decalogue, and justice according to the second. Polybius says that the desirable and stable condition of a commonwealth is one in which holy and blameless life is lived in private, and justice and clemency flourish in public.[26]

§29   Each part of this right of the realm about which we have spoken consists of universal symbiotic communion[27] and of its adminis-

§30   tration. We will first discuss this universal communion,[28] and later its administration.[29] Universal symbiotic communion is the process by which the members of a realm or universal association communicate everything necessary and useful to it, and remove and do away with everything to the contrary. And therefore this right of the realm pertaining to symbiosis and communion can be described as living lawfully, as nourishing life, and as sharing something in common.

---

[23] *The City of God,* XIX, 15. [XIX, 14 in the Modern Library edition.]
[24] Timothy 2:2.
[25] Titus 2:12.
[26] *Histories,* VI, 47.
[27] [*communio*: communication; sharing.]
[28] [The rest of this chapter and the whole of Chapters X–XVII.]
[29] Chapter XVIII and following.

Universal symbiotic communion is both ecclesiastical and *§31*
secular. Corresponding to the former are religion and piety, which
pertain to the welfare and eternal life of the soul, the entire first table of
the Decalogue. Corresponding to the latter is justice, which concerns
the use of the body and of this life, and the rendering to each his due, the
second table of the Decalogue. In the former, everything is to be
referred immediately to the glory of God; in the latter, to the utility and
welfare of the people associated in one body. These are the two *§32*
foundations of every good association. Whenever a turning away from
them has begun, the happiness of a realm or universal association is
diminished. . . .

Ecclesiastical communion of the realm[30] is the process by *§33*
which those means that pertain to the public organizing and conserving
of the kingdom of Christ (*regnum Christi*) are established, undertaken,
and communicated according to his will throughout the territory of this
universal association. This is done to the eternal glory of God and for
the welfare of the realm. Whence the ecclesiastical and sacerdotal right *§34*
of sovereignty of the realm is called the business of Jehovah. Within the
boundaries of the realm, this right guides the enjoyment of a pious life
by which we acknowledge and worship God in the present world. . . .

This sacerdotal or ecclesiastical right is properly instituted in *§35*
the territory of the realm when the same public and uncorrupted
worship of God is established, practiced, and conserved according to
the will of God in the individual cities and provinces or members of the
realm, and when the general care of it is expressed by the universal
association. This care is expressed, first and foremost, by the public *§36*
introduction, establishment, and conservation of religion and uncorrupted worship of God, as they are approved by sacred writings, in the
territory of the realm, and in all the cities and provinces thereof. "Seek
first the kingdom of God."[31] "For the fear of the Lord is the beginning
of understanding."[32] All members, both individually and collectively,

---

[30] [The rest of this chapter is devoted to ecclesiastical communion, and Chapters
XXVII to secular communion. Ecclesiastical matters will be discussed again in
Chapter XXVIII, but therein as an element of administration, not as part of the
discussion of communion. Note also that Althusius uses "communication" and
"communion" interchangeably.]

[31] Matthew 6:33.

[32] Psalm 111:10.

are obligated to the profession of this religion and divine worship. . . .

§37   The true and pure religion and worship of God are to be established not by a majority of the citizens, nor by the weight or vote of men, but by the Word of God alone, according to their agreement with faith.

§38   Public schools provide for the conserving of true religion and the passing of it on to later generations, for informing the life and customs of citizens, and for acquiring knowledge of the liberal arts. Schools are to be opened in the cities and provinces of the commonwealth in order that professors and instructors of liberal arts may publicly teach, that they may distribute prizes and honors for merit, and that they may confer upon their scholars the insignia of the master, the licentiate, and the doctor. In these schools the seeds of piety and virtue are adroitly poured into the youth from sacred writings and the more human liberal arts, so that good citizens may go forth as pious, manly,

§39   just and temperate persons. . . . Moreover, these schools are the custodians of the keys of science and doctrine, by which the resolution of all doubt is sought and the way of salvation is disclosed. Whatever the quality of rulers and citizens the school produces, of such is the commonwealth and church constituted. . . .

§41   Also pertaining to the conservation of religion, of divine worship, and of the church is their defense against all disturbers and scorners. Whence arises the right and power of restoring the uncorrupted worship of God, of expelling from the territory those alien to uncorrupted religion, and of compelling the citizens and inhabitants of the realm, by public ordinances and even by external force, to' worship God. . . . On the other hand, the worshipers of the true God are to be defended and protected in the realm, even if they are few in number and there are many who profess another religion. . . .

§42   Nevertheless, a schism should not be made, nor a separation from the church be granted, merely because of some error, sacramental reason, or other cause, provided the foundation of the true religion is retained and other human opinions merely added to it. . . . "Welcome the man who is weak in faith."[33] The Apostle Paul recognized as brothers those who came close to idolatry, profaned the supper of the Lord, and erred concerning the resurrection.[34] "If you bite and devour

---

[33] Romans 14:1.
[34] Corinthians 8:9 f.; 11:20 ff.; 15:12 ff.

one another, watch out that you are not in turn consumed by one another."[35] Christ suffered disciples who were weak, sinful, crude, inexperienced, and erratic.[36] The Gospel collects in its net not only good fishes, but others also.[37] It further advises that tares not be rooted out from good seeds.[38] "In a great house there are vessels of gold and of clay, and some perform with honor and others with dishonor."[39] The church is likened to a granary in which there are both grain and chaff,[40] to a banquet in which both good and evil feast together,[41] to the ten virgins,[42] and to a sheepfold in which there are both sheep and goats.[43]

Moderation should be observed, as Benedict Aretius says. The problem is to be handled in one way for authors of schisms and those who have openly separated themselves, and in another way for those who have been misled by a jealous piety and a certain simple ardor. It is indeed handled very badly when we demand a decision on all opinions in even the most minute matters, and, unless this decision is subscribed to in all particulars, we give way to thunderbolts, factions, sects, curses, even to prisons and deaths. For no mode of thought has ever come forth as so perfect that the judgment of all learned men would subscribe to it. Aretius concludes that if the principal articles of faith are preserved, nothing should stand in the way of disagreement on opinions in other Christian matters.[44] §43

To be sure, persons are not to be suffered who are openly and publicly atheists, who take action against the magistrate, who promote unnecessary wars, who support shameful acts in public, and who deny, break, or call into doubt the articles necessary for salvation. It is not permitted that everyone should be free to enjoy his religion in total opposition to the Christian faith. For as God is one, so there is one §44

§45

---

[35] Galatians 5:15.

[36] See Zachary Ursinus, *Dispositiones*, II, *in fine;* Benedict Aretius, *Problemata theologica*, I, loc. 9 and 58 f.

[37] Matthew 13:47.

[38] [Matthew 13:29.]

[39] II Timothy 2:20.

[40] Matthew 3:12.

[41] Matthew 22:1 ff.; Luke 14:16 ff.

[42] Matthew 25:1 f.

[43] Matthew 25:32 f.

[44] *Problemata theologica*, I, loc. 58.

formula for rightly worshiping him, which he has set forth for us, and outside of which it is not possible to please him. There is no communion of light with darkness, of Christ with Satan. And if Jehovah is your God, why do you not follow him? God wills that violators of orthodox religion be severely punished. He makes the magistrate the defender of his cause, and commends to him the protection and defense of the pious. . . . For this kind of liberty fights with faith and renders it uncertain. Many faiths, and many diverse churches, introduce idolatry and impiety. Moreover, diversity destroys unity. "Whoever is not with me is against me."[45] To what extent a magistrate in good conscience can tolerate men who stray from true religion in his realm will be discussed later.[46]

---

[45] Luke 11:23.
[46] Chapter XXVIII.

X–XVII

Secular Communication

X   **N**OW THAT WE HAVE DISCUSSED the ecclesiastical aspect of symbiotic communion in the universal association, we turn to its secular counterpart. Secular and political communion in the universal realm is the process by which the necessary and convenient means for carrying on a common life of justice together are communicated among the members of the realm. This communion is the practice of those things that relate to the use of this life or the public affairs of the realm. Whence arises the secular right of sovereignty (*jus majestatis*), and the employment of a king. This secular right of the realm (*jus regni*), or right of sovereignty, guides the life of justice organized in universal symbiosis according to the second table of the Decalogue. This right trains us how to live justly in the present world, as the Apostle says,[1] and so involves the practice of the second table of the Decalogue.

§1

This secular right of sovereignty is both general and special.[2] The general and secular right prescribes for members of the association the method and form for living and acting justly in each and all affairs of this symbiosis. Therefore, the various affairs of this universal association are to be tested by and accommodated to this right.

§2

We must here consider both the promulgation and the execution of the general right (*jus*).[3] Promulgation of this right is the process

§3

---

[1] Titus 2:12.

[2] [General right of sovereignty is common to all universal associations; special right of sovereignty is proper to each one according to its own requirements. The former, which is the common law (*jus commune*) as it pertains to the universal association, is discussed in Chapter X; the latter, which is the proper law (*jus proprium*) of the same, is discussed in Chapters XI–XVII.]

[3] [law.]

by which it is publicly announced and accepted as the rule and norm of
§4 all just actions in universal symbiosis. . . . This law and right (*lex et jus*)
is the rule of things to be done and to be omitted by members of the
realm individually and collectively, and is prescribed for the conservation of the life of justice and the universal association. It is called by
Seneca the bond that holds the commonwealth together, and a vital
spirit that the city breathes, which if withdrawn leaves the city as
nothing in itself except a burden and a prey.[4] This right is the guiding
light of civil life, the scale of justice, the preserver of liberty, a bulwark
of public peace and discipline, a refuge for the weak, a bridle for the
powerful, and a norm and straightener of imperium. It can be called
the public command of the people, as well as the promise and assurance
by the people that they will perform what is permitted and avoid what
is not permitted. It is also the precept by which political life is
instituted and cultivated according to a prescribed manner in the
realm, and by which duties to the fellow citizen or neighbor are
performed and things forbidden are omitted. Whence in Psalms and
other places of sacred scripture we find many times the notion, "Do
good and abstain from evil."[5] Hence the precepts of the Decalogue are
both affirmative and negative, a commanding and prohibiting, mandates and interdicts.

§5   Therefore, when we know the things that are to be vouchsafed
by us to our neighbor, it is easy to determine the things to be omitted
§6 and avoided. Those that are to be vouchsafed to our neighbor in this
civil and social life—which rightly are owed to him and are his so that
he possesses them as his own—are, first, his natural life, including the
liberty and safety of his own body. The opposite of these are terror,
murder, injury, wounds, beatings, compulsion, slavery, fetters, and
coercion. Secondly, the neighbor possesses his reputation, good name,
honor, and dignity, which are called the "second self" of man. Opposed
to them are insult, ill repute, and contempt. And here I also include
chastity of body, the contrary of which is any kind of uncleanness and
fornication. Also pertaining to this category are the right of family, and
the right of citizenship that belongs to some. Thirdly, a man has external

---

[4] *Clemency*, I, 4. [Seneca, however, ascribes these attributes not to law as such,
but to the emperor as the soul and intelligence of the people.]
[5] Psalm 34:14; 37:27; Isaiah 1:16; I Peter 2:11 f.; Romans 7:18 ff.

goods that he uses and enjoys, opposed to which are the corruption, damage, and impairing of his goods in any form, as well as their plundering or robbery, and any violation of their possession or artificial impediment to their use.

The laws of the Decalogue prescribe the duties vouchsafed to our neighbor. By acting according to them, we may live an honorable life, not injuring others, and rendering to each his due.[6] Above all, we vouchsafe and do to our neighbor what we wish to be done to ourselves.[7] Thus we render to him honor, authority, dignity, preeminence, and, indeed, the right of family; nor do we, on the contrary, despise him or hold him in contempt, the fifth precept of the Decalogue. His life is to be defended and conserved, and his body may not be injured, hurt, struck, or treated in any inhumane way whatever, nor may the liberty and use of his body be diminished or taken away, the sixth precept. His chastity is to be left intact, free from fornication, and may not be taken away in any manner whatever, the seventh precept. His goods and their possession, use, and ownership are to be conserved, and they may not be injured, diminished, or taken away, the eighth precept. His reputation and good name are to be protected, and they may not be taken away, injured, or reduced by insults, lies, or slander, the ninth precept. And so one may not covet those things that belong to another, either by deliberation or by passion, but everything our neighbor possesses he is to use and enjoy free from the passion of our concupiscence and perverse desire.

Other laws (*leges*) are prescribed for the inhabitants of the realm both individually and collectively. By them the moral law (*lex moralis*) of the Decalogue is explained, and adapted to the varying circumstances of place, time, persons, and thing present within the commonwealth. So Moses, after the promulgation of the Decalogue, added many laws by which the Decalogue was explained and adapted to Jewish commonwealth.[8] Such laws, because of circumstances, can therefore differ in certain respects from the moral law, either by adding something to it or taking something away from it.[9] But they ought not to be at all contrary

§7

§8

---

[6] [*Institutes* I, 1, 3; Digest I, 1, 10, 1.]
[7] Matthew 22:39; 7:12; Leviticus 19; Luke 13:24.
[8] Deuteronomy 6–8; Exodus 21–22.
[9] Digest I, 1, 6.

to natural law (*jus naturale*), or to moral equity. [10] As men cannot live without mutual society, so no society can be secure or lasting without laws (*leges*), as Plato says.[11] Aristotle says no commonwealth can exist where the laws do not exercise imperium.[12] For what God is in the world, the navigator in a ship, the driver in a chariot, the director in a chorus, the commander in an army, so law (*lex*) is in the city. Without law, neither house nor city nor commonwealth nor the world itself can endure. According to Papinian, "law is a common precept, a decree of prudent men, a restraint against crimes committed voluntarily or in ignorance, and a common obligation of the commonwealth."[13] According to Marcian, "law is the queen of all things human and divine. It should also be the watchman of both the good and the bad, the prince and leader of them, and accordingly the measure of things just and unjust, as well as of those living beings that are civil by nature. It is the preceptress of what ought to be done, and the restrainer of what should not be done."[14] "We are taught [. . .] by the authority and bidding of laws," says Cicero, "to control our passions, to bridle our every lust, to defend what is ours, and to keep our minds, eyes, and hands from whatever belongs to another."[15] "Through the law comes knowledge of things to be done and to be omitted,"[16] and in it is our wisdom.[17]

§9   The power of interpreting and explaining law is the means by which, in reference to those matters that are uncertain, clarification is provided from the system of law and the nature of the problem. This is done through the broad consideration of things, persons, time, place, and other circumstances. Thus the established rights (*jura*)[18] are accommodated to men's power of comprehension.

---

[10] *Institutes I, 2, 11.*

[11] Laws, III.

[12] *Politics*, 1292ᵃ 32.

[13] Digest I, 3, 1.

[14] Digest I, 3, 2. [Marcian in turn attributes this quotation to the Stoic philosopher Chrysippus.]

[15] *The Orator*, I, 43. [The passage from Cicero more accurately states, "We are taught *not by unending debates full of controversies, but* by the authority and bidding of laws, etc." Italics are added to indicate the words omitted without acknowledgment by Althusius.]

[16] Romans 3:20.

[17] Deuteronomy 4:20; Psalm 119:104.

[18] [laws.]

The execution of law (*lex*) pertains to the preserving of   §10
external public discipline. It is the responsibility (*jus*) of distributing
what is merited, the responsibility and power of punishing delinquents
and of rewarding doers of good. From another perspective it is the
administration of justice. . . .

The power of punishing delinquents involves the life, body,   §11
name, and goods of evildoers in proportion to the crime and its
circumstances. . . . It is publicly useful to the human association to
punish delinquents. First, the delinquent is corrected by the punishment imposed, and led to greater maturity. Secondly, the harm done to
the injured party may be repaired by the penalty imposed, so that the
injured party need not become carried away in the vindication of the
injury. Whence penalties are called reins and whips for the wicked,
preservers and defenders of the upright. Thirdly, a penalty is also
imposed as a warning to others, that they may be deterred from
transgressions by the fear of punishment such an example evokes.
Thereby social life is not thrown into disorder, and other persons are not
infected by crime. Fear of becoming delinquent leads to the control of
inordinate desire, which I have discussed elsewhere.[19] For as bolts of
lightning strike to the hazard of a few and the fear of all, so punishments
scare more persons than those who are actually punished for evil. When
punishment comes to one person, fear comes to others subject to
punishment for the same crime. Whence punishments are called remedies by which the illnesses of a commonwealth are overcome and cured.
Fourthly, a penalty consisting in a fine, or public appropriation of
goods, is turned to the use of the realm. For when through crime a
commonwealth is injured, it is fair that the penalty be applied to what
has suffered by evildoing. Whence the collection of penalties is relevant
to the conservation of peace, discipline, and public tranquillity in a
realm and commonwealth. For impunity in transgressing is a great
inducement to transgression, a mother of injury and insolence, a root of
impudence, a wet-nurse of sin, and a license that renders everything the
worse. Fifthly, the wrath of God is mitigated by the expiatory act of
punishment, and we obtain his benediction. . . .[20]

---

[19] *Dicaelogicae libri tres*, I, 98.

[20] [At the conclusion of Althusius' somewhat parallel discussion in the *Dicaeologica* of
the reasons for punishment, the reader is referred to Martin Bucer, *De regno Christi*, II,
60, which is a chapter on the management and moderation of punishment.]

§12   Corresponding to this power of punishing is the right of conferring rewards. For as punishment deters men from vices, so rewarding them inspires, fosters, and conserves the love of virtue and good works. And thus it is fair that "he who sows iniquity will reap trouble."[21] On the other hand, it is not wrong that he who seeks virtue and goodness receives reward and glory for his good works.[22]

§1   **XI**   SPECIAL AND SECULAR RIGHT of sovereignty indicates and prescribes the particular means for meeting the needs and wants of all symbiotes of this association, for promoting advantages for them, and for avoiding disadvantages. For as each member of the body was created and constituted for its duty, and yet each and every member has the same end, namely, the conservation of the whole body, so each of us has been ordained to his proper and individual role in life, but nevertheless all of us to the glory of God and the welfare of our §2   neighbor. This special right should be equitable, good, useful, and adapted to place, time, and persons. Whence it is called civil law (*jus civile*),[23] and is said to be peculiar to each polity.[24]

§3   This special right is twofold. The first part is devoted to the arrangement established for procuring the material necessities of life.[25] It informs the procedure for communicating advantages and upholding responsibilities in those things that have been agreed upon in the universal association for the supply of necessities and supports. §4   This part of the special right of the realm consists in (1) commercial regulations, (2) a monetary system, (3) a common language, (4) public duties in the realm, and (5) privileges and the conferring of titles of nobility.[26]

---

[21] Proverbs 22:8. *See also* II Thessalonians 1:6.

[22] Romans 2:7; 13:1–7; Proverbs 11:18, 21; Ezekiel 18:21–24; Hebrews 6:10; Deuteronomy 28; Psalm 101.

[23] [the positive law of a commonwealth, which may vary in part from commonwealth to commonwealth, as distinguished from divine law (*jus divinum*), natural law (*jus naturale*), and the law of nations (*jus gentium*), each of which is general and binding upon all commonwealths.]

[24] Digest I, 1, 6.

[25] [The second part pertains to the protection of the universal association. The first part is found in Chapters XI–XV; the second part in Chapters XVI–XVII.]

[26] [The first, second, and third are discussed in Chapter XI, the fourth in Chapters XI–XIV, and the fifth in Chapter XV.]

First, the right and responsibility for regulating public com-   §5
merce, contracts, and business on land and water belongs to the universal association. The free use and exercise of these functions in the
territory of the realm depends upon permission, prescription, and
current laws. It is called public trade. . . . Without commerce we   §7
cannot live conveniently in this social life. For there are many things we
need and without which no man can live with comfort. We can also be
underprivileged in many things that are for our good, even to the extent
of great inconvenience to us. Just as the human body cannot be healthy
without the mutual communication of offices performed by its members, so the body of the commonwealth cannot be healthy without
commerce. The necessity and utility of this life have therefore contrived
a plan and procedure for exchanging goods, so that you can give and
communicate to another what he needs and of which he cannot be
deprived, any more than can you, without discomfort, and on the other
hand receive from him what is necessary and useful to yourself. Indeed,
peace and concord are often acquired through commercial pursuits.
"They asked for peace because their country was nourished from the
country of the king."[27] . . .

The second right is of money, or the right of striking and   §13
engraving coins, which is established in material publicly selected by the
supreme magistrate with the approval of the people or realm. . . . For if   §14
there is no fixed valuation of gold, silver, and money among men and
neighboring peoples, commercial activity cannot be maintained. It
follows that an uncertain monetary system throws everything into
disorder, and makes intercourse and commerce with other peoples
difficult. . . .

The third right is the maintenance of a language, and of the   §16
same idiom of it, in the territory. The use of speech is truly necessary for
men in social life, for without it no society can endure, nor can the
communion of right. . . .

The fourth right is the power and responsibility for assigning   §17
and distributing duties that arise in the universal association. A duty is an   §18
office imposed upon a citizen or inhabitant in a territory of the realm
that he bears for the benefit of the associated body by its agreement and
permission. . . . Such duties are of two types: real and personal. A   §20

---

[27] Acts 12:20. *See also* II Chronicles 2 and 19.

double necessity is imposed upon the citizen, namely, to contribute things for the utility of the commonwealth,[28] and to provide services for rightly administering and conserving the commonwealth.[29] . . .

§23   Real duties are performed by the payment and collection of a tax. They accompany the possession of things, and are levied with reference to these things in relation to their value. Thus the inhabitant, after a declaration and appraisal of his possessions, pays something from them that is turned over to the use of the commonwealth. . . .[30]

§1   **XII**   THERE ARE TWO TYPES of tax collections. One is ordinary and
§2   the other extraordinary.[31] An ordinary collection is one that by provision of law has a fixed regular payment recurring one or more times each year. It is made from the goods that the possessor and inhabitant holds in the territory of the magistrate who makes the collection, and is devoted to the ordinary and everyday use and business of the republic. . . .

§1   **XIII**   AN EXTRAORDINARY COLLECTION or contribution is one that
        is declared and imposed because of the occurrence of a public necessity at a time when the public treasury composed of funds from ordinary collections is depleted. It is imposed principally upon persons, but in view of the things they have in greater or lesser measure. It prevails for a fixed time until the necessity for it has ceased. . . .

§1   **XIV**   PERSONAL PUBLIC DUTIES of the realm or universal association
        are those performed in the administration of its public affairs by the labor and industry of remunerated persons for the common welfare and utility of the associated bodies. The administrators of these
§2   affairs are called general officials of the polity. . . . As real duties bring together and communicate things and money for the conservation and defense of the universal association, so personal services communicate

---

[28] [real duties: Chapters XI–XIII.]

[29] [personal duties: Chapter XIV.]

[30] [One of the conditions Althusius says should be observed in levying taxes is that they be imposed upon "those things that can harm the poor people less," and upon "those less necessary things that are not used for the everyday necessities of life."]

[31] [Chapters XII and XIII respectively.]

assistance, help, counsel, industry, and labor by which the benefit and utility of the association are promoted, necessities obtained, and all inconveniences avoided. Whence the supreme necessity and utility of these public duties of the realm become apparent. They are the bonds and nerves by which so great a conjunction of diverse bodies is held together and conserved, and without which it is at once dissolved and ruined. Hence we observe the worth and excellence of these public duties that accommodate even real duties to the uses of the universal association. Those who perform these duties are of two kinds. Some are ministers of the realm or universal association, and others are ministers of the supreme magistrate. . . .   *§3*

XV   THE GRANTING OF PRIVILEGES[32] is the exemption for just and   *§1*
commendable reason of an inhabitant of the realm from the performance of some duty that other commonwealth citizens are expected to perform and communicate. A community (*universitas*)   *§2* cannot ordinarily grant immunity from taxes except in general council. Such a privilege is either personal or real. A personal privilege involves   *§3* only the person to whom it is granted, and does not extend beyond his person and property to his servants, family, and so forth. A real privilege,   *§4* on the contrary, embraces heirs, children, wife, and other related persons. . . . It is to be observed that in cases of great and extreme   *§13* necessity confronting the commonwealth all immunities and privileges cease and are annulled. For the private and special benefit and good of the citizen should not be preferred to the public utility and necessity of the commonwealth. . . . Also pertaining to this right is the conferring   *§14* of titles and privileges of nobility upon certain persons, such as the titles of dukes, princes, counts, and barons. These persons can be deprived of their privileges and rights and divested of their titles.[33]

---

[32] [This is the fifth right involved in the first part of the special and secular right of sovereignty.]

[33] [The authors Althusius has drawn most heavily upon in his discussion of the five rights of the first part of the special and secular right of sovereignty are the following: Petrus Gregorius, *De republica* and *Syntagma juris universi*; Henry Rosenthal, *De feudis;* Andreas Gail, *Practicarum observationum*; Jean Bodin, *The Commonweale*; Mark Antony Natta, *Consilia;* Joachim Mynsinger, *Centuriae*; Jacques Cujas, *Commentarii* (Code) and *Observationum et emendationum*; Eberartus a Weyhe, *De regni subsidiis*; William Budé, *Commentarii* (Digest and Code); André Tiraqueau, *De nobilitate*.]

§1   **XVI**   WE HAVE THUS FAR SPOKEN of the first part of special right of sovereignty, namely, the right established to procure the material necessities of life. We turn now to the second part, which pertains to the protection of the universal association and symbiosis. By this right everything necessary for avoiding or removing all difficulties, impediments, and obstacles to the universal association, and for avoiding any troubles, dangers, evils, and injuries to any distressed or needy member of the universal association, is offered with mutual feeling and concern by each and all members thereof. This second and latter right, therefore, is principally concerned with the arrangement established for protection and defense.

§2   This right of protection consists in (1) aid and (2) counsel. Aid is the assistance and prompt support provided by the communication of things and services to a distressed and needy member of this universal association. It consists, first, in defense and, then, in the care of goods belonging to the universal association. . . .[34]

§4   Defense is threefold. It is the safeguarding of the associated individual members when one of them—a province, city, village, or town—suffers violence and injury, or requires the commonwealth's support for its basic interests and needs. It is, furthermore, the guaranty of free passage and public security against those who disturb, plunder, or restrict commercial activity in the territory of the associated body. It is,

§17   finally, the conduct of war. . . . Just cause for waging war occurs when all other remedies have first been exhausted and peace or justice cannot otherwise be obtained. There are seven just causes for declaring and waging war. The first cause is the recovery of things taken away through violence by another people. The second cause is the defense against violence inflicted by another, and the repulsion of it. The third cause is the necessity for preserving liberty, privileges, rights, peace, and tranquillity, and for defending true religion. The fourth cause occurs when a foreign people deny peaceful transit through its province without good reason. The fifth cause occurs when subjects rise up against their prince and lord, do not fulfill their pledged word, and are not willing to obey him, although they have been admonished many times. The sixth reason is contumacy, which occurs when any prince, lord, or city has so

---

[34] [Defense is discussed in Chapter XVI, and the care of goods in Chapter XVII. In addition, there is a brief section at the end of the latter chapter devoted to counsel.]

contemptuously and repeatedly scorned the decisions of courts that justice cannot otherwise be administered and defended. The seventh just cause of war occurs when agreements are not implemented by the other party, when he does not keep his promises, and when tyranny is practiced upon subjects. . . .[35]

XVII   THE CARE OF GOODS of the commonwealth or associated   *§2*
body is twofold. First, it is the diligent and faithful conservation of those things necessary and useful to the commonwealth. Secondly, it is their augmentation and extension. This conservation is either of movable or immovable goods of the commonwealth. The care   *§3*
and management of movable goods centers in the treasury and other buildings. Monies are managed in the treasury; other goods, namely, armaments, grain reserves, and documents and chronicles are provided for in other buildings. . . .[36] The care and inspection of immovable   *§14*
goods belonging to the realm are committed to designated curators by the will and agreement of the universal association. . . . Such goods are   *§15*
navigable rivers of the realm, harbors, public roads, public pastures, and so forth. . . .

The augmentation and extension of the goods of the associ-   *§24*
ated body is accomplished through confederation or association with others, or through other legitimate means and titles. In such a confeder-   *§25*
ation other realms, provinces, cities, villages, or towns are received into and associated with the communion and society of the one body. By their admission, the body of the universal association is extended, and made stronger and more secure. This cannot be done, however, without the consent and authority of the body and its administrators. . . . Such   *§26*
confederation with a foreign people or another body is either complete or partial. A complete confederation is one in which a foreign realm,   *§27*
province, or any other universal association, together with its inhabitants, are fully and integrally coopted and admitted into the right and communion of the realm by a communicating of its fundamental laws

---

[35] [This discussion of the just causes of war is supported by numerous references to the Old Testament, especially to passages in Judges, I and II Samuel, and II Kings. Beyond these, three writings are referred to more than once: Diego Covarruvias, *Regulae peccatum,* II, sect. 9; Peter Martyr, *Commentarii* (I Samuel 30; Judges 11); Henry Bocer, *De jure belli,* I, 17.]

[36] [In the armory, the granary, and the archives.]

and right of sovereignty. To the extent that they coalesce and are united into one and the same body they become members of that one and same

§30   body. . . . A partial confederation is one in which various realms or provinces, while reserving their rights of sovereignty, solemnly obligate themselves one to the other by a treaty or covenant made preferably for a fixed period of time. Such a partial confederation is for the purpose of conducting mutual defense against enemies, for extending trust and cultivating peace and friendship among themselves, and for holding common friends and enemies, with a sharing of expenses. A commonwealth ought to be cautious in contracting and covenanting such treaties that it not be carried along by them into unjust or disastrous

§31   activities, nor destroyed by the downfall of a confederated ally. Therefore, it ought to ponder the might of the confederating ally, his faithfullness and constancy in previous transactions, the similarity of his customs to one's own, and the equity and honesty of the agreement among the confederates. . . .

§54   The universal association is also augmented by legitimate occasions and titles other than by confederation, as by testamentary succession . . . by donations and gifts of others, by legitimate war, by purchase, and by the marriage of the administrators of the commonwealth. . . .

§55   So much for the communication of aid. We turn now to the communication of counsel, which is performed by the members of an associated body in ecumenical and general councils within the universal

§56   association. These general ecumenical councils of the realm or associated body are meetings of its assembled members in which the utility and advantage of the commonwealth are considered, as well as common and special remedies for meeting common and particular evils, and something is decided for the common welfare by the communication of counsel. The difficult, grave, and arduous affairs of the realm or commonwealth are examined and determined in these general councils and assemblies of the entire universal association. These matters are the affairs and situations of interest to the entire imperium, or polity, and its members, such as those concerning the fundamental laws of the polity, the rights of sovereignty, the imposition of taxes and contributions, and other things that require the common deliberation and consent of the entire polity.

§57   This council or assembly is therefore the epitome of the realm or polity. All public affairs of the realm are referred to it and, after

examination and discussion by the members of the realm, decided by it.
The right of examining, deliberating, and coming to conclusions   §58
belongs to individual members of the realm or commonwealth. The
right of deciding rests indeed in the judgments and votes of a majority
of the members. . . .

There are five reasons for these councils. First, it is equitable   §60
that what touches all ought to be acted upon by all.[37] And what requires
the faculties, strength, aid, and enthusiasm of all ought also to be done
with their common consent. When the people has not been excluded
from the handling of public affairs, there is less ill-will should a poorly
launched project fail, and the people's benevolence and favor are
retained. Second, a project can be examined better by many persons,
and whatever is needed can more easily be supplied by many because
they know more and can be deceived less. Third, there are some affairs
that cannot be handled except by the people in such assemblies. Fourth,
those who have great might can be contained and corrected in office by
the fear of these assemblies in which the complaints of all are freely
heard. Fifth, by this means the liberty reserved to the people flourishes,
and public administrators are compelled to render account of their
administration, and to recognize the people, or the universal association, as their master by whom they have been constituted. . . .

---

[37] [Code V, 59, 5, 2.]

XVIII

The Ephors and Their Duties

§1 W E HAVE THUS FAR DISCUSSED the right of communion in the universal association. We now turn our attention to the administration of this right. This is the activity by which the rights (*jura*)[1] of universal symbiotic association are ordered, properly administered, and dispensed by designated public ministers of the realm for the welfare of its members, both individually and collectively. Whence it is called the *jus* ἐπιμελητικὸν[2] pertaining to the provision for proper management, or the *jus* εὐτακτικὸν[3] pertaining to good ordering.

§2 This administration is the bond by which the commonwealth holds together, and its vital spirit by which the various and diverse human functions of the association are directed, ordered, and referred to the welfare of all. Whence it is evident that such administration does not execute or perform these functions, but only establishes, orders, and directs them, which it does by ruling, commanding, forbidding, and impeding.

§3 These public ministers of the realm are elected by the united and associated bodies or members of the realm for the purpose of properly and honestly attending to, administering, governing, and conserving the body and rights of this universal association. They are invested with the necessary power and authority, and are bound by oath

§4 of office to the realm. Whence they are called custodians, presiding officers, defenders of the commonwealth, and prudent and diligent

---

[1] [laws.]

[2] [the principle and practice of administration.]

[3] [the principle and practice of ordering something well.]

executors of right and law (*jus et lex*). Any such community (*universitas*) can indeed constitute these administrators, as Losaeus proves.[4]

In the election and establishment of these public ministers, some have the task of electors, others of elected ministers. Electors assign, confer, and entrust to suitable ministers, according to certain laws and conditions, the care, government, and administration of the rights (*jura*)[5] of the realm, and obligate these ministers to the realm by oath of office. Elected ministers undertake the care and administration entrusted to them for the utility and welfare of the association, according to the law by which the administration has been conferred. "He is a minister of God to you for good."[6] They are therefore called rectors, governors, directors, administrators, regents, pastors, leaders, deliverers, and fathers, and are adorned with other honorific titles. §5 §6

It is evident that the power of administering the commonwealth and its rights is entrusted to the elected ministers and curators by agreements made in the name of the whole people, or by the body of the universal association. These ministers are expected to do good and not evil in their delegated administration of the commonwealth, and to serve the utility and welfare of the associated political body by devoting to it all their intelligence, zeal, labors, work, care, diligence, indeed all their wealth, goods, strength, and resources, and by not withholding them for pursuit of their private advantage. . . . For the commonwealth or realm does not exist for the king, but the king and every other magistrate exist for the realm and polity.[7] By nature and circumstance the people is prior to, more important than, and superior to its governors, just as every constituting body is prior and superior to what is constituted by it. . . . §7 §8

The people first associated itself in a certain body with definite laws (*leges*), and established for itself the necessary and useful rights (*jura*) of this association. Then, because the people itself cannot manage the administration of these rights, it entrusted their administration to §10

---

[4] *De jure universitatum*, I, 3.

[5] [laws.]

[6] Romans 13:4.

[7] *See* Fernando Vásquez, *Illustrium controversiarum*, I, 1; I, 42; I, 44. [The following discussion refers to Vásquez and to Diego Covarruvias more than to any other writers. Three books by Covarruvias are employed: *Practicarum quaestionium*; *Regulae peccatum*; and *Variarum resolutionum*.]

ministers and rectors elected by it. In so doing, the people transferred to them the authority and power necessary for the performance of this assignment, equipped them with the sword for this purpose, and put itself under their care and rule. "Because the plebs began to experience difficulty in meeting together, and the people even more difficulty in so great a crowd of men, necessity itself brought the care of the common-

§11   wealth to the senate."[8] Such administrators and curators therefore represent the whole people, and their actions are considered to be actions of the community.

For this reason, the citizens and inhabitants of the realm are collectively but not individually, like a ward or minor, and the consti-tuted ministers are like a guardian in that they bear and represent the

§12   person of the whole people. Just as a ward, although he is master of the things he has yielded to a guardian for care and administration, cannot act in any matter nor incur an obligation without the authority and consent of the guardian, so the people, without the authority and consent of its administrators and rectors, cannot administer the rights of the realm (*jura regni*), although it is the master, owner, and beneficiary

§13   of them. What a guardian rightfully does regarding the things and person of his wards, ministers of a commonwealth for the most part perform for the united inhabitants of the realm, together with their goods and rights.

§14   In relation to their ownership and delegation of supreme right the united subjects and members of a realm are masters of these ministers and rectors; indeed, these administrators, guardians, and rec-

§15   tors are servants and ministers to these very members of the realm. But in relation to the entrusted administration that has been approved by the people—that is, outside this delegating of right—the individual inhab-itants of a realm are themselves servants and subjects of their administra-tors and rectors. They serve them by performing and carrying through with their entrusted responsibility, and in so doing extend to them their services, abilities, and obedience.

The administrators of these individual subjects are called lords, guardians, and overseers, who are expected, however, to regard their subjects not as slaves and bonded servants, but as brothers.[9] Before

---

[8] Digest I, 2, 2, 9.

[9] *See* John 8:33, where the Jews pride themselves that they have never been slaves

undertaking this administration, and after relinquishing it, such rectors and administrators are equal and similar to other private men. Indeed, as the rights of sovereignty (*jura majestatis*) arise from the associated body, so they adhere to it indivisibly and inseparably, nor can they be transferred to another. Kings certainly cannot make themselves equal to or greater than the associated body. . . .

    The rector and administrator of this civil society and commonwealth cannot justly and without tyranny be constituted by any other than the commonwealth itself. For "by natural law (*jus naturale*) all men are equal"[10] and subject to the jurisdiction of no one, unless they subject themselves to another's imperium by their own consent and voluntary act, and transfer to another their rights, which no other person can claim for himself without a just title received from their owner.[11] In the beginning of the human race there were neither imperia nor realms, nor were there rectors of them. Later, however, when necessity demanded, they were established by the people itself. We see examples of this in India and among the Ethiopians, as historians report. For the people of Israel, however, there was in this matter a special procedure. For God marvelously governed this people for about four hundred years, just as if he himself were king. He led the people first through Moses out of Egypt, then through Joshua, and afterwards through a long series of vigorous judges. Then, when the people requested a king, he was indignant and gave it Saul, who was designated and chosen immediately by himself through the service of a prophet. When he afterwards rejected Saul because of his sons, he substituted David in the same manner, and by his word established the descendants of David in the control of the realm. These actions, however, were so performed by him that the consent and approval of the people were not excluded from the process of designating these kings and putting them in control of the realm. Rather the matter was so handled that the kings were considered to be chosen by the people as well, and to receive therefrom the right of kingship (*jus regis*).

§18

§19

---

of anyone. *See also* Deuteronomy 1:16; 17:20; I Kings 4:5, 9:22; I Chronicles 13:1 f.; 28:2.

[10] Digest L, 17, 32.

[11] *See* I Peter 2:13, where the magistracy is called a human institution that is to be properly obeyed.

§20   This can be discovered in sacred history by anyone willing to inspect it, and to study it with care. Indeed, it is evident that the supremely good and great God has assigned to the political community this necessity and power of electing and constituting. "You shall establish judges and moderators in all your gates that the Lord your God gave you through your tribes, who shall judge the people with a righteous judgment."[12] "I will establish a king over me."[13] "So you shall establish a king over you."[14] This ordination of a political magistrate, however, God ascribes in various places to himself. "Through me kings rule, and framers of laws discern what is just."[15] "You shall be subject to your lords, whether to the king as the one who is pre-eminent, or to leaders who are sent by him for the punishment of evil-doers and the praise of the upright."[16] "Let every person be subject to the governing powers. For there is no power except from God, and those powers that exist have been ordained by God. Therefore anyone who opposes such powers resists the ordination of God."[17] From this it can be concluded that God has formed in all peoples by the natural law itself the free power of constituting princes, kings, and magistrates for themselves. This means that in the measure in which any commonwealth that is divinely instructed by the light of nature has civil power, it can transfer this power to another or others who, under the titles of kings, princes, consuls, or other magistrates, assume the direction of its common life.

§21   Nature has also expressed in other created things a certain likeness and image of this political domination and government. Just as the mind reveals and performs all its actions in one physical body by the joining together and concord of its members, and unifies these members under one spirit, so also one imperium under the power of one person or a united group directs and rules in the commonwealth for the convenience of the members, declares laws, seeks the things necessary for human society, communicates concord and makes it firm, and directs actions and friendships by suitable rules that either nature or

---

[12] Deuteronomy 16:18.

[13] Deuteronomy 17:14.

[14] Deuteronomy 17:15. *See also* II Samuel 5:3; I Kings 1:34, 40; 6; 12:1 f.

[15] Proverbs 8:15.

[16] I Peter 2:13 f.

[17] Romans 13:1 f.

necessity recommends should be kept inviolate. When God as Lord of everything created the world, he prescribed for all creatures, even for trees, springs, rivers, and other created things, princes appropriate to their kind. Thus bees acknowledge and follow their queen, cranes have §22 a leader of their order, and the whale acknowledges his leader and rector. Moreover, for angels God established a prince of angels, for birds a bird, for beasts a beast, and for men a man. And even in man the soul dominates in the body, and the mind in the appetite. It is also necessary that in any combination of elements one of them dominate. Therefore, "to rule, to direct, to be subjected, to be ruled, to be governed are agreeable to the natural, divine, and human law". . . .[18]

The power of administering the rights of the realm originates §25 in the election of these ministers and in their undertaking the office entrusted to them.[19] The administrators and rectors of the universal §26 symbiosis and realm represent the body of the universal association, or the whole people by whom they have been constituted. They bear its person in those things they do in the name of the commonwealth or realm. They are held to be less in authority and power than those by whom they have been constituted and from whom they received their power. For however much the imperium and right that is conceded to another, it is always less than the conceder has reserved to himself. It also §27 cannot be denied that the power and strength of the whole is always greater than that of one man, or the body than that of a member thereof. On the other hand, these administrators are rightly called superior in authority and power to individual members of the realm. The sole §28 power of administering and directing the body and rights of this universal association according to just laws is transferred to these administrators and rectors by the members of this universal association. Such §29 governors by no means have the ownership of these rights, nor superiority in them. These rights remain under the control of the political body of this association. Whence the customary formula in the decrees, §30 orders, and rescripts of the Emperor of the Germans is *Uns und dem heiligen Reich*,[20] or *In unser und des heiligen Reichs statt*.[21] Here in the word

---

[18] [Petrus Gregorius, *De republica*, VI, 1, 1. *See* page 25, footnote 32.]

[19] *See* Lupold of Bebenburg, *De jure regni et imperii*, I, 6 and 16.

[20] [ourselves and the holy realm.]

[21] [in our and the holy realm's behalf.]

Uns is indicated the dominion of protection and general jurisdiction that the rector has; in the words *des Reichs statt* is expressed the dominion

§31   of the community. The less the power of those who rule, the more lasting and stable the imperium is and remains. For power circumscribed by definite laws does not exalt itself to the ruin of subjects, is not dissolute, and does not degenerate into tyranny.

§32   An administration is said to be just, legitimate, and salutary that seeks and obtains the prosperity and advantages of the members of the realm, both individually and collectively, and that, on the other hand, averts all evils and disadvantages to them, defends them against violence and injuries, and undertakes all actions of its administration according to

§40   laws. . . . This power of administering that these ministers and rectors established by the universal association have is bound to the utility and welfare of the subjects, and is circumscribed both by fixed limits, namely, by the laws of the Decalogue and by the just opinion of the universal association. Therefore, it is neither infinite nor absolute. . . .

§41   Administrators are not permitted to overstep these limits. Those who exceed the boundaries of administration entrusted to them cease being ministers of God and of the universal association, and become private persons to whom obedience is not owed in those things

§42   in which they exceed the limits of their power. . . . These administrators exceed the limits and boundaries of the power conceded to them, first, when they command something to be done that is prohibited by God in the first table of the Decalogue, or to be omitted that is therein commanded by God. They do so, secondly, when they prohibit something that cannot be omitted, or command something that cannot be committed, without violating holy charity. The former commands and prohibitions are called impious, the latter wicked. The limits of their power are transgressed, thirdly, when in the administration entrusted to them they seek their personal and private benefit rather than the common utility and welfare of the universal association. . . .

§43   The reason for refusing obedience to these administrators, as well as for denying absolute power to them, is their general and special vocation in which as Christian men they promised otherwise to God in baptism, which they are bound to fulfill. Moreover, administrators do not themselves have such great power, for no one gave them the power and jurisdiction to commit sin. Nor did the commonwealth, in constituting administrators for itself, deprive itself of the means of self-protection, and thus expose itself to the plundering of administrators. Besides, whatever power the people did not have it could not transfer to its administrators. Therefore, whatever power and right the administrators did not receive from the people, they do not have, they cannot exercise over the people, nor ought they to be able to do so. Finally, the wickedness of administrators cannot abolish or diminish the imperium and might of God, nor release the administrators from the same. For the power and jurisdiction of God are infinite. He created heaven and earth, and is rightly lord and proprietor of them. All who inhabit the earth are truly tenants, vassals, lessees, clients, and beneficiaries of his. "The earth is the Lord's and the fulness thereof,"[22] and is so by the right of creation and conservation. God is therefore called "King of kings and Lord of lords." . . .[23]

§44

We require love and ability in these administrators and directors. We require love toward the association that is committed to them so that all its hardships may be lighter; and we require ability of governing and administering so that the commonwealth may not suffer damage by the deficiency of administrative competence. An abundance of good counselors, however, can serve as a supplement in meeting this latter requirement.

§47

ADMINISTRATORS OF THIS UNIVERSAL ASSOCIATION are of two kinds: the ephors and the supreme magistrate.[24] Ephors are the representatives of the commonwealth or universal association to whom, by the consent of the people associated in a political body, the supreme responsibility has been entrusted for employing its power and right in constituting the supreme magistrate and in assisting him with aid and counsel in the activities of the associated body. They also employ its power and right in restraining and impeding his freedom in undertakings that are wicked and ruinous to the commonwealth, in containing him within the limits of his office, and finally in fully providing and caring for the commonwealth that it not suffer anything detrimental by

§48

---

[22] Psalm 24:1.

[23] [I Timothy 6:15].

[24] [The remainder of this chapter is devoted to the ephors, and the next two chapters to the commissioning of the supreme magistrate by the ephors. Following thereafter are eighteen chapters devoted to administration by the supreme magistrate, and one concluding chapter on types of rule.]

the supreme magistrate's private attachments, hatreds, deeds, negligence, or inactivity.[25]

§49   These ephors, by reason of their excellence and the office entrusted to them, are called by others patricians, elders, princes, estates, first citizens of the realm, officials of the realm, protectors of the covenant entered into between the supreme magistrate and the people, custodians and defenders of justice and law (*jus*) to which they subject the supreme magistrate and compel him to obey, censors of the supreme magistrate, inspectors, counselors of the realm, censors of royal honor, and brothers of the supreme magistrate.

§50   From these things it is apparent that ephors, as the critical supporters and upholders of the universal society or realm, are the means by which it is sustained and conserved during times of interregnum and peril, or when the magistrate is incapable of exercising imperium, or when he abuses his power, as Botero says.[26] They do this in order that the commonwealth may not become exposed to dangers, revolutions, tumults, seditions, and treacheries, or occupied by ene-

§51   mies. For the ephors establish the head of the political body, and subject the king or supreme magistrate to law (*lex*) and justice. They establish the law, or God, as lord and emperor when the king rejects and throws off the yoke and imperium of law and of God, and ceasing as a minister of God, makes himself an instrument of the devil. These ephors, together with the supreme magistrate, are said to carry the weight and burden of the people.[27]

---

[25] [The ephors are mentioned by Althusius even in his major work on law, wherein is assigned to them the responsibility for taking legal action against those who abuse public power, or against tyrants. *Dicaeologica*, III, 16, 6.]

[26] *Practical Politics*, IV, 3. [Botero, however, does not consider ephors to be an unmixed blessing, as he says in this chapter cited by Althusius. They are good insofar as they provide stability and continuity in a realm during times of emergency; they are bad insofar as they weaken the power of the king and provide a force in being for potential mutiny.]

[27] [Althusius refers to the following biblical passage here and at several other points in this discussion of the ephors: "And the Lord said to Moses, 'Gather for me seventy men of the elders of Israel, whom you know to be the elders of the people and officers over them; and bring them to the meeting tent, and let them take their stand there with you. And I will come down and talk with you there; and I will take some of the spirit which is upon you and put it on them; and they shall bear the burden of the people with you, that you may not bear it yourself alone.' " Numbers 11:16 f. R.S.V.]

In the Golden Bull of Emperor Charles IV the electors, who   §52
are the general ephors of the German imperium and realm, are called
the bases and pillars of the German imperium, and a part of the body of
Caesar. . . . Other realms also recognize such ephors, and have been   §53
more enduring and fortunate for that reason. Among them are the
Persian, Greek, Roman, French, British, Danish, and Polish imperia.

It is the nature of polities that they degenerate easily, nay, that   §54
they are even transformed in nature and pass from one type to another,
unless custodians are appointed in them by whom their administrators
and kings are curbed and held within limits, and by whom the petu-
lance, license, insolence, luxury, and pride of kings are restrained.
Whence polities have often been freed from their greatest dangers and
disorders by these ephors and orders. For the ephors either abolish or   §55
overcome the wicked actions or tyranny of the supreme magistrate.
They also compensate for his sloth by their own vigilance and diligence,
and fully provide and make sure that the commonwealth does not suffer
anything to its detriment by the actions of the king. Unless the ephors
have done all this, they themselves are held liable and are rightly said to
be betrayers of the commonwealth, especially when they secretly con-
spire or connive in the wicked and impious actions of the king.[28]

The ephors, by the communication of their strength, abilities,
labors and counsels, make the king strong and wise. They defend him
against all perils and difficulties, and conserve the healthy, well-ordered,
and well-guarded condition of the commonwealth. If the prince en-
gages in dissensions and hostilities against them, from whom can he
expect aid, counsel, and defense? And furthermore, how can an association and polity exist in which private persons oppose themselves to
these orders, and reject their curators and defenders? For the people has   §56
committed itself to these ephors for safety, and transferred all its actions
to them, so that what the ephors do is understood to be the action of the
entire people. The people does this because of utility and necessity. For
it would be most difficult, as Diego Covarruvias says,[29] to require
individual votes of all citizens and parts of a commonwealth. For this
reason it is agreed that the multitude of the plebs so conducts its public

---

[28] Emmanuel Meteren cites examples and arguments from the Belgian polity. *A General History of the Netherlands*, XIV.

[29] *Practicarum quaestionum*, 1, 4.

transactions through its optimates that these transactions are accomplished safely and without tumults or seditions in the commonwealth. The votes, therefore, of these optimates are determined according to the same law by which the consensus of all citizens, which they represent, is determined. And therefore it is rightly said that "inhabitants are understood to decide what these persons decide to whom the supreme responsibility of the public weal has been entrusted,"[30] and that what they do through them is regarded as if it had been done by them all and to pertain to all.[31]

§57   For this reason, Covarruvias says that the seven princes of the Germans, upon whom has been conferred the responsibility for the election of the emperor of the Christian world, jointly represent the people itself and the Christian community that is governed by this emperor. They employ its delegated power, and act in its place in this election. Whence it happens, he says, that the election of the emperor belongs to the seven electors as a collegium, not as individuals. . . .[32]

§59   These ephors are elected and constituted by the consent of the entire people. This consent is given by tribes, by centurial or curial divisions, by individuals, or by lot, according to the nature and custom of each realm. In other words, ephors are constituted by the votes of the entire people collected through the centuries, tribes, or collegia in which the people has been distributed, or, as I say, through the votes and divisions of individuals, or by lot. . . . Sometimes even the prince, supreme magistrate, or optimates have the power of electing an ephor, or of substituting another in place of one who has died. They do this by the favor and concession of the people.[33] The nomination and establishment of an ephor is correctly considered to be among the royal functions when the administration of this function has been conceded to the prince by the people or universal association.

§60   Those persons should be elected ephors who have great might and wealth, because it is in their interest that the commonwealth be healthy, and they will act as custodians of the public welfare with greater love, concern, and care. A few should be elected from the many. For

---

[30] Digest L, 1, 14.

[31] Digest L, 1, 19; L, 17, 160.

[32] *Variarum resolutionum*, III, 1, 4. Lupold of Bebenburg demonstrates the means by which this is best done. *See* his *De jure regni et imperii*, I, 6.

[33] Moses constituted seventy elders by the mandate of God. Numbers 11:24 f.

nothing is more useful in avoiding civil wars and factions of seditious men than to take away from the multitude the creation of magistrates and princes, and to impart it to a very few.

These elected ephors pledge themselves to care for the utility §61 of the realm, commonwealth, or universal association, and to perform faithfully and diligently the functions of the office entrusted to them. . . . The collegium of ephors proceeds with all things according to the §62 regular procedure of office, and decides these things through majority vote. And therefore the election of the magistrate pertains to it as a collegium, not as individuals. The greater and more powerful part of the people prevails in electing the king. By this means the collegium, not individual members of the collegium, represents the universal association or polity. This collegium has greater power and authority than the supreme magistrate, as all the sounder political theorists, jurists, and theologians teach.

THE DUTIES OF THESE EPHORS are principally contained under five §63 headings. The first duty is that they constitute the general and supreme magistrate. The second is that they contain him within the limits and bounds of his office, and serve as custodians, defenders, and vindicators of liberty and other rights that the people has not transferred to the supreme magistrate, but reserved to itself. The third is that in time of interregnum, or of an incapacitated administration of the commonwealth, the ephors become a trustee for the supreme magistrate and undertake the administration of the commonwealth until another supreme magistrate is elected. The fourth is that they remove a tyrannical supreme magistrate. The fifth is that they defend the supreme magistrate and his rights. Each and all of these duties are considered to be entrusted to the ephors for execution, who are not able to fulfill their office except by them.

The first duty of the ephors is to constitute the supreme §64 magistrate and rector of the universal association. For this task the ephors have received public power and authority from the united people of the universal association that they may elect such a rector and administrator in its name. This matter is discussed more fully in the next chapter.

The second duty of the ephors is that they contain the su- §65 preme magistrate and general administrator that they have constituted within the prescribed and accepted limits of his universal administration. They do this in order that the commonwealth or universal association may not suffer anything detrimental, and that its rights and even those of the king or supreme magistrate, are not violated or diminished, but may always remain unharmed, well ordered, and well protected. Peter Heige says that for this reason requests for the alleviation of oppressions, and complaints concerning violation of the imperial rights (*jura imperii*), are frequently brought to the ephors.[34] Nothing is as apt for conserving the imperial right (*jus imperii*)[35] as constraint of power brought about by others, by which such power is contained within its boundaries. For great power cannot contain itself within boundaries without some coercion and constraint entrusted to others.

§66   For this purpose the ephors have the power of helping the general and supreme magistrate by counsel and aid, and of admonishing and correcting him when he violates the Decalogue of divine law, or the sovereign rights and laws of the realm. Therefore, they have received the right of the sword (*jus gladii*) for the sake of discharging this required responsibility. . . .[36]

§68   Whence it is said to be the duty of the ephors to oppose unjust decrees of the supreme magistrate, to mitigate them by their counsels, and to impede them when they are contrary to the common welfare and laws of the universal association. Without the ephors' approval, an enactment or general decree of the supreme magistrate is not valid. So great is the authority and power of these ephors in the French realm that the official letters of the king have no authority unless they are countersigned by the secretary of the realm, nor his rescripts unless they are signed and sealed by the chancellor of the realm. Other matters concerning the realm take effect only when the ephors or optimates of the

§69   realm have been consulted and approve. Whence it is evident that Jean

---

[34] *Quaestiones juris*, I, quest. 3, num. 1 f. and 73; I, quest. 4, num. 50.

[35] [the imperial right, law, and power; in a more general sense as applying to any association, the right, responsibility, and structure of rule.]

[36] [Althusius refers to the following writers for support for this position: Junius Brutus, *Defence of Liberty Against Tyrants*, quest. 3; Francis Hotman, *De antiquo jure regni Gallici*, I, 12 f.; Georg Obrecht, *De bello*, thes. 161; Zachary Ursinus, *Dispositiones*, III, 44 and ult.; Lambert Daneau, *Politices christianae*, VI, 2 and 3; Otto Cassman, *Doctrinae et vitae politicae*, 10; David Parry, *Commentarius* (Romans 13); Juan de Mariana, *The King and His Education*, I, 8; Emmanuel Meteren, *A General History of the Netherlands*, XIV and XX.]

Bodin greatly errs in attributing absolute and all-encompassing power to the king of France, and in hardly recognizing the optimates.[37] He thinks that when optimates have power, the sovereignty and power of the king are either destroyed or shared with colleagues. Peter Heige calls attention to this error.[38] Indeed, jurists state that a prince who harms his subjects, and who does not maintain them inviolate, is not maintained by his contract with them.[39]

Even should the king or emperor concede kingly functions to dukes and counts of the imperium, or to the vassals and optimates of the realm, imperial superiority and pre-eminence are understood to be reserved to him. Whence it is that such optimates can by no means be considered colleagues of the king, or of equal power with him.[40] For only special and restricted power and administration have been given to these optimates. Indeed, the king or supreme magistrate has general power, sovereignty, and pre-eminence over individual optimates, and everything else depends upon his power and administration. However great may be the imperium that is assigned to another, it is always less than what the conceder has reserved to himself, as is the common judgment of the jurists. The supreme ruler cannot constitute an equal to himself.[41] The whole has greater power than one man, and whatever anyone has more than other men, he has received it from the whole. Nor can the power of the king be said to be diminished because ephors and optimates exercise some power, as the hand is not weaker because it has been divided into fingers, but is more agile in action. So power is more useful when deployed among a large number, and the affairs of the commonwealth are more readily expedited when communicated among many.

Moreover, these ephors as a whole are superior to the supreme magistrate to the extent that, representing the people, they collectively do

§70

§71

§72

§73

---

[37] [*The Commonweale*, I, 8.]

[38] *Questiones juris*, I, quest. 2, num. 22 f.

[39] Henry de Suge, *Summa aurea* (Decretals I, 33, 12); Nicolaus Tudeschi, *Commentaria* (Decretals II, 1, 13); Vincent Cabot, *Variarum juris*, II, 12.

[40] [A distinction is implied by Althusius between the optimates as inferior administrators of the realm, and the same optimates as ephors of the realm. In the one role, they are not "colleagues of the king, or of equal power with him"; in the other role, they are collectively "censors of the supreme magistrate," and superior in power to him.]

[41] Henry Rosenthal, *De feudis*, I, 5, 10.

something in its name; individually and separately, however, they are
§74   inferiors of this magistrate. The supreme prince is bound by oath to the
commonwealth as an officer of it, and is less than the entire commonwealth or realm itself. Julius Caesar bears witness that the ruling arrangements of the kings of France in his time were such that the people when
rightly convoked had no less authority over the king than the king had
over the people.[42] So the synod is superior to its bishop, the council to a
pope, the chapter to its agent, and the community (*universitas*) to its syndic.
§75   To these ephors, rather than to the supreme magistrate, the supreme
power of the commonwealth has first been entrusted by the people.
Therefore, because the power was first conferred upon such ephors, it
could not afterwards be given by the people to any magistrate. . . .

§83   We see in the power and authority conceded to these few
ephors for defending the rights of the people or universal association that
the people has not transferred these rights to the supreme magistrate, but
has reserved them to itself. For the universal association entrusted to its
ephors the care and defense of these rights against all violators, disturbers,
and plunderers, even against the supreme magistrate himself. The Dutch
Wars of Independence offer examples of this care and defense by ephors
§84   during forty years of conflict against the King of Spain. Whence the
office of these ephors is not only to judge whether the supreme magistrate has performed his responsibility or not, but also to resist and impede
the tyranny of a supreme magistrate who abuses the rights of sovereignty,
and violates or wishes to take away the authority (*jus*) of the body of the
commonwealth. So the theologians and jurists assert.[43] "For we have no

---

[42] *The Gallic War*, V and VII. [*See* especially V, 11; VII, 14 and 15.]

[43] Among the theologians are Zachary Ursinus, *Exercitationes theologicae*, II, exer.
44; Lambert Daneau, *Politices christianae*, VI, 3; III, 6; John Calvin, *Institutes of
the Christian Religion*, IV, 20, 24 f.; Peter Martyr Vermigli, *Commentarii* (Judges
3); David Parry, *Commentarius* (Romans 13); William Rose, *De justa reipublicae
christianae auctoritate*, 2; Juan de Mariana, *The King and His Education*, I, 7.
Among the jurists are Francis Hotman, *De antiquo jure regni Gallici*, I, 2;
Francis Zoannet, *De tripartitione defensionis*, III, num. 28 f. and 95 f.; Fernando
Vásquez, *Illustrium controversiarum*, I, preface, num. 102 f.; Edigio Bossi, *De
principe et ejus privilegiis*, num. 55 f.; Charles Dumoulin, *Consuetudines Parisienses*,
tit. 1, art. 1, glos. 7, num. 9; Tobias Paurmeister, *De jurisdictione*, I, 21, 19 and 42;
Paris de Puteo, *De syndicatu*, 3, rub. "de excessibus regis"; Prospero Farinacci,
De crimine laesae majestatis, quest. 112, num. 24; [Nicolas Barnaud], *Dialogi in
Gallorum*, dial. 2; [Theodore Beza], *Concerning the Rights of Rulers*; Junius
Brutus, *Defence of Liberty Against Tyrants*.

fellowship with a tyrant, but only the greatest parting of ways. Nor is it contrary to nature to depose [. . .] a man whom it is morally right to destroy."[44] The Digest says that he has not committed a crime who has killed a tyrant. . . . [45] Ephors resisting the tyranny of a supreme magistrate who misuses the rights of sovereignty, or endeavors to plunder or deprive a universal association of its authority, are not thereby said to abandon the communion of the realm and the rights thereof, but rather to condemn their abuse and to avoid approval and communication of the sins of the supreme magistrate. . . .

§85

The third duty of these optimates is to constitute themselves guardians, trustees, and administrators of the realm upon the supreme magistrate's captivity, death, madness, imbecility, minority, prodigality, or other disorder and impediment rendering him incapable or harmful in administration.[46] So Hotman demonstrates from historical materials that in France trustees were appointed by the estates of the realm for kings who were mad, underage, or in any other manner incapacitated for governing the realm.[47] Many examples of this are mustered by Froissart.[48] René Choppin says that today in France a regent is appointed by the king or estates of the realm for a widow and mother of the royal ward, which regency is ended when the royal ward has attained the age of fourteen.[49] But in my judgment this arrangement, which stems from the Salic law barring a female from the administration of the realm, is unfortunate. . . . Such a trustee is assigned from the ephors

§86

---

[44] Cicero, *Duties*, III, 6. [The words omitted by Althusius are "if you can."]

[45] Digest XI, 7, 35. [This passage from the Digest paraphrased by Althusius does not actually mention a tyrant, but rather anyone who comes forward "to destroy the fatherland."]

[46] *See* examples in II Kings 10:5–7; 12; 15:5; I Kings 22:47.

[47] *De antiquo jure regni Gallici.*

[48] Chronicles, I, 107 and 171; II, 58 and 60; III, 134; IV, 44. [Froissart probably did not himself divide his four books into chapters. The many manuscripts from which printed editions were later made divided the books variously into chapters, and even rearranged and abridged some materials. Consequently, it is impossible to obtain complete accuracy in chapter citation from the *Chronicles* unless one knows precisely which of the numerous manuscripts and printed editions was used. Nevertheless, the point Althusius is making would seem to find support from historical incidents reported in the following book and chapter divisions of the English translation by Thomas Johnes: I, 170 and 171; II, 57 and 59; III, 135; IV, 45.]

[49] *De dominio regis*, III, tit. 5.

(1) when the king is unable to defend the realm, (2) when he is negligent, (3) when he is incorrigibly profligate, (4) when he is unable to administer justice or maintain peace, (5) when he is out of his mind, and (6) when he is unfit in any other manner whatever.

§87   It is part of this duty that in time of interregnum these same ephors are the rectors and administrators of the realm and universal association. They have the right of administering and of acting in place of the supreme rector and general magistrate until a new one shall have been elected and constituted. So in German polity when a Caesar dies and there is interregnum, the power of administering the imperium is assigned to two of the seven imperial electors—namely, to the electors of the Palatinate and of Saxony—who act in place of the emperor in certain of his functions, as the Golden Bull of Emperor Charles IV holds.[50] In other polities these functions are entrusted for the most part to all the ephors, or to the principal one among them. . . .

§88   The fourth duty of the optimates is to resist a supreme magistrate who abuses the rights of sovereignty, and to discharge and remove him when he scorns and violates the rights and laws of the realm, and practices tyranny. When, how, and with what considerations this ought to be done, we will discuss later.[51]

§89   The fifth duty of the ephors consists in the defense of the supreme magistrate and his rights against the ambitions, conspiracies, and plots of subjects, against the pride of nobles, the factions and seditions of the mighty, against those who act improperly towards the supreme magistrate's royal power, weakening or impeding it, depriving him of it, or inflicting force and violence upon him. . . .

§90   This right that we have said the ephors have as ephors in the administration of the whole realm differs greatly from the right they have as dukes, princes, and counts in the administration of particular provinces

§91   and regions. The former is general, the latter special and restricted. It is to be observed that the duty of the ephors is to take care that the supreme magistrate not degenerate by doing or omitting something contrary to his office. So also the duty of the supreme magistrate is to take care that none of the ephors misuses his limited imperium to the ruin of his subjects or

---

[50] [This edict or constitution was issued in 1356. It fixed the method of holding elections and coronations in the Holy Roman Empire, and assigned duties and privileges therein to specified electors.]

[51] Chapter XXXVIII.

the realm. This mutual watchfulness, censure, and correction between the king and the estates or ephors keeps the condition of the realm sound, in good repair, and well protected, and frees the realm from all dangers, evils and inconveniences. . . .

WILLIAM BARCLAY ATTEMPTS TO DEPRIVE the ephors and the realm of this right that we have said is appropriate to the ephors over against the supreme magistrate.[52] He considers this right to be entirely yielded and transferred, nay, even alienated, by the people to the king. I will repeat his arguments, and refute them in a few words, before I turn to a discussion of types of ephors. The power of a guardian or trustee, he says, is greater than that of a ward or minor. Therefore, the power of the king, who is the trustee of a commonwealth, is greater than that of the ward or of the ephors representing the people. Against this I reply according to the rule that greater is the authority and power of the proprietor who constitutes a trustee for his things and affairs than of the constituted trustee. Therefore, greater is the authority and power of the ephors and the people who constitute the king than of the constituted king. This is most true. Even if against this rule a guardian or trustee has greater authority and power than the ward or minor, this happens because of a defect in the volition and judgment of the ward, who in this period of his life cannot have a proper and adequate volition. However, as soon as he reaches a proper age, he assumes and maintains this authority and power, just as any proprietor maintains the direction of his own things.

§92

Thus the guardian bears the person of the ward, and integrates it in those actions of life pertaining to the administration of the ward's person and things. In considering and examining the nature of care, guardianship, and any other administration for another, we are compelled to acknowledge that these types of administration manifest a certain service and ministry, which are exhibited and performed by such administrators for wards needing their works, aid, and counsel. Accordingly, such administrators are what they are by reason of the wards, minors, and others whose affairs they administer; wards, minors, and others are not what they are by reason of their administrators.

Moreover, in searching out the source and cause of administration, we discover that they proceed from the commission of the propri-

---

[52] *The Kingdom and the Regal Power*, IV, 10; VI.

etor. The person who commissions or enjoins another with the oversight of his things resembles one who summons or approves; the person who undertakes such administration resembles one who obeys, serves, and performs his duty toward another. I ask precisely whose authority and power is greater, the person who commissions and enjoins, or the person who is commissioned and who ministers and undertakes the administration?

§93   Barclay, however, says that those who constitute others under themselves are known to be greater and more powerful than the ones constituted. So Potiphar in constituting Joseph, Nebuchadnezzar in setting up Daniel, and Darius in establishing prefects under himself are each rightly called greater in authority and power than those they constituted.[53] Doubtless, he continues, the people constitutes a king above itself, not under itself. "I will constitute a king over me."[54] "We will have a king over us."[55] "But constitute a king over us."[56] "You shall

---

[53] [These examples from the Bible came originally from Junius Brutus, whom Barclay was attempting to refute along with George Buchanan, Jean Boucher, "and other monarchomachs." The passage in Brutus is the following: "Now seeing that the people choose and establish their kings, it follows that the whole body of the people is above the king; for it is a thing most evident, that he who is established by another, is accounted under him who has established him, and he who receives his authority from another, is less than he from whom he derives his power. Potiphar the Egyptian sets Joseph over all his house; Nebuchadnezzar, Daniel over the province of Babylon; Darius the six score governors over the kingdom. It is commonly said that masters establish their servants, kings their officers. In like manner also, the people establish the king as administrator of the commonwealth." *Defence of Liberty Against Tyrants*, quest. 3.

The nature of Barclay's refutation of Brutus is to observe that "examples of this sort do not sufficiently suit the conclusion. . . . For the examples plainly demonstrate that you mean this conclusion about those who constitute others under themselves, as Potiphar Joseph, Nebuchadnezzar Daniel, and Darius prefects under himself. But your discussion before was about a king whom a people set up, not indeed under itself, as Pharaoh or Potiphar set up Joseph, and the others that you mention, but plainly above itself and promised that it would obey him. Have you ever learned that it has been handed down to memory that any nation set up a king under itself?" Thus the significance of the four biblical passages that follow, which Barclay first produced and Althusius reproduced. *The Kingdom and the Regal Power*, IV, 10.]

[54] Deuteronomy 17:14.

[55] I Samuel 8:19.

[56] I Samuel 10:19.

appoint a king over Israel."[57] Whence to be over (*praeesse*) and to be subjected (*subjici*), Barclay says are opposites that cannot be attributed to the same king at the same time in the same relationship and with reference to the same interpretation, which is the nature and true meaning of opposites.

Barclay presses this argument vigorously. But he does so wrongly. For the king is constituted over affairs that belong to another, namely, over the affairs of the people and the universal association, the administration, direction, government, and care of which have been granted to him. He certainly is not constituted over the proprietary right (*jus proprietatis*) in these affairs. An example is that of a guardian or trustee who is constituted over the affairs of his ward or minor, or of a servant, minister, or overseer whom the proprietor constitutes over his affairs, and who nevertheless does not for this reason have greater authority and power than the proprietor who does the constituting. So the people or universal association constitutes the king over its affairs as director, governor, and trustee, but notwithstanding under itself. This is to say that the people has committed to the king, under definite conditions and restrictions, power and authority to rule it, and has retained to itself, under definite conditions, power and authority over a degenerate king. This direction and administration of the king is not plenary, absolute, and §94 unrestricted to the detriment and ruin of subjects, but is limited and circumscribed for their welfare by definite laws. When a king, rector, or governor oversteps these laws, he can no longer be said to be constituted over the affairs of the people, nor can the subjects be said to be under (*subesse*) him. The subjects individually are ordinarily under the king; collectively they are above the king, who administers the affairs not of individuals, but of the whole body. He who administers tyrannically does not so much care for and direct as destroy. Therefore, the king is over and the king is subjected.

He is over individuals in order to administer rightly, to which extent he is the executor, preserver, and minister of law. Properly speaking, therefore, law is thus over everyone. It is the superior above all, and each and every man recognizes it as the superior. The king who §95 governs the commonwealth according to law is over and superior to the commonwealth so far as he governs by the rule of law (*praescriptum*

---

[57] I Kings 19:16.

legis) presiding as the superior. Therefore, if he governs against the rule of law, he becomes punishable by the law, and ceases to be superior. In this unfortunate event, he begins to be under the executors of law. Whence it happens that when he exercises tyranny, he is under the united body. When he abuses his power, he ceases to be king and a public person, and becomes a private person. If in any way he proceeds and acts notoriously or wickedly, any one may resist him, as we have said above.[58]

§96   Furthermore, Barclay says an equal cannot have imperium over an equal. Therefore, a magistrate is not bound by the decrees of his predecessors. Indeed, I say that God, the law of nature and of nations, and the ephors of the realm are all greater than the king, and hold imperium over him. In addition, the obligation that the prince takes upon himself at the time of his initiation binds him. And he cannot be said to be equal who was not a prince when his predecessor was living. . . .[59]

§98   It is not absurd or contrary to nature that a king as the greater is subjected even to an inferior. For he who is greater or equal to another can be subjected to the jurisdiction of the other. Litigating parties can thus submit themselves to the decision of inferiors,[60] and inferiors can judge in the case of superiors.[61] So Caesar has the elector of the Palatinate as judge in cases that others bring against him, as the Golden Bull of Charles IV teaches. The king of France is under the judgment of the Parliament of Paris, and the princes of the German imperium are under the judgments of other princes, of counts, or even of their

---

[58] [This right of resistance receives further definition and limitation in Chapter XXXVIII.]

[59] [Althusius neglects to develop this idea at this point, but apparently had in mind his belief that while rulers change and are mortal, the people is immortal. In a similar vein, Junius Brutus wrote that "The commonwealth never dies, although kings be taken out of this life one after another: for as the continual running of the water gives the river a perpetual being, so the alternative rotation of birth and death renders the people immortal." *Defence of Liberty Against Tyrants*, quest. 3.]

[60] Digest II, 1, 14. ["It is accepted in our system of justice that if anyone submits himself to the jurisdiction of someone of inferior or equal rank, the latter can administer justice for and against him."]

[61] Digest V, 8, 6. ["Indeed, it is said that the son of a family can be the arbiter in a matter relating to his father, and it seems proper to many that he can also be the judge."]

counselors.[62] Bartolus asserts that a king also can be subjected to someone less than himself or to his equal.[63] Therefore, these persons— Caesar, king, and prince—are over (*praeesse*) in one relationship and are under (*subesse*) in another, but not over and under in the same relationship; they are, nevertheless, over and under at the same time and with reference to the same interpretation. The king is over and rules in those things for which he receives the power of ruling and governing, not in those things that have been reserved to the power and judgment of the ephors. He is over when he governs and administers lawfully, justly, and piously; that is, he ceases to be the administrator when he does not care what happens, but loses, squanders, and destroys, and ceases to be a living law, just as a pastor ceases to be a pastor who flays, divides, and loses his sheep.   *§99*

Barclay continues by developing his argument from examples. Thus he says cardinals constitute a pope above them, priests a bishop above them, and monks an abbot above them. Whence the former are inferior in power and authority, and the latter are superior. The former are devoid of the imperium and power that the latter have. But I say that such persons—the pope, bishop, abbot, or anyone else—can be removed for just reasons by those who constituted them, and can be deprived of their power. For what if such a pope, bishop, or abbot should become a heretic, or in any manner become unfit or untrustworthy in office? Canonical laws (*jura canonica*) pronounce such persons to be restrained from the authority and administration of the office entrusted to them.[64] And often such persons have been deprived of their office, as history bears witness and practical experience teaches. For who, to the detriment of the church and to the damage and loss of man's salvation, would long endure such unfit men, heretics, schismatics, sorcerers, incapacitated persons, those who live a shameful life and provide not at all for the functions of their office, or those who do not tend their sheep but flay them? If they lose their mind or develop another disorder of soul or body, so that henceforth they become altogether unfit or incapacitated, will not the church be committed to the government of other ministers? Or does the church so fall into their   *§100*

§101

---

[62] Matthew Stephani, *De jurisdictione*, II, pt. 2, num. 3.

[63] *Commentarii* (Code III, 13).

[64] Conrad Lancellot, *Templum omnium judicum*, II.

power, care, and protection that while they are living its government never can be committed to another? Or in emergencies is the order, authority, and power of one man—of a pope, bishop, or abbot— greater and stronger than that of the church, the cardinals, or the monks? Or is the power of one greater than the power of many? No one will maintain this. Or in these emergencies is the right of one pope, bishop, or abbot greater, stronger, and in better condition than that of all the cardinals and monks of the entire church? Nor will anyone affirm this. For whatever the right, power, and authority such ecclesiastical overseers have, it is not their property, nor do they derive it from themselves. Rather they have received it from the church, the collegium of cardinals, and the chapter of monks. Those who die or lay aside their office resign this right, power, and authority into the hands of the church, collegium, or chapter by which they were constituted. They restore this right to its owners, so that these overseers are considered to be nothing more than usufructuaries of it, and the collegia indeed to be

§102   its proprietors. Whence it is that the right of these overseers is temporal. On the other hand, the right of the collegia is permanent and immortal to the extent that these collegia, because of their constant succession of persons in place of those who depart, are considered to be immortal.

When we consider the office and administration of kings, we find that their nature and constitution are not unlike those of ecclesi-

§103   astical overseers. The right of a king consists in the faithful and diligent care and administration of the commonwealth entrusted to him by the people. For this reason the people transfers to him as much authority and power as it judges necessary. By the communication, sharing, and contribution of individual persons from the people, the king becomes rich and powerful. By their counsel he becomes wise. By the aid of his subjects he excels in strength, vigor, and might. If the people denies these to the king, he again becomes weak, poor, needy, and a private person. The king holds, uses, and enjoys these riches— and this might, wisdom, and authority—as a usufructuary. When the king dies, or is denied the regal throne by any legitimate means, these rights of the king, as we have said, return to the people as to their proprietor. The people then reassigns them as it thinks wise for the

§104   good of the commonwealth. Therefore, the right of the king is one thing, and the right of the people is another. The former is temporal and personal; the latter is permanent. The former is the lesser; the latter is the greater. The former is a precarium given by contract to the commissioned king, and undertaken by him; the latter is an incommunicable property.

Moreover, Barclay says that as the husband who is constituted over his wife is her superior, so the king is superior to the commonwealth and realm. But I say that the superiority and power the husband has over his wife he derives from the marriage. And this is only for a time and with a condition, namely, that it lasts as long as the marriage endures, that is, as long as the marriage is not dissolved by adultery, desertion, or death. When the marriage is dissolved, every marital power he exercises over his wife is ended. Of equal seriousness with desertion is the intolerable cruelty of a husband that makes it impossible to live with him. Because of incurable cruelty, and its hazard to life and health, theologians concede a dissolution of marriage, and defend divorce by the authority of sacred scripture.[65] Is there not equal reason for conceding divorce between a king and a commonwealth because of the intolerable and incurable tyranny of a king by which all honest cohabitation and association with him are destroyed? No bond is considered to be stricter than that of matrimony, which is ordained by divine authority to be indissoluble. However, for the previously mentioned causes it is dissolved. Cannot the bond between magistrate and subjects likewise be dissolved for equally serious reasons? §105

All power is limited by definite boundaries and laws. No power is absolute, infinite, unbridled, arbitrary, and lawless. Every power is bound to laws, right, and equity. Likewise, every civil power that is constituted by legitimate means can be terminated and abolished. §106

Barclay is likewise wrong when he says that all functions of the commonwealth are entrusted to the king.[66] For the function of electing, constituting, and defending a king, the function of resisting tyranny, and many other functions that I have listed in this chapter as entrusted to the ephors cannot be committed to the king.

THUS FAR WE HAVE SPOKEN of the office of the ephors, and we have refuted the things that have been alleged against their power by Barclay. We will now speak of the types of ephors. Ephors are permanent §107

---

[65] Theodore Beza, *De divortiis et repudiis.* [No other theologian is mentioned by Althusius in this connection.]

[66] *The Kingdom and the Regal Power,* IV, 25.

(rendered hereditary by the consent of the universal association), or temporal. Permanent ephors have their responsibility so assigned to them that they may even transfer it to their heirs. Temporary ephors, on the other hand, perform this office for a prescribed time only, after which they lay it aside. . . .

§108   Such ephors and estates, or orders of the realm, are also of two kinds. Some are ecclesiastical, and others are secular. Ecclesiastical ephors are those who have been constituted from among ecclesiastical

§109   persons, and bear the responsibility for ecclesiastical things. Secular ephors are those who have the knowledge and care of public things. These latter are, in turn, either nobles or commoners. Nobles are chosen from the order of the nobility; commoners are selected from the remaining persons of the villages, towns, and cities of the realm.

All these ephors and orders of the realm are distributed among

§110   two species. Some are general, and others special. General ephors are those to whom is entrusted the guardianship, care, and inspection of the whole realm and of all its provinces. Such are imperial senators, counselors, syndics, chancellors of the realm, and so forth.

Such general optimates and ephors in the Israeli realm were the seventy elders. "And the Lord said to Moses, 'Gather for me seventy men of the elders of Israel, whom you know to be the elders of the people and officers over them; and bring them to the tent of meeting, and let them take their stand there with you. And I will come down and talk with you there; and I will take some of the spirit that is upon you and put it upon them; and they shall bear the burden of the people with you, that you may not bear it yourself alone.' "[67]

In the Roman imperium there first were in the democracy the tribunes of the people who checked the consular power so that the consuls might not abuse the imperium, nor become accustomed to excessive boldness or savagery. Later in the Roman monarchy the general ephors were the senators of Rome, as Xenophon, Aristotle, Plutarch, and others have testified.[68]

---

[67] Numbers 11:16 f. [R.S.V.]

[68] [Presumably the testimony of these writers refers to various periods of Roman history, and not merely to the monarchical period. Or was Althusius simply careless at this point in his historical attributions? He also mentions in this connection the sixteenth-century historian Alexander ab Alexandro, *Genialium dierum*, I, 3; IV, 6; V, 2; VI, 24.]

In the German polity such general ephors are the electors, or the seven men of the imperium, of which three are ecclesiastical and four secular. The ecclesiastical are the archbishop of Mainz, who is also the arch-chancellor of the imperium, the archbishop of Cologne, and the archbishop of Treves. The secular ephors are the king of Bohemia, the prince of the Rhenish Palatinate, the duke of Saxony, and the duke of Brandenburg. The Palatinate elector, in accord with the Golden Bull of Emperor Charles IV, is the judge from among them in cases instituted against the emperor. Likewise, he and the Saxon prince are trustees and vicars of the imperium in time of interregnum. The archbishop and elector of Mainz, as the arch-chancellor of the German imperium, has the right of calling together the electoral colleagues in this collegium of electors, of proposing matters to them, and of soliciting their judgments.

Philip Honorius and other historians agree that in the French realm there are three orders; the ecclesiastical order, the nobility, and the commons. . . .[69] The general optimates of France are the chancellor of France, the French princes born with royal blood from their fathers, the major courtiers, who today are called equestrian counts, marshals, admirals, the keeper of the seal, quaestors, and others accepted by the Parisian senate. . . .[70]

Special ephors are those that undertake the guardianship and care of a province, region, or certain part of the realm. They recognize the supreme magistrate or commonwealth as their immediate superior, and are inscribed on the roles of the imperium. Such are dukes, princes, margraves, counts, barons, castellans, nobles of the realm, imperial cities (as they are called in Germany), and others that are named according to the province entrusted to them. They recognize the commonwealth or universal association, of which they are ephors, as their immediate superior, as I have said. There may be some dukes, counts, nobles, and cities that are mediately under the supreme magistrate of the common-

§111

---

[69] *Thesauri politici*, II, apos. 54.

[70] [Here follow brief discussion of ephors in England, Poland, Belgium, and ancient Sparta, and even briefer mention of them in Hungary, Sweden, Denmark, Spain, ancient Babylon, and ancient Philistia. The historical sources acknowledged by Althusius are Sir Thomas Smith, *De republica Anglorum*, II; Martin Cromerus, *De republica Polonici*, II; Lodovico Guicciardini, *Omnium Belgii descriptio*; Niels Krag, *De republica Lacedaemoniorum*; Daniel 3:3 f. and 27; 5; 6; Esther 1; 3; 4; I Samuel 5:8, 11; 6:4, 12.]

wealth, but immediately under other princes, dukes, or counts as intermediate magistrates who are themselves ephors, estates, or orders of the commonwealth or realm. But these counts and cities that are subject only mediately to the commonwealth are not estates or orders of the realm.[71]

§112   A special ephor has the same right and power in the province entrusted to his care and protection that the supreme magistrate has in the whole realm. He exercises in his territory those things that have been reserved to the emperor under the sign of the imperial crown. . . . [72]

§113   It is advisable that these general and special orders, and particularly the special ones among them, be bound together by definite procedures and structures, that they depend one upon the other, and that each need the aid and counsel of the other. Each order should also be kept within its own boundaries so that it cannot injure another, and should have definite remedies by which it can be protected against wrongs from another. It should have these remedies so that the ambition of the ecclesiastical order, the insolence of the nobility, and the license of the commons may be restrained, and that injuries of one order to another may be prevented. Whence there arises a certain interdependent and sober plan for governing the commonwealth—so greatly praised by philosophers—that is the preserver of public tranquillity and the bond of human society. . . .

§123   If to the contrary in a realm or universal association there are no ephors (who nevertheless in my judgment are most necessary for properly constituting a commonwealth, for reasons I have stated at the beginning of this chapter), then these duties that otherwise have been entrusted to ephors are arranged for by the consent of the entire people, proposed or obtained by tribes, by curial or centurial divisions, or individually, so that no prescription or encroachment contrary to liberty or to the right of the realm (*jus regni*)[73] can be undertaken by the
§124   magistrate. And if there are encroachments for a season, they take nothing away from the right of the people, but only add to the wrongs of the king, as Junius Brutus learnedly explains.[74] If the people, circum-

---

[71] *See* Chapter VIII, and Matthew Stephani, *De jurisdictione*, II, pt. 1, chap. 4.

[72] [Does Althusius mean "have *not* been reserved to the emperor"?]

[73] [law of the realm.]

[74] *Defence of Liberty Against Tyrants*, quest. 3.

vented by fraud, or constrained by fear and force, has sold itself to be reduced to slavery, it has a proper claim to complete restitution, as Buchanan correctly asserts.[75] Indeed, if a people is conquered in war, placed under a yoke, and received into the society of one commonwealth by the victorious people, then it also uses the same right (*jus*)[76] as its conqueror. And if by chance the people has consented to wicked conditions by the constraint of excessive fear, these are to be considered invalid.[77] But if these conditions are harsh and yet not repugnant to the natural law (*jus naturale*), they are to be observed.[78]

Moreover, by the negligence, perfidy, deceit, fraud, or betrayal of ephors and optimates, or by their conspiracy or collusion with a prince, nothing is taken away from the right of a people, and nothing is added to the license of a tyrant. For it is wicked and absurd to affirm that ephors are able to transfer to a tyrant what they themselves have never possessed, and that they can disperse and alienate these rights of the associated body to the disadvantage of the universal association. They would thereby set themselves in opposition to the fundamental laws of the realm—to which the supreme magistrate swore allegiance—that infuse spirit and soul into the commonwealth and that distinguish and separate the commonwealth from a band of robbers and evil men. Thus they would act from the assumption that the right and ownership of the commonwealth is under the control of the ephors rather than the people. We have already spoken against and refuted this assumption.

---

[75] *The Rights of the Crown in Scotland.* [*See also* the Roman law titles "De in integrum restitutionibus—Concerning Complete Restitution," and "Quod metus causa gestum erit—Where an Act Was Performed Because of Fear." Digest IV, 1 and 2.]

[76] [legal order.]

[77] The author [Theodore Beza] of *Concerning the Right of Rulers*, quest. 6. For examples of wicked conditions, *see* I Samuel 11:2; I Maccabees 1:55 [1:54?].

[78] *See* the example of the Gibeonites. Joshua 9:25–27.

XIX–XX

The Constituting of the
Supreme Magistrate

§1   **XIX**   S O MUCH FOR THE EPHORS of the universal association. We turn now to its supreme magistrate. The supreme magistrate is he who, having been constituted according to the laws (*leges*) of the universal association for its welfare and utility, administers

§2   its rights (*jura*) and commands compliance with them. Although the rights of the universal association belong to the body of the universal association, or to the members of the realm, by reason of ownership and proprietorship, they also relate to its supreme magistrate to whom they have been entrusted by the body of the commonwealth by reason of administration and exercise. . . .

§4   The magistrate is called supreme because he exercises not his own power, but that of another, namely, the supreme power of the realm of which he is the minister. Or he is so called in relation to inferior and intermediate magistrates who are appointed by and depend upon this supreme power, and for whom he prescribes general laws. Whence he is said to have supereminence over all other superiors.[1] Moreover, he is called supreme in relation to individuals. But he is not supreme in relation to his subjects collectively, nor to law, to which he is himself subject. . . .

§5   Three matters are henceforth to be considered; the constitut-
§6   ing, the administration, and the types of the supreme magistrate.[2] The constituting of the supreme magistrate is the process by which he

---

[1] So Joshua was constituted supreme prefect by Pharaoh (Genesis 41:43 f.), Daniel was called supreme among his colleagues (Daniel 2:48; 5:29), and some priests were said to be supreme (Matthew 27:1, 6, 12, 20; Acts 7:1).

[2] [Chapters XIX–XX, XXI–XXXVIII, and XXXIX respectively.]

assumes the imperium and administration of the realm conferred by the body of the universal association, and by which the members of the realm obligate themselves to obey him. Or it is the process by which the people and the supreme magistrate enter into a covenant concerning certain laws and conditions that set forth the form and manner of imperium and subjection, and faithfully extend and accept oaths from each other to this effect.

There is no doubt that this covenant, or contractual mandate *§7* (*contractum mandati*) entered into with the supreme magistrate, obligates both of the contracting parties, so much so that it is permitted to neither magistrate nor subjects to revoke or dishonor it. However, in this reciprocal contract between the supreme magistrate as the mandatory, or promiser, and the universal association as the mandator, the obligation of the magistrate comes first, as is customary in a contractual mandate. By it he binds himself to the body of the universal association to administer the realm or commonwealth according to laws prescribed by God, right reason, and the body of the commonwealth.[3] According to the nature of a mandate, the obligation of the people, or members of the realm, follows. By it the people in turn binds itself in obedience and compliance to the supreme magistrate who administers the commonwealth according to the prescribed laws.

• The supreme magistrate exercises as much authority (*jus*) as has been explicitly conceded to him by the associated members or bodies of the realm. ʻAnd what has not been given to him must be considered to have been left under the control of the people or universal association. Such is the nature of the contractual mandate. The less the *§8* power of those who rule, the more secure and stable the imperium remains. For power is secure that places a control upon force, that rules willing subjects, and that is circumscribed by laws, so that it does not become haughty and engage in excesses to the ruin of the subjects, nor degenerate into tyranny. . . . Absolute power, or what is called the *§9* plenitude of power, cannot be given to the supreme magistrate. For *§10* first, he who employs a plenitude of power breaks through the restraints by which human society has been contained. Secondly, by absolute power justice is destroyed, and when justice is taken away realms

---

[3] "Let him not turn aside from this precept." Deuteronomy 17:20. "To be instituted for the utility of the realm." II Samuel 23:3.

become bands of robbers, as Augustine says.[4] Thirdly, such absolute power regards not the utility and welfare of subjects, but private pleasure. Power, however, is established for the utility of those who are ruled, not of those who rule, and the utility of the people or subjects does not in the least require unlimited power. Adequate provision has

§11   been made for them by laws. Finally, absolute power is wicked and prohibited. For we cannot do what can only be done injuriously. Thus even almighty God is said not to be able to do what is evil and contrary to his nature.[5] The precepts of natural law (*jus naturale*) are to "live honorably, injure no one, and render to each his due."[6] Law is also an obligation by which both prince and subjects are bound. . . .[7]

§14   The forms and limits of this mandate are the Decalogue, the fundamental laws of the realm, and those conditions prescribed for the supreme magistrate in his election and to which he swears allegiance when elected.

§15   Wherefore Fernando Vásquez and Lambert Daneau rightly say, and refute those who disagree, that the people is prior in time and more worthy by nature than its magistrate, and has constituted him.[8] And so no realm or commonwealth has ever been founded or instituted except by contract entered into one with the other, by covenants agreed upon between subjects and their future prince, and by an established mutual obligation that both should religiously observe. When this obligation is dishonored, the power of the prince loses its strength and is

§16   ended. Whence it follows that the people can exist without a magistrate, but a magistrate cannot exist without a people, and that the people

§17   creates the magistrate rather than the contrary. Therefore, kings are constituted by the people for the sake of the people, and are its ministers to whom the safety of the commonwealth has been entrusted. The magistrate or prince is mortal and an individual person; the realm or

§18   community (*universitas*) is immortal. Upon the death of the king, the right of the realm returns to the estates and orders of the realm.

---

[4] [*The City of God*, IV, 4.]

[5] Friedrich Pruckmann, *De regalibus,* 3, 51; Aymon Cravetta, *Consiliorum,* I, cons. 241.

[6] [Digest I, 1, 10, 1.]

[7] Digest I, 3, 1; Code I, 14, 4.

[8] *Illustrium controversiarum,* I, preface, num. 108; I, 1; *Polites christianae,* I, 4. *See* Genesis 36, where the chiefs are listed last among the descendants of Esau.

There are many precepts, examples, and rational evidences of this constituting a supreme magistrate by such a covenant or contract between the supreme magistrate and the ephors who represent the entire people of the associated bodies. . . .[9]

THIS COVENANT OR CONSTITUTION by which the supreme magistrate is constituted by the ephors with the consent of the associated bodies has two parts. The first is the committing of the realm and its administration to a governor; the second is the promising of obedience and compliance by the people.[10] The committing of the realm is the process by which the ephors, in the name of the people or associated body, confer and entrust the administration of the realm to the supreme magistrate.[11] This is accomplished by two actions, namely the election of the supreme magistrate, and his inauguration or initiation. . . .

§23

§24

The election, which is called ἀρχαιρεσία by the Greeks, is the process by which the ephors or magnates of the realm choose and designate, according to the laws and customs of the commonwealth, the supreme magistrate of the associated bodies or realm, and—invoking the name of God—offer and entrust to him, under fixed conditions and laws, the care and administration of the realm in accord with the established order of piety and justice. . . . The estates or ephors of the realm united together exercise this right of electing collectively, not individually, unless certain ones among them hold this right by the common consent of all. . . . In this election conducted in the name of the associated people as the mandator, certain laws and conditions

§25

§27

§29

---

[9] [Here follows an extended discussion of these precepts, examples, and rational evidences. Although this discussion adds nothing new to what has already been said, it nevertheless illustrates Althusius' use of theology, history, and philosophy respectively in support of his political theories. Precepts are passages from the Bible setting forth God's ordination of rulership as arising from the people or as being for the good of the people. (Deuteronomy 16:18; 17:14–20; Romans 13:1, 5.) Examples are alluded to from the histories of Israel, Sparta, Persia, Rome, Germany, France, England, Denmark, Sweden, Spain, Portugal, and Belgium. Rational evidences are, for the most part, the same arguments for rulership that Althusius employed in Chapter I, which arguments draw heavily upon Cicero and Petrus Gregorius.]

[10] [Chapters XIX and XX respectively.]

[11] A community (*universitas*) can elect and constitute its own curators and administrators. Digest III, 4, 6, 1; I, 2, 13 and 22; Nicolaus Losaeus, *De jure universitatum*, I, 3.

concerning subjection, and the form and manner of the future imperium, are proposed to the prospective magistrate as the mandatory. If he accepts these laws, and swears to the people to observe them, the election is considered firm and settled. This agreement entered into between magistrate and people is known as a mutually binding obligation. . . .

§30 　　　　The conditions and laws of subjection, or the form, manner, and limits of the entrusted imperium, are customarily defined in certain articles that are publicly read and proposed by one of the ephors to the magistrate to be elected. Then this ephor asks whether the magistrate is willing to abide by these articles in the administration of the realm, and solemnly binds his assurances by a written oath. . . .

§33 　　　　But if no laws or conditions have been expressed in the election, and the people has subjected itself to such a magistrate without them, then whatever things are holy, fair, and just, and are contained in the Decalogue, are considered to have been expressed, and the people is considered in the election to have subjected itself to the imperium of the magistrate according to them.[12] Indeed, there is no instance in which a people has conferred upon a prince the unrestrained licence to bring about its own ruin.[13] For a people when questioned could have doubtlessly responded that it had granted no power to accomplish its own ruin. . . .[14]

§35 　　　　If the people or commonwealth has conferred all its right and imperium upon the supreme magistrate, as it is said in the Digest,[15] or yields to him supreme power free from laws and without any reservation, exception, or condition, then the general wording is to be closely interpreted according to the subject matter—to the extent that the subject matter manifestly permits—so that whatever is the nature of imperium or reign, such is to be the interpretation of this general wording. The nature of magistracy and imperium is that they regard the utility of subjects, not the benefit of the one who exercises the imperium, and they administer the commonwealth according to right reason

---

[12] *See* Francis Hotman, *Franco-gallia,* 6, 25; George Buchanan, *The Rights of the Crown in Scotland;* Fernando Vásquez, *Illustrium controversiarum,* I, 1; Junius Brutus, *Defence of Liberty Against Tyrants,* quest. 1–3.

[13] Code I, 55, 4.

[14] Alberico Gentili unreasonably dissents from this position in *De potestate regis absoluta.* I have responded to his arguments in Chapter XXXVIII.

[15] I, 4. 1.

and justice. For, as Augustine says, when justice is taken away, what are realms other than large bands of robbers?[16] And so absolute power and the jurisdiction of sinning cannot be given to the supreme magistrate. Therefore, even a concession made with the most general wording is to be interpreted in support of the welfare and utility of the conceding people. For the mind of the conceding people was surely that which restricts and limits the general wording. Indeed, the people in constituting a prince by no means intended to elect a tyrant to the ruin of itself, or to lose the capacity to protect itself. For a prince can easily degenerate into a tyrant or do what is contrary to nature, so that the power of the one may then be greater than the power of the whole. So even in a general mandate or concession, things are not included that anyone would not have conceded in a special mandate, especially those things that tend toward the ruin of the conceder, the destruction of human society, and the violation of divine law.

§36

I add that no one can renounce the right of defense against violence and injury. And the power of correcting an errant king, which the ephors have, has not been transferred to the king and cannot be so transferred. Nor can the supreme right in a commonwealth be transferred, because it is by nature incommunicable, and remains with the body of the universal association. Moreover, there is no power for evil or for inflicting injury. There is only power for good and for giving support, and thus for the utility and welfare of subjects. Therefore, the power that the people has, not a power that the people does not have, is considered to be given by this general wording. . . .[17]

§37

The laws and conditions by which Charles V swore allegiance when elected emperor are recorded by Jean Sleidan.[18]

§39

---

[16] [*The City of God*, IV, 4.]

[17] *See* Friedrich Pruckmann, *De regalibus,* 3; Fernando Vásquez, *Illustrium controversiarum,* I, 2; I, 3; I, 15; I, 26; I, 43; Marius Salomonius, *De principatu,* V. The following writers unreasonably dissent: Alberico Gentili, *De potestate regis absoluta*; Jean Bodin, *The Commonweale,* I, 8; William Barclay, *The Kingdom and the Regal Power,* III, 4; IV, 2.

[18] *De statu religionis et reipublicae,* I, ann. 1519. [This reproduction of material from Sleidan is retained in this translation to provide an historical illustration of what Althusius has in mind when he writes about fundamental laws of a realm. This German illustration should be sufficient for the purpose, however, and it therefore seems unnecessary to retain the comparable material that follows on the fundamental laws of France, England, Spain, Sweden, Poland, and Brabant.]

"1. He (Caesar) shall defend the Christian commonwealth, the pope, and the Roman church, of which he shall be the protector.

2. He shall administer law (*jus*) fairly, and seek peace.

3. He shall not only confirm all the laws (*leges*) of the imperium, and especially what they call the Golden Bull, but with the counsel of the electors he shall also amplify these laws when there is need to do so.

4. He shall convene a senate chosen from Germans in the imperium, which will oversee the commonwealth.

5. He shall not in the least rescind or diminish the rights, privileges, and dignities of princes and orders of the imperium.

6. He shall permit the electors, when there is need, to convene among themselves and to deliberate concerning the commonwealth; and he shall not place any impediment whatever before them, nor shall he annoy them.

7. He shall abolish leagues of the nobility and of the masses, or societies entered into against princes, and prohibit them by law so that they may not arise later.

8. He shall make no league or covenant with foreign nations concerning things pertaining to the imperium, except with the consent of the seven electors.

9. He shall neither sell nor pledge the properties of the imperium nor impair them in any other manner; and as soon as he can he shall recover those lands that have been occupied by other nations, and those goods that have been removed from the imperium, but without injury to those who by right or privilege depend upon them.

10. If he or any member of his family possesses something not legitimately acquired that belongs to the imperium, he shall restore it when requested to do so by the seven electors.

11. He shall cultivate peace and friendship with neighboring and other kings; and he shall not undertake any war on behalf of the affairs of the imperium, either within or beyond the boundaries of the imperium, without the consent of all orders, and especially of the seven electors.

12. He shall bring no foreign soldier into Germany except with their consent; however, when he or the imperium is assaulted in war, it is permitted to him to do so, as it would be to any defenders.

13. He shall summon no assembly of the imperium, nor demand any tax or tribute, except by the consent of the electors.

14. There shall be no assembly beyond the boundaries of the imperium.

15. He shall not place foreigners in charge of public affairs, but Germans selected from the nobility; and all documents shall be prepared either in Latin or the language of the people.

16. He shall summon no estate to a court of law outside the boundaries of the imperium.

17. Because many things happen at Rome against the agreements entered into with popes in former times, he shall arrange with the pope that there be no injury to the imperial privileges and liberty.

18. He shall form a plan with the electors by which the merchant monopolies so greatly damaging to Germany may be restrained, and he shall carry the plan through to its conclusion.

19. He shall impose no duty or tax upon imported goods unless the electors consent, nor shall he lessen by letters of recommendation the tax of electors who are near the Rhine.

20. If he has reason for action against any order, he shall proceed by law, and he shall apply no force against those who place themselves under the judgment of law; [. . .][19]

21. He shall confer upon no one the goods of the imperium that have been accidentally vacated, but shall restore them to the public patrimony.

22. If he acquires a foreign province with the support of the orders, he shall add it to the imperium; and if he recovers some public property by his own strength and virtue, he shall restore it to the commonwealth.

23. He shall ratify what the electors of the Palatinate and Saxony have performed in their public capacity during the time of interregnum.

24. He shall not scheme to make the dignity of the imperium hereditary and proper to his family, but shall permit the free and unimpaired power of election to the seven electors, according to the law

---

[19] [The unacknowledged—and perhaps inadvertent—omission from this law and condition as found in Sleidan reads as follows: "and he shall punish no one without a hearing, but proceed therein by due process of law (*jus*)."]

(*lex*) of Charles IV and the prescript of pontifical law (*jus*); and if anything shall have been done to the contrary, it shall have no effect.

25. As soon as he shall be able, he shall come to Germany for the inauguration." . . .

§49   In the election of the supreme magistrate, the highest concern must be had for the fundamental law of the realm (*lex fundamentalis regni*). For under this law the universal association has been constituted in the realm. This law serves as the foundation, so to speak, of the realm and is sustained by the common consent and approval of the members of the realm. By this law all the members of the realm have been brought together under one head and united in one body. It is indeed called the lodestone (*columna*) of the realm.

This fundamental law is nothing other than certain covenants (*pacta*) by which many cities and provinces come together and agree to establish and defend one and the same commonwealth by common work, counsel, and aid. When common consent is withdrawn from these covenants and stipulations, the commonwealth ceases to exist, unless these laws are rejected and terminated by common consent, and new ones established, without harm to the commonwealth or impairment to its rights of sovereignty. Lambert Daneau sets forth an important difference between these fundamental laws and the rights of sovereignty.[20] A commonwealth or realm can be constituted and continue to endure, he says, without these fundamental laws. But without rights of sovereignty no commonwealth can be established or, if already established, conserved and passed on to posterity. . . .

§70   The election of the supreme magistrate is in accord with either of two types. One is entirely free, and the other is restricted to persons of a certain origin from whom the choice is to be made. For rulers are to be elected either from all persons or from men of a certain kind, namely, from the nobility or from a certain family.

§71   The entirely free election is one that rests upon the free choice
§72   of the ephors who do the electing.[21] In this unrestricted election, it is

---

[20] *Politices christianae*, III, 6.

[21] You will find examples of this in Petrus Gregorius, *De republica*, VII, 15; Vincent Cabot, *Variarum juris,* I, 8 and 10; I Samuel 8; 16; II Samuel 5:3 f.; Judges 11:10 ff.; I Chronicles 29:22–24. The kings of Poland and Denmark are so elected, so far as I have been able to gather from historical writing.

allowed to change the earlier polity, or to annul it and to establish another and new one. For the people, or body of the associated communities, retains for itself the free power to establish and change the commonwealth. The people is not obligated to anyone concerning the succession and continuation of imperium and administration, but upon the death of the last supreme magistrate as administrator of the commonwealth, it regains its authority (*jus*) undiminished, which it can transfer to any other person whatever according to its own preference.[22] However, an atheist, an impious or wicked man, or one who is a stranger to true and orthodox religion should not be elected. Nor should a man from an ignoble or servile station in life. Nor should a bastard, for reasons provided by Petrus Gregorius.[23] Nor should one who is given to drunkenness, or inclined to vices and crimes. Nor should one who is unappreciative toward a good predecessor. But concerning the election of a woman, see my earlier comments[24] as well as those later in this chapter.

§73

There should be a regard for piety and virtue in the election to this indispensable office, however much at other times some men have been elected because of wealth, as historical examples testify,[25] others because of force and might, others by plots and stratagems, others by promises made and broken, and still others by lot. Such elections, however, are not without the consent of the people, and they are rightly permitted when neither regard for piety and virtue, nor counsel concerning them, can be exercised.

The restricted election is one that has been limited by the agreement of the people and realm, or universal association, to persons of a certain origin. By established law, the right to be elected has been obtained for these persons, and it cannot later be withdrawn or transferred to another against their will, without injury and violation of trust. And so in this election a change in the polity once established and accepted by the people is not permitted to the ephors or to the people.

§74

§75

---

[22] Vincent Cabot musters examples of this. *Variarum juris,* I, 10. But he is in error when he says that if no arrangement has been prescribed, then the king has free disposition concerning the realm, a statement that he himself contradicts at another place. I, 14.

[23] *De republica,* VII, 8.

[24] [Chapter VII, footnote 6.]

[25] Petrus Gregorius records them. *De republica,* VII, 13–19.

The reason is that the people has obligated itself to certain persons, to whom it promised to continue the administration of this polity, and gave its word to them, which it is not later permitted to break. And this obligation passes over into the fundamental law of the commonwealth. The right of succession even attaches itself to the descendants of the first supreme magistrate while still in the loins of their parents, so far as they are not incapable of ruling because of defect or other disabilities. Therefore, they ought not to be rejected and excluded from imperium. . . . This restricted election, which leads political theorists to refer to a successive realm, is preferred by many to the free election.[26] For by this procedure every occasion is cut off for factions and conspiracies, which the ambition to exercise domination often excites, and many perils are averted that would ordinarily happen in a time of interregnum. The occurrence of much confusion and disturbance that accompanies an interregnum is also avoided, and imperium is continued without interruption. When, however, the persons become extinct to whom this election is limited, then this restricted election becomes a free one.

The restricted election, by which they call a realm hereditary or successive, is either of two kinds. It may be limited to a certain nation and the nobles thereof, or to the heirs of the deceased supreme magistrate. In an election restricted to a certain nation, it is permitted to elect a supreme magistrate only from those having their origin within the realm. So among the Jews it was not permitted by the fundamental law of the realm to establish a king unless he came from an Israelite family. For this reason the female Athaliah, a foreign-born queen, was cast down from the imperium.[27] So it is established in a fundamental law of the German imperium that no one who is not from the German nation may be elected emperor and caesar.

§76

§77   An election restricted to the heirs of the deceased magistrate is in turn limited either to any heirs whatever, even foreign ones, or else to his family and blood relatives. . . . An election of the first kind, namely, one that is limited to testamentary heirs, even foreigners, is servile and

§78   pernicious. . . . An election of the other kind, namely, one that is restricted to the family and offspring, is also twofold. It is either limited

---

[26] Jean Bodin, *The Commonweale*, VI, 4; Petrus Gregorius, *De republica*, VII, 4 f. and 15; Eberartus a Weyhe and Justus Lipsius [no references provided].
[27] II Kings 11.

to persons of both masculine and feminine sex, or to masculine heirs only. In the former, living masculine agnates of the deceased exclude females who are even closer in degree of relationship. But if no such males are living, females related by blood to the deceased are admitted. Vincent Cabot disagrees.[28] He considers it to be general in all realms in which females are able to succeed to the supreme magistracy that women who are descendant from the deceased in a straight line are to be preferred to men related in a lateral line, which he confirms by the opinion of Spaniards. But the previous judgment is approved by Jean Bodin,[29] and more nearly agrees with Mosaic law.[30] It also has greater regard for the commonwealth because it keeps the government thereof in the family of the deceased, and does not transfer this government to another family.[31] Such is the example of the Jewish polity, which is the best of all. . . .[32]

In the election restricted to male heirs of the same family and clan, which excludes females as ineligible, the closest living males of the same family as that of the deceased are elected to the administration of the realm. So according to the fundamental law of the Jewish polity, kings from the family of David were elected continuously until the fall of Jerusalem under Nebuchadnezzar. . . . In this election according to hereditary succession carried out in keeping with the fundamental laws of the realm, the first-born (*primogenitus*) from a legitimate matrimony is preferred, and the others are excluded. However, the first-born should make provision for his brothers that they may be able to maintain themselves decently. . . .

This first-born is to be elected even if he is deaf, mute, of a different religion, or in any other manner awkward for ruling. . . . For once such a law of primogeniture has been established, the people has obligated itself to the supreme magistrate and to his descendants, and has even elected his descendants who are still in the loins of the parent. This promise once made cannot be withdrawn without a violation of

§80

§81

§83

§85

---

[28] *Variarum juris,* I, 15.

[29] [*The Commonweale,* IV, 1.]

[30] Numbers 27.

[31] [Althusius apparently fears that the marriage of a female supreme magistrate, or of a female in the line of succession to the supreme magistracy, may introduce a foreign influence and royal house into the realm.]

[32] Deuteronomy 17. [*See* especially verse 15.]

§87   trust and justice. . . . Wherefore, if a prince of a different religion is
called to administer the realm, then the orders will undertake to instruct
him in the true and orthodox religion. If this cannot be done, they will
require him to grant the exercise of pure religion to the remaining
members of the realm, as we see done in the German, Polish, French,
English, and Swiss polities. . . .

§90   Election by the people is not excluded, however, in these
hereditary realms. . . . The reason is that the person elected receives the
realm not from his dead father, but from the universal association. This
practice is customarily even more useful and favorable to the magistrate
than it is pleasing to the people and worthy of respect to outsiders. For
because of it obedience can much less be denied to him. Whence I
consider it best that even in this case the people and members of the
realm shall have reserved to themselves the election, so that they shall be
permitted to choose the one from the many children of the deceased
magistrate, or from his entire family, that they have judged best fitted for
the administration of the realm. . . .

§92   THE INAUGURATION OF THE MAGISTRATE, which is also called a coro-
nation, is the process by which he who has been elected by the
magnates, after he has executed an oath that he will administer the realm
according to the prescribed laws, is publicly confirmed and proclaimed
magistrate in the presence of the people and with the invocation of the
name of God. Thus he is inducted and put into possession of the realm,
with the granting and handing over to him of the insignia and customary symbols by which the administration of the realm is represented.
And, with the favorable and joyful acclamation of the people, he is
§93   greeted as supreme magistrate. The inauguration, therefore, is a renewal
of the preceding election, and a solemn confirmation for stabilizing the
authority of the magistrate and for making his person known to each
and all. The inauguration, to be sure, does not add anything to the
newly elected supreme magistrate. . . .

§98   These supreme magistrates bear and represent the person of
the entire realm, of all subjects thereof, and of God from whom all
power derives. They bear, as it were, the form of divine might, majesty,
glory, imperium, clemency, providence, care, protection, and government. For this reason they use in their titles, "We by the grace of God,"
§101   and other similar formulas. . . . Such an elected and inaugurated su-

preme magistrate does not need the approval and confirmation of the pope. . . .[33]

XX   THE PROMISE OF OBEDIENCE and compliance that follows the   §1
election and inauguration is the event in which the members of the realm—or the people through its ephors, and the ephors in its name—promise their trust, obedience, compliance, and whatever else may be necessary for the administration of the realm. This promise, which pertains to things that do not conflict with the law of God and the right of the realm, is made to the magistrate who receives the entrusted administration of the commonwealth, and is about to undertake his office and to rule the commonwealth piously and justly. . . .

The oath that the magistrate first swears to the subjects, and   §5
the subjects then offer to the magistrate, is properly called a homage (*homagium*) from ὁμοῦ, which means "at the same time" (*simul*), and ἅγιον, which means "sacred" (*sacrum*), so that, as it were, what is common, or a common oath, should be sacred. Those subjects who have upheld this oath are called faithful.

Because of this trust, compliance, service, aid, and counsel that   §6
the people promises and furnishes to its supreme magistrate, he is said to have innumerable eyes and ears, large arms, and swift feet, as if the whole people lent him its eyes, ears, strength, and faculties for the use of the commonwealth. Whence the magistrate is called mighty, strong, rich, wise, and aware of many things, and is said to represent the entire people. . . .

Such service and aid consist above all in works of occupational   §7
skill and in works of allegiance. Works of occupational skill consist in material services extended and performed for the welfare and utility of the realm and magistrate according to the function, trade, and office that each is able to perform. . . . Works of allegiance consist in obedi-   §10
ence and reverence. Obedience is the compliance that is shown to the   §11
just commands of the magistrate, and is required even if he should be an impious or wicked man. For the life of the magistrate does not take away his office, and whoever disparages the magistrate scorns God. . . .
However, obedience is not to be extended to impious commands of the   §12
magistrate. For obedience to God is more important than obedience to

---

[33] Lupold of Bebenburg, *De jure regni et imperii,* I, 8.

§13   men. . . .[34] Reverence is that honor, veneration, and adoration that the subject with fear and trembling owes to the magistrate because of the lofty position to which the magistrate is elevated by God, and because of the many and great benefits that God dispenses to us through the hand of the magistrate. Whence the deeds of the whole realm are attributed wisely and happily to the virtue and administration of the prince, and we honor no one in preference to him. . . .

§19   If the people does not manifest obedience, and fails to fulfill the service and obligations promised in the election and inauguration— in the constituting—of the supreme magistrate, then he is the punisher, even by arms and war, of this perfidy and violation of trust, indeed, of

§20   this contumacy, rebellion, and sedition.[35] But if the supreme magistrate does not keep his pledged word, and fails to administer the realm according to his promise, then the realm, or the ephors and the leading men in its name, is the punisher of this violation and broken trust. It is then conceded to the people to change and annul the earlier form of its

§21   polity and commonwealth, and to constitute a new one.[36] In both cases, because a proper condition of the agreement and compact is not fulfilled, the contract is dissolved by right itself. In the first case, the prince will no longer treat such rebels and perfidious persons as his subjects, and is no longer required to perform toward them what he has promised. In the other case, likewise, the people, or members of the realm, will not recognize such a perfidious, perjurous, and compact-breaking person as their magistrate, but treat him as a private person and a tyrant to whom it is no longer required to extend obedience and other duties it promised. The magistrate loses the right to exact them justly. And it can and ought to remove him from office. Thus Bartolus says that a legitimate magistrate is a living law, and if he is condemned by law he is condemned by his own voice.[37] But a tyrant is anything but a living law. . . .

---

[34] Acts 5.

[35] Andreas Gail says that it is permitted to a lord to take and hold the goods of subjects until the subjects are brought back into the obedience that they owe. *Practicarum observationum,* I, obs. 17.

[36] How this is to be done is discussed in Chapter XXXVIII below, where I have explained how, when, and by what persons a supreme magistrate who has become a tyrant against the original covenant and compact may be resisted.

[37] *De tyrannia.*

XXI–XXVII

Political Prudence
in the Administration
of the Commonwealth

XXI T HE CONSTITUTING OF THE SUPREME MAGISTRATE has §1
thus far been discussed. We turn now to his administration, which is conducted according to the agreement by which it was
bestowed. In keeping with the agreement, this administration pertains
not to individuals, but to the members of the realm collectively. . . .
The administration of the commonwealth or realm, which is granted by §2
the people and conducted by the magistrate, is the wise, diligent, and
just care, management, oversight, and defense of the rights of sovereignty (*jura majestatis*), that is, of the affairs and goods of the realm and
its subjects, in accord with their nature and condition. It is directed to
the glory of God and to the welfare of the realm and its subjects. . . .

The order, rule, and norm of this administration should first §5
be understood, and then its types.[1] The order and rule of this adminis- §6
tration consist in political prudence, in which no administration of a
magistrate ought to be lacking. . . . This political prudence is, accord- §8
ing to the authority of Justus Lipsius,[2] the understanding and choice of

---

[1] [The order, rule, and norm of administering here mean the entire teaching on
political prudence (Chapters XXI–XXVII). Later, political prudence will be
divided into its members (political understanding and political choice) and its
kinds (proper prudence and borrowed prudence). Political understanding in
turn will be divided into doctrine and practice. Doctrine still again will be
divided into the rule of living and administering, the nature of the people, and
the nature of rule or imperium. It is important, therefore, that the order, rule,
and norm of administering (or political prudence in general) not be confused
with the rule of living and administering (one of the subdivisions of political
prudence), which will be discussed very soon.

The types of administration refer to the ecclesiastical administration (Chapter
XXVIII) and secular administration (Chapters XXIX–XXXVII).]

[2] [*Politicorum sive civilis doctrinae.*]

those things that publicly and privately are to be done or to be omitted in the administration of a commonwealth. Understanding is to be likened to the eye, and choice to the hand. I accept the word "prudence" in the broad sense, as does Cicero.[3]

Seneca describes this political prudence when he says that it orders the present, provides for the future, and remembers the past.[4] King David exercised this prudence in his government and administration. "God chose his servant David . . . who tended the peoples of Israel with a sound mind, and guided them with a prudent hand."[5] "The people is without judgment and prudence; would that they were sensitive to the past, understood the present, and provided for the new or the future."[6] "Wisdom resides in venerable things, and prudence in what has stood the test of time."[7] "The governor will consider the events of past years in his own and other commonwealths, what was done well and what was done badly, what in those events was laudable and what was reprehensible; and in judging individual persons, he will consider how they lived in those periods of their lives already completed. The affairs of the present gain prudence from past affairs"[8] when memory, discretion, and judgment are exercised. "Foresight regards future affairs by considering the outcome of past events.[. . .] For when a ship is still safely in port, it should be equipped with necessary things before it is sent out to sea."[9]

§9   "Most miserable is that commonwealth, therefore, in which its governor is imprudent or ignorant in the art of governing, in which he learns for the first time from his own experience those things that were necessary from the beginning."[10] "An uninformed king destroys his people, and a city shall be inhabited through the intelligence of

---

[3] *Duties,* I, 4. [Cicero relates prudence to wisdom, and understands them both to seek the essential truth of any given matter.]

[4] [The Four Virtues.]

[5] Psalm 78:70, 72.

[6] Petrus Gregorius, *De republica,* X, 4, 5. [Gregorius presents this passage as a statement by Moses in Deuteronomy 32. Althusius retains the reference to Deuteronomy 32, but does not mention Moses.]

[7] Job 12:12. [This Biblical reference is also to be found in Gregorius, *De republica,* X, 4, 5.]

[8] Gregorius, *De republica,* X, 4, 5. [Gregorius then proceeds with brief comments on memory and discretion, but does not mention judgment.]

[9] *Ibid.,* X, 4, 6. [There are slight variations in wording in this quotation and others here employed from Gregorius.]

[10] [Gregorius, *De republica,* X, 3, 3.]

rulers."[11] A wise king is called a pillar of the people.[12] For what the eye is in the body, and the sun in the heavens, so is the magistrate in the commonwealth. He ought to be attentive to everything, and to keep many things secret. "Certain rulers are to be found who are not in the least evil, and who would like to rule well and to benefit their subjects, but do not know how. Indeed, even when they wish to do so and make the attempt, they instead inflict injury upon themselves and others as they pursue their intention. Thus the proverb is true, that a sword should not be given to a child."[13] Nor should a wild and stubborn horse be given to one who is not skilled in ruling him. But no animal is more capricious than man, and none requires greater art to handle.[14] For this reason God requires men for the administration of a commonwealth who excel in the practice and experience of things. . . .[15]

There is a twofold division, as I have said,[16] in this political   §10
prudence: one into its members, and the other into its kinds.[17] The members of this prudence are two in number: namely, political understanding (*intellectus*) and choice (*delectus*) of things to be done and to be omitted in the administration of the commonwealth.[18] By political understanding a magistrate sees, recognizes, knows, and comprehends the things that he is to do or to omit by reason of his office. . . . A complete political   §11
understanding is composed of doctrine (*doctrina*) and practice (*usus*).[19] They are therefore considered to be the parts of a perfect knowledge.[20]

Doctrine of things salutary and necessary for administration is   §12
supplied by the knowledge that comes through reading and listening.

---

[11] Ecclesiasticus 10:3.

[12] Wisdom 6:26.

[13] [Gregorius, *De republica,* X, 3, 3.]

[14] [This same comparison of man with an animal, although not in the same words, is found in Gregorius, *ibid.,* X, 3, 4.]

[15] Exodus 18:21; Deuteronomy 1:13–15; Numbers 11:16.

[16] [Actually he has not said this before. But he has spoken earlier in this chapter of the division in the next sentence, namely, the distinction he has borrowed from Lipsius between political understanding and political choice.]

[17] [Chapters XXI–XXVI and XXVII respectively.]

[18] [Political understanding is discussed in Chapters XXI–XXV and the first part of XXVI, and political choice in the latter part of XXVI.]

[19] [Doctrine is discussed in Chapters XXI–XXV, and practice in the first part of XXVI.]

[20] Whence practice (experience) begot me, and memory brought me forth; the Greeks call me *sophia,* and you *sapientia.*

But he is rightly to be praised who is productive and useful to the commonwealth, not he who merely knows many things. The origin of intemperance is the wish to know more than enough, as Seneca declares. As we incline towards intemperance in all things, so in literary matters. And in so doing we learn not of life, but of learning. "The reading of many things is a weariness of the flesh."[21] The best way to learn is to listen to a teacher in person. It is to be sought in the experience and practice of the learned through conversation with distinguished men among them; with theologians, jurists, philosophers, historians, generals, soldiers, and others. A prince can learn more in a brief time in colloquies around a table with these men—while wandering about and consulting them—than he would be able to gather in a

§13   longer period of time in schools. . . . The means of learning from the voice of the dead, or from silent instructors, is provided principally by the reading of histories. For by them it is possible without peril or expense to observe others, to look upon their journeys, calamities, perils, wars, customs, virtues, vices, governments, life and death, joy and sadness, fortune and adversity, the beginning, middle, and end of imperia, as well as the causes, effects, foundations, accessories, conflicts,

§14   and relations of all events. . . . But in this matter Cicero advises that "two errors are to be avoided. One is that we must not consider the unknown as known, and thus accept it without adequate investigation. [. . .] The other is that we ought not to devote excessive study and great pains to obscure and difficult matters that are not necessary."[22]

§15   Three things are properly and unavoidably to be learned and known by the supreme magistrate in the administration of the commonwealth. The sinews and bond of imperium and commonwealth depend upon them. First is the rule of living and administering; the second is the nature of the people; and the third is the nature of rule (*regnum*).[23] We will consider each of these in order.[24]

---

[21] Ecclesiastes 12:12.

[22] *Duties,* I, 6. [The unacknowledged omission from this quotation reads, "and he who wishes to avoid this error, as all should, will apply both time and diligence to the weighing of evidence." Althusius also makes other minor changes in wording.]

[23] [The word *regnum,* which is consistently rendered as "realm" in this translation unless otherwise noted, conveys in this instance much more the meaning of "rule." For *regnum* is here used interchangeably with *imperium,* and will be dropped by Althusius in favor of *imperium* when he turns to a discussion of the nature of rule or imperium in Chapters XXIV–XXV.]

[24] [Chapters XXI–XXII, XXIII, and XXIV–XXV respectively.]

THE RULE OF LIVING, OBEYING, AND ADMINISTERING is the will of God   *§16*
alone, which is the way of life, and the law of things to be done and to be
omitted. It is necessary that the magistrate rule, appoint, and examine all
the business of his administration with this law as a touchstone and
measure, unless he wishes to rule the ship of state as an unreliable vessel
at sea, and to wander about and move at random. Thus the administration and government of a commonwealth is nothing other than the
execution of law. Therefore, this law alone prescribes not only the order   *§17*
of administering for the magistrate, but also the rule of living for all
subjects. . . .

    This rule, which is solely God's will for men manifested in his   *§18*
law, is called law in the general sense that it is a precept for doing those
things that pertain to living a pious, holy, just, and suitable life. That is to
say, it pertains to the duties that are to be performed toward God and
one's neighbor, and to the love of God and one's neighbor. . . . It is
evident from these things that laws or rights in human society are as
fences, walls, guards, or boundaries of our life, guiding us along the
appointed way for achieving wisdom, happiness, and peace in human
society. When laws are taken away, human society, which we call
symbiotic, is changed into a brutal life. . . .

    This law, as we have said, is twofold. It is either common or   *§19*
proper.[25] Common law (*lex communis*) has been naturally implanted by
God in all men. "Whatever can be known about God has been
manifested to men, because God has made it manifest to them."[26] As to
knowledge (*notitia*) and inclination (*inclinatio*), God discloses and
prescribes the reason and means for worshiping him and loving one's
neighbor, and urges us to them. "For there was reason derived from the
nature of the universe," Cicero says, "urging men to do right and
recalling them from wrong-doing, and this reason did not first become
law at the time it was written down, but at its origin."[27] It is commonly
called the moral law (*lex moralis*).

    By the knowledge imprinted within us by God, which is   *§20*
called conscience, man knows and understands law (*jus*)[28] and the

---

[25] [There is another treatment of common law and proper law in Althusius'
Dicaeologica, I, 13 and 14.]

[26] Romans 1:19.

[27] *Laws*, II, 4.

[28] [In this discussion of common and proper law Althusius usually employs *jus*
interchangeably with *lex*. Consequently, both Latin words will be translated as

means to be employed or avoided for maintaining obedience to law. By this innate inclination, or secret impulse of nature, man is urged to perform what he understands to be just, and to avoid what he knows to be wicked. "When gentiles who do not have the law do by nature what the law requires, they are a law unto themselves, even though not having the law, because they show forth service to a law written on their hearts. Their conscience bears witness to it, and their thoughts alternately accuse and even excuse them."[29] Other witnesses of scripture also make clear that conscience duly excuses a man when he acts uprightly, and disturbs and accuses him when he deserves condemnation for acting wickedly. . . .[30] In this common law (*jus commune*) is set forth for all men nothing other than the general theory and practice of love, both for God and for one's neighbor.[31]

§21   There are different degrees of this knowledge and inclination. For law is not inscribed equally on the hearts of all. The knowledge of it is communicated more abundantly to some and more sparingly to others, according to the will and judgment of God. Whence it is that the knowledge of this law may be greater in some than in others. Nor does God urge and excite all persons to obedience of this law in the same manner and to an equal degree. Some men exert themselves more strongly, others less so, in their desire for it.[32]

§22   Christ set forth two headings of this common law.[33] The first heading pertains to the performance of our duty immediately to God,
§23   and the second to what is owed to our neighbor. In the former are the mandates and precepts that guide the pious and religious life of acknowledging and worshipping God. These are in the first table of the Decalogue, where they instruct and inform man about God and the
§24   public and private worship of him. . . . In the latter table are those

---

"law" except where noted. The reader should also observe that Althusius here employs common law (*jus commune*) in a different sense from that of Chapter IV where it refers to the fundamental law of a particular association.]

[29] Romans 2:14 f.

[30] I Corinthians 1:12; 4:4; 5:1 f.; 11:14; Acts 23:1; Psalm 26:1–3; I Timothy 1:19; Proverbs 28:1; Romans 2:15; 9; Ecclesiastes 7:22.

[31] *See* Benedict Aretius, *Problemata theologica,* "De cognitione Dei naturali," loc. 1.

[32] *See* Romans 7:15–13; Psalm 10:4; 36:2; Romans 1:24, 28; I Timothy 4:2; Jeremiah 31.

[33] Matthew 22:34–40.

mandates and precepts that concern the just, and more civil and political, life. Man is informed by them that he may render and communicate things, services, counsel, and right (*jus*) to his symbiotic neighbor, and may discharge toward him everything that ought to be rendered for alleviating his need and for living comfortably. Properly speaking, however, they are not called mandates and precepts, as the previous ones are, but rather judgments, statutes, and witnesses. They are contained in the second table of the Decalogue.

Affirmative precepts of the Decalogue are about duties to be performed that are owed to God and one's neighbor. Negative precepts are about prohibited things that are to be omitted or avoided.

The first precept of the first table is about truly cherishing and *§25* choosing God through the knowledge of him handed down in his word, and through unity with him accompanied by a disposition of trust, love, and fear. Forbidden by this precept are ignorance of God and of the divine will, atheism, errors concerning God, and enmity or contempt towards God.

The second precept is about maintaining in spirit and in truth a genuine worship of God through prayers and the use of the means of grace. In this precept a false or feigned worship of God is forbidden, whether through images, idolatry, hypocrisy, human traditions, magic, or anything else.

The third precept is about rendering glory to God in all things through the proper use of the names of God, oaths of allegiance to him, respect for what has been created by the Word of God, and intercessory prayers. Negatively this precept is about not taking away from the glory of God by perjury, blasphemy, cursing, abuse of the creation, superstition, a dissolute life, and so forth.

The fourth precept is about sanctifying the sabbath in holy services through hearing, reading, and meditating upon the Word of God, and through use of the sacraments. Negatively, it is about not violating the sabbath through occupational employment, marketing, physical labors, games, jokes, frolics, feasts, or the mere form of piety.

Whatever is in conflict with these precepts of the first table is *§26* called impious. And for that reason these precepts are always, absolutely, and without distinction binding upon all, to such a degree that the second table of the Decalogue ought to yield precedence to the first table as to a superior law. Therefore, if a precept of God and a mandate of the magistrate should come together in the same affair and be contrary to each other, then God is to be obeyed rather than the magistrate. And in like manner private utility ought to give way to public utility and the common welfare. Whence it is that these precepts of the first table can never be set aside or relaxed, and not even God himself is able to reject them.

§27 　　The precepts of the second table are those that contain duties to be performed toward our neighbor. These are either proper or common. Proper duties are comprehended by the fifth precept, which is about those things that inferiors are expected to perform towards superiors, and vice versa. The dignity, honor, authority, and eminence of superiors are to be upheld through respect, obedience, compliance, subjection, and necessary aid. These are owed to more distinguished persons because of the gifts, talents, or services they bring to public or private office in the commonwealth, or because of their origins. And when a man fulfills these duties, he is at the same time upholding reason and order in the social life. Negatively, this precept is about not despising, scorning, or depreciating our neighbor by word or deed. It is also about not destroying order among the various stations in human society, and not introducing confusion into them.

Common duties, which are to be performed toward everyone, are treated in the remaining precepts. Of these the sixth requires the defense, protection, and conservation of one's own life and that of the neighbor. The conservation of one's own life comes first, and consists in defense, conservation, and propagation of oneself. . . . [34] Conservation of the neighbor's life is his protection through friendship and other duties of charity, such as provision for food, clothes, and anything else he needs for sustentation. Negatively, this precept prohibits enmity, injury to the human body, assault, mutilation, blows, murder, terror, privation of natural liberty,[35] and any other inhuman treatment.

The seventh precept concerns the conservation of the chastity of one's own mind and body, and that of one's neighbor, through

---

[34] [By propagation of oneself Althusius means "the legitimate union of man and wife, and the honorable procreation and education of children."]

[35] I have spoken more extensively about this in my *Dicaeologicae libri tres* [I, 25].

sobriety, good manners, modesty, discretion, and any other appropriate means. Negatively, it pertains to the avoidance in word or deed of fornication, debauchery, lewdness, and wantonness.

The eighth precept concerns the defense and conservation of one's own goods and those of one's neighbor, and their proper employment in commerce, contracts, and one's vocation. Negatively, it forbids the disturbance, embezzlement, injury, seizure, or impairment of another's goods, or the misuse of one's own. It condemns deceit in commerce and trade, theft, falsehood, injury, any injustice that can be perpetrated by omitting or including something in contracts, and an idle and disordered life.

The ninth precept concerns the defense and conservation of the good name and reputation of oneself and one's neighbor through honest testimony, just report, and good deeds. Negatively, it prohibits hostility, perverse suggestions, insults of any kind, defamations, and slander, either by spoken or written words or by an act or gesture.

The tenth precept concerns concupiscence, and exerts influence on each of the other precepts of the second table. "We are taught [. . .] by the authority and bidding of laws to control our passions, to bridle our every lust, to defend what is ours, and to keep our minds, eyes, and hands from whatever belongs to another."[36]

Not only the fifth precept of the second table, but also the sixth, seventh, eighth, ninth, and tenth precepts concern the political society and the magistracy of the commonwealth, both as to persons and as to the goods of the subjects. Whatever is in conflict with these precepts of the second table is called unjust. What is commanded or prohibited by them ought to be done or omitted by each person in keeping with his public or private vocation and out of love for his neighbor. God sometimes relaxes the fifth, sixth, and eighth precepts, and out of his great wisdom sets aside the things that ought to be done according to them. Thus he ordered Abraham to kill and sacrifice his son contrary to the sixth precept of the Decalogue. And Ehud, by special command of God, killed Eglon, and Jehu killed Joram. Thus he permitted to the Jewish people polygamy, divorce, marriage with the surviving widow of a deceased brother, and many other things that had

§28

---

[36] Cicero, *The Orator,* I, 43. ["not by unending debates full of controversies, but" is the unacknowledged omission.]

been specifically prohibited in the second table. But his power of dispensation has not been given to men. . . .

§29   The Decalogue has been prescribed for all people to the extent that it agrees with and explains the common law of nature for all peoples. It has also been renewed and confirmed by Christ our king. Jerome Zanchius says that this is the common judgment of theologians. . . . [37]

§30   Proper law (*lex propria*) is the law that is drawn up and established by the magistrate on the basis of common law (*lex communis*) and according to the nature, utility, condition, and other special circumstances of his country. It indicates the peculiar way, means, and manner by which this natural equity among men can be upheld, observed, and cultivated in any given commonwealth. Therefore, proper law (*jus proprium*) is nothing other than the practice of this common natural law (*jus naturale*) as adapted to a particular polity. It indicates how individual citizens of a given commonwealth are able to seek and attain this natural equity. Whence it is called the servant and handmaiden of common law (*jus commune*), and a teacher leading us to the observance of common law.

§31   Proper law is established for two principal reasons, as Zanchius says.[38] The first reason is that not all men have sufficient natural capacity that they are able to draw from these general principles of common law the particular conclusions and laws suitable to the nature and condition of an activity and its circumstances. The second reason is that natural law is not so completely written on the hearts of men that it is sufficiently efficacious in restraining men from evil and impelling them to good. This is because it merely teaches, inclines, and accuses men. It is therefore necessary that there be a proper law by which men who are led neither by the love of virtue nor by the hatred of vice may be restrained by the fear of punishment that this law assigns to transgressions of common law. In this sense, it is said that "law is set forth not for the just, but the unjust."[39]

§32   There are two parts of this law. The first is its agreement with common law, and the second is its difference, as Francis Junius ob-

---

[37] *De redemptione,* I, 10, 1 [actually thesis 1 of the second section ("De legibus humanis") of Chapter 10].

[38] [*De redemptione,* I, 11, 1.]

[39] I Timothy 1:9.

serves[40] and the jurists teach.[41] For if this law were to teach nothing other than what common law does, it would not constitute a new specie. If it set forth something entirely contrary to common law, it would be evil in that it would make mutable an otherwise immutable common law. It is truly necessary, therefore, that it not entirely depart from common law, that it not be generally contrary to it, and that it not completely combine with it and thus be identical with it.

Its agreement (*convenientia*) with common law is in those matters common to each law, namely, in the starting point from which analogical deductions are made, in the subject under consideration, and in the purpose. The starting point is the right and certain reason upon which both laws rely, and by which each decides what is just and declares it. The subject under consideration is the joint business and action to which both laws relate themselves and give directions. The purpose of each is justice and piety, or sanctity, and the same equity and common good in human society.

Its difference (*discrepantia*) from common law arises from the fact that, in accommodation to particular and special circumstances, it departs somewhat from common law, adding or subtracting something from it. Proper law differs for two reasons, each of which provides a necessity for adding or subtracting something from common law. And so mutability, or the possibility and necessity of just changes, is introduced. One reason is that, because of a better understanding by the legislator of order and utility, a law that for a long time was looked upon as just is changed. The other is the nature and condition of an activity so far as persons, things, circumstances, place, or time are concerned. Since the nature and condition of these circumstances may be diverse, inconstant, and changeable, it is not possible for proper law to acknowledge one and the same disposition of common law for everything and in everything, as Junius and Zanchius, together with the jurists, say.

Therefore, this law is rightly said to be mutable or subject to §33 change with respect to circumstances and its consequent difference from common law. But it is altogether immutable with respect to its agreement with common law. So the jurists assert, together with Junius, Zanchius, Martyr, and Bucer. Thus common or moral law concludes

---

[40] *De politicae Mosis observatione.*
[41] In commentaries on the Digest I, 1, 6.

from its principles that evildoers ought to be punished, but proposes nothing concerning the punishment. Proper law determines specifically that adulterers, murderers, and the like are to be punished by death, unless the punishment should be mitigated because of further circumstances. Various punishments, for example, exist in the Mosaic law for these crimes. Common law requires that God be worshipped. Proper law determines that this is to be done each seventh day. Therefore, common law commands in general. Proper law makes these commands specific, and accommodates them to the experience and utility of the commonwealth and the circumstances of each activity. For this reason, the moral precepts of the Decalogue, having no certain, special, and fixed punishment attached to them, are general. The forensic and political law then makes specific determinations, which it relates to the circumstances of any act.

§34   This proper law is one thing among the Jews, another among the Romans, another among the Germans today, and still another among other peoples. However, almost all European polities use the Roman Law (*jus Romanum*), which is described in the Digest, Code, Novels, and Institutes.

§35   Jewish proper law is twofold. It is in part ceremonial, and in part forensic or judicial. The ceremonial law, because of its emphasis, was directed to the observance and support of the first table of the Decalogue through certain political and ecclesiastical actions and

§37   things; or it was devoted to piety and divine worship. . . . The forensic law was the means by which the Jews were informed and instructed to observe and obey both tables, or the common law, for the cultivation of human society among them in their polity, according to the circum-

§40   stances of things, persons, place, and time. . . . It should be observed that often one and the same law of the Jews could be said in varying respects to be moral (or common), ceremonial, and forensic, and to this extent mixed. What is moral in such a law is perpetual; what is judicial can be changed by the change of circumstances; and what is ceremonial is considered to have passed away. . . .

§41   At this point we encounter the controversy over what we maintain to be the political doctrine of the Decalogue. In the judgment of others the Decalogue should instead be considered theological.[42]

---

[42] [For another discussion by Althusius of the respective uses of the Decalogue in

Some persons consider that we thus sin against the law of homogeneity. Whence there is a deep silence among them about the role of the Decalogue in politics. But this is wrong in my judgment. For the subject matter of the Decalogue is indeed political insofar as it directs symbiotic life and prescribes what ought to be done therein. For the Decalogue teaches the pious and just life; piety toward God and justice toward symbiotes. If symbiosis is deprived of these qualities, it should not be called so much a political and human society as a beastly congregation of vice-ridden men. Therefore, each and every precept of the Decalogue is political and symbiotic. The contemplative and practical life in every respect is embraced and completed in them, although the first and last precepts have the sole purpose of building up the souls of men and are merely speculative. If you would deprive political and symbiotic life of this rule and this light to our feet, as it is called,[43] you would destroy its vital spirit. Furthermore, you would take away the bond of human society and, as it were, the rudder and helm of this ship. It would then altogether perish, or be transformed into a stupid, beastly, and inhuman life. Therefore, the subject matter of the Decalogue is indeed natural, essential, and proper to politics.

If the external and civil life of words, deeds and works is accompanied by true faith—together with holiness of thought and desire, and with a right purpose, namely, the glory of God—then it becomes theological. So therefore, when the works of the Decalogue are performed by the Christian to the glory of God because of true faith, they are pleasing to God. But if, to the contrary, they are performed by an infidel or heathen, to whom the Apostle Paul indeed ascribes a natural knowledge of and inclination towards the Decalogue,[44] these works are not able to please God. But in political life even an infidel may be called just, innocent, and upright because of them.

Jurists and moralists also handle the concerns of both tables of the Decalogue, but in a manner fitting and proper to each art and profession, so that neither is confused with the purely theological or political. As the general doctrine of the Decalogue is therefore essential, homogeneous,

---

politics and theology, *see* the preface to the third edition. Actually, the discussion of the Decalogue here is somewhat out of place and should have come earlier. For the Decalogue is not proper law, Jewish or otherwise, but common law.]

[43] Psalm 119:105.

[44] Romans 1; 2.

and necessary in politics, so the special and particular doctrine of the Decalogue accommodated to individual and separate disciplines is proper to jurisprudence. And theology rightly claims for itself the pious and salutary doctrine of the Decalogue, which ought to be a teacher leading to Christ, so far as the Decalogue pertains to life eternal. . . .

§3   **XXII**   FROM THESE THINGS[45] it follows that the magistrate is obligated in the administration of the commonwealth to the proper law of Moses so far as moral equity or common law are expressed therein. This is to say, he is required to conform to everything therein that is in harmony with common law. But he is by no means required to conform in those things in which the proper law of Moses, in order to be accommodated to the polity of the Jews, differs from common law.

§4   For if the magistrate should establish as absolutely necessary these proper Jewish laws, which by their nature are either changeable or obsolete, he would destroy Christian liberty, which has been given for edification to him and to others, and would entangle himself and others in the yoke of slavery. Thereby he would make a necessity of something free, and impede consciences by a grievous and dangerous snare. He would obtrude mortal laws, which were promulgated in former times only for the Jewish people and are by their nature subject to change for a variety of reasons, as if they were immortal. And unless proper laws are changed with the changing circumstances because of which they broadly exist, they become wicked and attain neither to the equity of the second table of the Decalogue nor the piety of the first. Thus they cease to contain the common foundation of right reason. Accordingly, the magistrate who makes the proper law of Moses compulsory in his commonwealth sins grievously. For those particular circumstances and considerations because of which the Jewish proper law was promulgated should bear no weight in his commonwealth. . . .

§1   **XXIII**   THUS FAR WE HAVE SPOKEN about the law, rule, and norm of living and administering. We turn now to the nature and attitude of the people and the associated body, the knowledge of which

---

[45] [Althusius returns here (Chapter XXII) to the matters he was discussing prior to his raising of the controversy over the theological and political uses of the Decalogue.]

is indeed necessary to the magistrate in the highest administration of the realm. Here I mean by the people the common multitude and crowd, and by the associated body the members of the realm united in one body.

The character, customs, nature, attitude, and viewpoint of the people are to be sought and learned from the nature and location of a region, and from the age, condition, circumstances, and education of the people therein.[46] One learns about the nature of men from the location of the region. He does this by considering whether the region is situated in the east, north, west, south, or wherever in relation to the rising and setting of the sun, and whether it is flat, mountainous, windy, or calm. Oriental peoples are by nature more humane and polite than others. Peoples located midway between north and south, because they enjoy a mean between coldness and hotness, are gifted in strength both of mind and body. And for that reason they are to be ruled with moderate freedom. Such are Romans, Greeks, Poles, Hungarians, Frenchmen, and others. Northern peoples are by nature spirited, courageous, and sincere, but not astute or diligent. They are truly straightforward, guileless, corpulent, sluggish, faithful and constant, cheerful, addicted to drink, and uncultivated. The Transylvanians, certain Poles, the Danes, Swedes, and others are considered to be of this sort. They are to be held more loosely by the reins of government, for they delight in greater liberty and indulgence. Southern peoples, to the contrary, are clever, ingenious, unreliable, inconstant, addicted to love-making, and melancholy. Such are the Saracens and other Arabs, the Egyptians, Ethiopians, Persians, Gedrosians, Indians, and many others.

Those who live in open and windy regions are turbulent, restless, and unsteady. Those living in calm places, to the contrary, are peaceful and steady. Mountainous peoples are hardy, robust, and austere. They are more cheerful, and seek enjoyment in liberty and licence. Inhabitants of valleys, on the other hand, are faint of heart, gentle, and effeminate. Those who live in barren places are skillful, industrious,

§2

§3
§4

§5

§6

§7

§8

§9
§10

---

[46] *See* Jean Bodin, *The Commonweale, V, 1; and Method for the Easy Comprehension of History,* 5; Justus *Lipsius, Politicorum sive civilis doctrinae,* IV, 5; Hippolytus a Collibus, *Princeps,* 8; Theodore Zwinger, *Theatrum vitae humanae,* vol. XXI, lib. 1; Alexander ab Alexandro, *Genialium dierum,* IV, 13; Petrus Gregorius, *De republica,* IV, 4; X, 3 and 6; Giovanni Botero, *Practical Politics,* II, 3 f.; Scipio Ammirato, *Dissertationes,* IV, disc. 7.

§11   diligent, and strict, and they consider that the stubborn and cruel life of man should be held together by close bonds. The inhabitants of fertile regions, to the contrary, are leisurely and addicted to pleasure. Those who live in seaports or river towns, because of contacts and conversation with a wide variety of men are astute, addicted to money, and full of cunning. . . .

§14   Then, as the customs of regions often express diverse interests and discernments, so persons born in these regions hold diverse patterns in their customs. Accordingly, they are unable to come together at the same time without some antipathy toward each other, which when once aroused tends to stir up sedition, subversion, and damage to the life of the commonwealth. . . .

§15   The magistrate should know the nature and attitude of his own people, of neighboring peoples, and of people in general. The nature, condition, and attitude of his own people, or the people subject to him, ought to be perceived, explored, and learned by him in order that he may know in what things and by what means he may lead, motivate, offend, and rule his people, and what sort of laws and manner

§16   of governing are consequently most appropriate. . . . It is necessary that he know the nature, character, and propensities of neighboring peoples because treaties, commercial arrangements, wars, and other transactions often develop with them, or because he has need of their

§17   services in social life. . . . Bad neighbors are inflicted by God upon some realm or other in order to reprimand and correct its vices, or to

§19   constrain it within its duties. . . . It is important that the magistrate understand the nature, character, tendencies, and propensity of people in general, especially what are the common attitudes exercised by subjects everywhere toward the superior who rules them. He will be able to learn this by no better means than by being a subject for a while in a foreign realm. For from this experience he can reflect upon what he liked or disliked under another prince, and how you as the one who

§20   obeys would like or dislike a ruler to act toward you. . . . Then it is advisable that the magistrate accommodate himself for a time to the customs and character of the people that he may learn what things are fitting and appropriate to them, and may propose suitable laws. In this way he will rule for a longer time and with less effort. . . .[47]

---

[47] [Here follows an extended discussion first of thirteen characteristics of people

XXIV SUCH IS THE NATURE and temperament of the people toward   §1
          its magistrate. We turn now to the attitude of the universal
association or the associated body toward the magistrate arising from the
nature of imperium, and from the exercise and administration of it. . . .
This attitude is twofold. One aspect of it is intrinsic, natural, and
constant; and the other is acquired, extrinsic, and changeable. By reason
of the natural and constant attitude, imperium is exposed to misfortune,
hostility, and modification. I say that it is naturally subject to misfortune   §2
because it wavers and is unstable when unexpected events occur, and
because it quickly falls prostrate and totally collapses when any part of it
is taken away. . . .

          Imperium is said to be exposed to hostility because it is by its   §3
nature hateful to subjects for two reasons. These are the habits of the
rulers and the temperaments of the subjects, that is, the faults of both
rulers and subjects. It is rendered hateful by the habits of rulers because   §4
power and imperium, when accompanied by the rulers' lack of self-
restraint, make them more readily and decidedly inclined to sin. For this
reason rulers tend to be unbridled, obstinate, and prideful persons who
consider it no less shameful to be bent than to be broken, as Seneca
says.[48] They are often extravagant and immoderate men, injurers of
others, and tyrants who overthrow law (*jus*) under the guise of upholding law. They love informers, defend mischief-makers, and drive honest
men away. Because they live in fear, they case to converse with others,
and are suspicious of everyone. They become greedy, harsh, rigid,
thoughtless, and negligent in their duties. . . .[49] Imperium is exposed to   §6
hostility also by the habits and temperament—or the faults—of subjects. This is because imperium finds it naturally difficult to provide for
the people, which is a many-headed monster that cannot be satisfied
even with a good magistrate. . . .

---

in general, then of eighteen characteristics of courtiers, and finally of the
distinction between friends and flatterers. This presentation refers to a number
of works, but especially to the following: Scipio Ammirato, *Dissertationes;*
Gregory Richter, *Axiomata politica;* Petrus Gregorius, *De republica;* Francesco
Patrizi, *De regno.*]

[48] *Benefits,* VI, 3.

[49] [Althusius observes that there are three stages in the fortunes of such magistrates. The first is one of security arising from successful ventures. The second is
one of pride arising from security, in which they admire themselves and trust in
their own powers. And in the third they sink into ruin and destruction.]

§8   Imperium is subject to modification in respect either of its quality or quantity. The reason of quality is that when an imperium is very new, established by vote, force, or law, the harmony among its members suffers from mutual dissensions, enmities, and deceptions. The royal scepter must be accommodated to these conditions, and the reins of imperium thereby relaxed or tightened, as Lipsius says. . . .[50]

§14   Imperium is subject to modification by reason of quantity when it is very small and is allied with no others, or when it has dispersed its resources. Its proper potential ought to be known to the magistrate; how much ordinary and extraordinary revenue can be raised, how, when, and from whom; how many troops he has available, and how long he can maintain them; and what allies may be obtained. On the other hand, the more extensive the imperium, the more persons must be admitted to the direction of the commonwealth. Thus the need becomes greater for prudence, order, and public and private justice in ruling the commonwealth that it not fall increasingly into ruin. . . .

§15   The acquired and extrinsic attitude toward imperium is one
§17   either of benevolence or reverence. . . .[51] This benevolence, as defined by Lipsius,[52] is the manifest love and respect of subjects for their magistrate and his position. . . . The magistrate obtains this benevolence from subjects by his own gentleness, kindness, indulgence, and
§18   desire to serve the commonwealth well. Gentleness consists in courteous and humane words and deeds by which he calls forth the duties of subjects with affability and encouragement, but without impairing the dignity of the magistrate. Tempering severity with leniency, he exercises a just, restrained, and quiet imperium over his subjects, who are able to endure neither complete servitude nor complete liberty, and are to be won over to the magistrate not as slaves but as subjects. Thereby a moderate subjection and a moderate liberty may prevail, and hence peace and security.[53] The advantages of this gentleness are great. For a clement prince enjoys more obedient subjects, as we have said. Clemency also confirms his position and influence, and strengthens impe-

---

[50] *Politicorum sive civilis doctrinae,* IV, 6.

[51] See Giovanni Botero, *Practical Politics,* I, 8–11.

[52] *Politicorum sive civilis doctrinae,* IV, 8.

[53] For examples of this humane attitude, *see* Artaxerxes (Nehemiah 2:4–9), David, who called his subjects brothers (I Chronicles 28:2), Augustus, Anthony Pius, and others.

rium. Indeed, he rules without difficulty those whose will to obey has been freely obtained. There is nothing that more impels men to obey than the confirmed equity of an imperium; and there is nothing that makes the magistrate more beloved and pleasing to others than clemency. For numerous punishments are no less scandalous to a prince than many funerals are to a doctor. . . .   §19

Kindness is liberality exercised with judgment. "Nothing," as Cicero says, "is more appropriate to human nature than kindness,"[54] which generates friendship and affection. . . . Kindness is not exercised with judgment when it is extended without distinction toward those who are undeserving and unworthy. Rather it should be extended to associates in war, partners in time of trouble, those who serve the commonwealth extensively and well, or those who are capable of doing so. . . .   §26 §27

Indulgence is the means by which the magistrate, without corrupting morals, makes provision for the alleviation and pleasure of his subjects. He makes provision for their alleviation in the necessities of life so that the multitude is not oppressed by the price of food, and is not in distress because of the want of other things that are indispensable. "A good prince should attend to his subjects and citizens as if they were his own children."[55] He makes provision for their pleasure by games and other honorable public diversions and amusements that, without debauchery or excess, subdue and allay the harsh passions of subjects, and distract them from harmful meddling with imperium. . . .   §31

The desire to serve the commonwealth well is the characteristic by which the magistrate undertakes his imperium and administration for the common utility of the realm and the advantage of its citizens. He conducts his administration on behalf of the associated body, and renders to each his due, with rewards for the good and punishments for the wicked. . . . The magistrate gives evidence of this desire to serve well by a twofold course of action. He gives evidence of it, first, when he shows by his deeds that he is not the proprietor of the goods and rights of the realm and its subjects, but their faithful steward and defender constituted by the general mandate of the associated body, and that as he became magistrate by the grace of the universal association so he continues to be dependent upon it. He gives evidence of this   §32 §33 §34

---

54 [*Duties,* I, 14.]
55 Pliny [Pliny the Younger, *Panegyric on Trajan*].

desire, secondly, when he shows that his government and administration are directed to the glory of God and the welfare and benefit of subjects and citizens. By these two actions, a good, pious, and faithful magistrate is known. He is loved by his subjects because he first loves them. . . .

§1   **XXV**   THIS COMPLETES the discussion of benevolence, the first aspect of the acquired and extrinsic attitude toward imperium. We turn now to the second aspect of an acquired authority, which is reverence. A reverent attitude toward the magistrate derives from imperium and a favorable opinion about the magistrate's exercise of authority. Giovanni Botero, however, distinguishes between reverence and authority.[56] Respect for authority, Lipsius says, is a reverent opinion of the supreme magistrate and his position that has been received and impressed on the minds of subjects and aliens by the magistrate's administration of

§3   the realm. . . . [57] This respect for authority is composed of the admiration and fear that arise from the ruler's form of imperium, his greatness, and his moral qualities. The form of imperium ought to be austere, constant, and well managed if respect for authority is to be obtained. . . .

§15   The greatness of the ruling magistrate, who doubtless has sufficient resources available for conserving what he has and securing others, should be a means for obtaining firm respect for authority that is both straight-

§16   forward and befitting a king.[58] This greatness is conferred by wealth,

§24   arms, counsel, treaties, and the success of his ventures. . . . Through his life and moral qualities, too, the magistrate may acquire respect for his authority, as Lipsius says.[59] This may be accomplished through inward and

---

[56] [Botero's point, which is not explained by Althusius, is that reverence (*reverentia*) resides in the people, but the means of producing reverence, namely authority (*auctoritas*), resides in the magistrate. Henceforth Althusius will follow Botero and speak not of reverence but of authority, by which he will mean, however, not what Botero means by *auctoritas*, but something much closer to *reverentia*, namely, respect for authority. Therefore, in this chapter the word has been translated as "respect for authority," except where Botero's or some other special use would seem to be intended.

Botero's point is made in one of the supplements of *Practical Politics*, that is, in Book I of "The Authority of the Prince." George A. Moore, Botero's translator, entitles this supplement "The Reputation of the Prince."]

[57] [*Politicorum sive civilis doctrinae*, VI, 8.]

[58] Nebuchadnezzar excelled in this greatness. Daniel 5:19 f.

[59] *Politicorum sive civilis doctrinae*, IV, 9.

outward strengths, especially those that are contrary to the weaknesses toward which rulers are most easily impelled because of their ruling power: licence, flatterers, and other irritations. The inward strengths consist of piety, foresight, courage, fidelity, modesty, temperance, self-restraint, and self-confidence. . . . [60]

§25

XXVI So much for doctrine and knowledge of those things that are necessary to the magistrate in the administration of the commonwealth. We have called this doctrine the first part of political understanding. We turn now to the other part, namely, to its practice. This is the experience of things known through one's own attempts and examples. "My mind has discovered and digested many things."[61] . . .

§1

Practice and experience can teach the magistrate about things to be done and to be omitted by which the position of the commonwealth and its security are conserved.[62] He learns that he should not confide too much in a friend or relatives; that he should attempt to meet every evil and problem at the beginning so that evil does not have time to increase and gather strength; that in the greatest extremities and perils he should withdraw for a season, for with time everything changes; that, on the other hand, he should not directly oppose the strength of the multitude, but accommodate his sails to the wind as a skillful sailor does, and permit for a time what he cannot prevent; that he should not neglect small disorders that are likely in time to become greater; that he should not handle at the same time many grave and arduous enterprises that cannot be expedited at the same time; that he should undertake no new enterprises in the first year of his magistracy and imperium, especially unexpected ones; that he should not commit himself to chance and misfortune, but prepare himself for each particular time and

§3

---

[60] [Outward strengths are discussed, oddly enough, as the second part of modesty, and include dignity, urbanity, and facility in speech, and discipline and refinement in body. After discussing these inward and outward strengths that produce respect for authority, Althusius then turns to contempt for authority, which is the result of corrupt forms of the magistrate's imperium, the failure of his ventures, and unfortunate moral qualities.]

[61] Ecclesiastes 1:13.

[62] [The following discussion of the things that practice teaches is an unacknowledged restatement and abridgment of Giovanni Botero, *Practical Politics*, II, 6.]

occasion;[63] that he should prefer the old to the new, peace and tranquillity to war, the certain to the uncertain, the safe to the perilous; that he should apply no force where it is not proper, especially that he should cause no injury to the church; that he should not engage in continuous wars with neighboring countries, nor with subjects, who would thereby become ever more provoked with him and alienated from him; that he should never be militarily unprepared, since an unarmed peace may be precarious and brief; that he should seize the opportunities offered in any enterprise, and not neglect them; and that he should not

§4   trust anyone he has injured. Experience of this kind is required in a magistrate.[64]

§5   WE TURN NOW TO CHOICE, the other member of political prudence. This is the right judgment by which the magistrate discerns and separates the upright, useful, and good from the dishonorable, useless, illicit, and harmful, and aptly accommodates the former to the

§6   business at hand. . . . This choice or judgment should be tempered by a certain distrust and concealment. It should be tempered by distrust so that the magistrate may be slow in giving his confidence and approval, may believe nothing easily, and may be on his guard in

§8   all matters. . . . Concealment pertains to those things we know and learn. It is a reticence practiced in the present place and time by which we hide our feelings and cover our thoughts. And for this reason it is called a distinguished art that eludes the arts of others as if they were not even perceived, as Scipio Ammirato points out with many examples. . . . [65]

§1   **XXVII** HAVING COMPLETED the members of prudence, we turn now to the kinds of prudence. Civil prudence has two kinds. One is

§2   proper to the magistrate, and the other is borrowed or alien. . . . Proper prudence is what a magistrate has himself been furnished with. But it is an exceedingly rare thing, even though it is more necessary than wealth

---

[63] "A wise man sees evil and flees from it." Proverbs 2 [12:26?]

[64] This experience was present in Moses, Joshua, David, Samuel, and Jehoshaphat, and others. For they did not come to the principate until after they had been involved in many adversities.

[65] *Dissertationes,* I, disc. 4.

and greatness. . . . An alien or borrowed prudence is what is sought   *§3*
and obtained from counselors, attendants, and friends. . . .[66]

Counselors are faithful persons skilled in respect to men and   *§6*
affairs who supply helpful advice, and who, just as skillful sailors in
stormy seas, help to guide the ship. However, they are without power,
imperium and jurisdiction. Three things should be considered regarding these counselors: their qualifications, their selection, and their
counsel. The qualification of a good counselor is that he should be a   *§7*
friend to the magistrate and imperium who is wise in the customs and
sentiments of the subjects of the realm, and well acquainted with public
affairs. . . . A good counselor's requisites are prudence, a liberal mind, a   *§9*
sound disposition and fidelity towards the commonwealth, and a capacity for silence. . . .

In the selection of a counselor, the magistrate should not act in   *§27*
haste, but only after a careful investigation of the prospect's habits,
temperament, doctrine, strengths, age, and whatever qualities I have
said to be required in a counselor. He should examine all of these
matters, and hear accusations and denunciations, but treat them with
judgment and discretion. . . . After the worth and ability of the coun-   *§30*
selor have been determined, he is selected with a commendation and a
warning. The commendation is in anticipation of the rewards he ought
to expect if he performs his office well, and the warning in anticipation
of punishment if he discharges it badly. . . .

The third thing we have said ought to be considered in a   *§40*
counselor is the form of the deliberation or consultation, the manner of
consulting. In this activity the subject matter, the inquiry, the weighing   *§41*
of what has been said, and the conclusion belong to the one who
consults. Only the opportunity to speak pertains to the counselor or the
one giving counsel.

The prince or magistrate ought to communicate with his   *§42*
council and counselors in all private and public matters. . . . The most   *§43*
difficult matters, however—those of great moment that concern the
whole realm, or one or more leaders or estates of the realm—he should
handle and communicate not only with his own council and counsel-

---

[66] [The discussion of counselors that follows refers most often to Innocent
Gentillet, *Against Nicholas Machiavell*; Gregory Richter, *Axiomata Politica*; Petrus
Gregorius, *De republica* and *Syntagma juris universi*.]

ors, but also with the counselors of the realm, namely, with the great men and ephors of the whole realm. He should do this in general and universal assemblies and councils of the realm. Such matters are the welfare of subjects, the exercise of divine worship, the abolition of idolatry, the establishment of laws, the making of war or peace, and the collection of extraordinary taxes. . . .

XXVIII

Ecclesiastical Administration

THIS COMPLETES the discussion of political prudence as a rule and norm employed in the administration of the commonwealth and entrusted imperium. We turn now to the types of administration. There are two types: one is universal, and the other particular.[1] The former is public administration, and the latter private. In the former the supreme magistrate is concerned with the whole body of the commonwealth, and in the latter with the members and parts of it.

Universal administration is the process by which the public functions and goods in the entire territory of the realm, commonwealth, and universal association are handled, directed, and diligently managed for the utility and welfare of the total commonwealth.[2] This universal administration is twofold. One aspect of it pertains to public functions, and the other to public things.[3] The administration of the public functions of the realm is either ecclesiastical or secular.[4] John Piscator says that what is just is known from the second table, and ruling in fear of God is understood according to the first.[5] Both are of

§1

§2

§3

---

[1] [Chapters XXVIII–XXXVI, together with the first and larger part of XXXVII, and the latter part of XXXVII respectively.]

[2] "For if anyone does not take responsibility for his own, and especially those of his household, he has denied the faith, and is worse than an infidel." I Timothy 5:8. "Whoever presides, let him preside with care." Romans 12:2.

[3] [Chapters XXVIII–XXXVI and the first part of XXXVII respectively.]

[4] [Chapters XXVIII and XXIX–XXXVI respectively. In this translation, however, Chapter XXXVII will also be presented as a part of "Secular Administration," largely because its discussion of the administration of things, both public and private, is almost entirely civil or secular in nature.]

[5] *Commentarii* (II Samuel 23:3).

concern to the magistrate, as can be demonstrated by examples of pious kings, namely, of David, Solomon, and others who followed them.[6]

§4   Ecclesiastical functions are the means whereby the kingdom of God (*regnum Dei*) is introduced, promoted, cared for, and conserved in the commonwealth or political realm.[7] Ecclesiastical administration is the process by which these ecclesiastical functions are administered

§5   according to what is prescribed in the Word of God. This ecclesiastical administration by the supreme magistrate consists in his inspection, defense, care, and direction of ecclesiastical matters. But the execution and administration of ecclesiastical offices belong to the clergy (*personae ecclesiasticae*). . . . There is therefore a twofold administration of ecclesiastical matters. One part pertains to the magistrate, and the other to the clergy. Each directs and obeys the other, and each helps the other in the distinct administration entrusted to it, according to the example of Moses and Aaron. The administration of the supreme magistrate directs the clergy as long as he enjoins them to perform the parts of their office according to the Word of God, and orders and arranges for other things that are necessary for establishing, conserving, and transmitting to posterity the true worship of God.[8] On the other hand, the supreme magistrate is subject to the administration and power of the clergy with respect to censures, admonitions, and whatever concerns eternal life

§6   and salvation.[9] In the administration of ecclesiastical matters the magistrate does nothing without the counsel and consent of the clergy based on the Word of God.

§7   This administration is imposed upon the magistrate by the mandate of God, as we have said, and is supported by examples of pious men and by arguments from reason. . . . So Moses began his magistracy with this administration, which he later confirmed by a paschal

---

[6] I Chronicles 23 ff.; I Kings 4 ff.; II Chronicles 2:12; 14; 15; 17; 19; 23; 30 f.; 34 f.; II Kings 12; 18; 22.

[7] We have identified the ecclesiastical functions in Chapter VIII above.

[8] We will discuss the magistrate's role more specifically and extensively in this chapter. In his performance of this role the clergy and all others are expected to obey the magistrate. Romans 13.

[9] So teach the examples of David (II Samuel 12; 24), Hezekiah (II Kings 20:19), Asa (II Chronicles 16), Jehoshaphat (II Chronicles 20), Jeroboam (I Kings 13), Jehu (I Kings 16), Ahab (I Kings 21), Ahaziah (II Kings 1), and Manasseh (II Kings 21). *See also* Jeremiah 1:10; Ezekiel 3:2 ff.; and Hebrews 13:17.

lamb.[10] Gideon began his with the erection of an altar.[11] David brought the ark of the covenant to Jerusalem at the beginning of his reign.[12] Joash restored the house of the Lord at the beginning of his administration,[13] as did Hezekiah and Josiah.[14] And every supreme magistrate should admonish his subjects to the worship of God. . . .[15]

The arguments from reason over and beyond the mandate of God and the examples given are weighty and significant. For a sound worship and fear of God in the commonwealth is the cause, origin, and fountain of private and public happiness. On the other hand, the contempt of God, and the neglect of divine worship, are the causes of all evil and misfortune. Moreover, the Christian religion not only subordinates the bodies and goods of pious subjects to the magistrate, but even lays their souls and consciences under obligation to him, and shapes them to obedience. It nourishes peace and concord, disapproves all scandals, and makes men pious and just. For this reason, even though the Christians in the early church suffered the gravest persecutions, they nevertheless did not forsake or oppose their magistrate, but are known to have devoted themselves constantly to peace. That the profession and practice of orthodox religion are the cause of all public and private happiness is evident from the fact that piety holds the promise of benediction that supporters of it will receive in this life and the next. . . . Furthermore, the advantages that derive to the entire commonwealth from these subjects who are worshipers of God—and, on the other hand, the evils and perils into which the commonwealth is precipitated by the ungodly—ought to lead the magistrate to a love and zeal for ecclesiastical administration. Even an evil commonwealth is supported and sustained by the pious. The reason is that because of their presence it suffers less from the just wrath of God, and thus avoids punishments that it deserves. . . .

§8

§9

---

[10] Exodus 12.

[11] Judges 6.

[12] II Samuel 6. *See also* Solomon (I Kings 2 f.; 6 f.; II Chronicles I), and Asa (I Kings 15:12–15).

[13] II Chronicles 24.

[14] II Chronicles 29; II Kings 22.

[15] *See* the following examples: Deuteronomy 32; Joshua 23 f.; I Chronicles 29; I Kings 8; II Chronicles 14; 20; 30; 34; I Samuel 12:14 ff.; Ezra 3:1 ff.; Nehemiah 3; Psalms 22; 122; 132; Leviticus 8; 10:16 f.; Numbers 4:15 ff.

§10   Consequently, the magistrate before anything else, and immediately from the beginning of his administration, should plant and nourish the Christian religion as the foundation of his imperium. If he does this, all the virtues will flourish among his subjects, and he will be prospered in his actions. . . .

§13   This ecclesiastical administration is performed chiefly through two duties. The first is the introduction of orthodox religious doctrine and practice in the realm. The other is the conservation, defense, and

§14   transmission to posterity of this doctrine and practice. The former duty is employed in seeing that God is rightly known and worshiped, and the latter that the true understanding or comprehension of God thrives throughout the realm, and the right worship of God is maintained freely and publicly by each and all in the whole realm, without any fear or peril. By these two duties of the magistrate, the kingdom of God is raised up and preserved among men in this political society.

§15   By a religious covenant (*pactum religiosum*) the magistrate, together with the members of the realm commonly and solemnly consenting in councils of the realm, promise to God the performance of this twofold duty. They agree assiduously to perform this service by which God may be constantly and truly known and worshiped by each and all in the entire realm. And in this agreement they recognize their realm to be under God, and they promise to him fidelity and obedience as subjects and vassals. "For the earth and the fullness thereof are God's."[16] "He is the Lord of lords, and the King of kings."[17] He is the proprietary lord of all creatures, and concedes their administration to him whom he wills. But he does not thereby lose his own authority (*jus*), as we have said concerning the ephors.

          Examples of this religious covenant are readily to be found. "You have made a promise to Jehovah this day that he will be your God, that you will walk in his ways, that you will observe his statutes, his precepts, and his judgments, and will give heed to his voice. Jehovah has made a promise to you this day that you will be a special people to him, as he said to you, provided you observe all his precepts, and that he will lift you up above all peoples that he has made, with praise, renown, and glory, and that you will be a holy people to Jehovah your God, as he has

---

[16] Psalm 24:1.
[17] [I Timothy 6:15.]

spoken."[18] At the present time, as well, kings are bound by agreements to care for the approved religion, and to remove unapproved religion.[19]

$§16$ This religious covenant may be confirmed by the oath of the promisers—the people and supreme magistrate—in which they swear that they will devote themselves to those things that pertain to the conservation of the church and the kingdom of God.[20] The debtors in this $§17$ religious covenant are those who make the promise, or the supreme magistrate of the realm and its ephors together with the entire people. The creditor is God to whom the promise is made. The debtors jointly obligate themselves by indicating that they intend to render to God the things that are his, namely, the cultivation of the true knowledge and pious worship of him in the realm according to the Word of God, not according to the pleasure or mandate of men. . . . The supreme magistrate of the realm $§18$ and the ephors representing the people are the debtors in such a manner that the fulfillment of their promise can be entirely and continuously demanded of both magistrate and ephors as if each were the principal obligant.[21] For God does not will that the church, or the responsibility for acknowledging and worshiping him, be committed to one person alone, but to the entire people represented by its ministers, ephors, and supreme magistrate. These administrators represent the people as if they corporately sustain the church as one person, and yet as if anyone from among them were obligated for the entire responsibility. . . .[22]

$§19$ God makes a promise to the magistrate and people in this religious covenant concerning those who perform these things, as well as a threat to those who neglect or violate this compact (*fedus*). He promises to those who perform them that he will be to them a benevolent God and a merciful protector. He threatens those who disobey and violate this compact that he will be a just and severe exactor of punishments. . . .

---

[18] Deuteronomy 26:17–19.

[19] *See* the imperial German constitutions of 1555 [when Ferdinand I was elected emperor], and Chapter XIX above [which presents the laws and conditions under which Charles V was elected emperor in 1519].

[20] For this reason many kings wished to be priests and pontiffs, as Petrus Gregorius says. *De republica,* VIII, 2, 6–9. Such were Melchizedek (Genesis 14), Samuel (I Samuel 3 ff.) and Eli before Samuel (I Samuel 2).

[21] Code VIII, 39, 3.

[22] Digest XLVI, 1, 22.

God is the vindicator of this covenant when it is violated by the magistrate or by the ephors representing the people. One debtor is held responsible for the fault of the other, and shares his sins if he does not hold the violator of this covenant to his duty, and resist and impede him so far as he is able. "He will cast Israel down because of the sins of Jeroboam."[23] For this reason the ephors are expected to remind a deviating magistrate of his duty, and to resist him. Therefore, if the ephors do not do this, but by remaining silent, defaulting, dissembling, permitting, or submitting they do not obstruct the violation of this covenant by the supreme magistrate, they are deservedly punished by God for this fault and surrender, as many examples indicate. . . .[24]

§23   William Barclay disagrees with the things we have said about this covenant and compact.[25] He asserts that such a compact was employed among the Jews in a time of interregnum and in a democratic state of affairs, and accepts it only in this sense. But he greatly errs in this. For the texts prove most conclusively that such a compact also occurred among prince and people under the monarchy.[26] And they demonstrate that the nature and purpose of this compact is such that it is useful and necessary in any type of commonwealth.

Concerning this compact entered into by the king and people with God, Barclay furthermore adds that he thinks any party whatever can individually uphold it by not allowing itself to be led away from true

[23] I Kings 14:16. See also Junius Brutus, *Defence of Liberty Against Tyrants*, quest. 2.

[24] [Althusius here quotes or refers to the following Biblical material: I Samuel 12:17, 25; 13:14; Ezekiel 7:23 ff.; Deuteronomy 28:45 ff.; 29:12 ff.; II Kings 25:9; 17; II Chronicles 21:14; 24:20, 23; 15; I Kings 11:33; Judges 2:20; I Samuel 15:26; II Samuel 21:1 ff.; 24:2 ff.; Jeremiah 15:4 ff.; 17:20 ff.; I Kings 16:2 ff.; II Chronicles 21:13 f.; 34:23 f.; I Kings 14:16; II Kings 17:34–41; Psalm 82; II Kings 25:9; 17; Isaiah 60:12; Psalm 73:27; 2:10 f.; 94:15, 20; I Kings 12:23 ff.; Ezra 6:12; Joshua 24:11, 20; Judges 6:6. For profane examples he calls attention to Petrus Gregorius, *De republica*, VIII, 2; XIII, 10; Lambert Daneau, *Politices christianae*, III; Junius Brutus, *Defence of Liberty Against Tyrants*, quest. 1 and 2; Melchior Junius, *Politicarum quaestionum*, I, quest. 6. He also notes that "the entire Florentine realm was overthrown because of the violation and rupture of this covenant, and the idolatry and sins of the inhabitants."]

[25] *The Kingdom and the Regal Power*, IV, 6.

[26] I Chronicles 11:3–5; II Samuel 5:3; I Samuel 10:17 ff.; II Chronicles 23:3; II Kings 11:17; 14:21; and other evidences that we have mentioned above.

religion. And this the people can do.[27] He says this compact in itself grants no right and imperium, neither to the people over the king, nor to the king over the people. It merely makes both debtors to God alone. Barclay says something important here, and omits something else.[28] For no one can doubt that such a compact or covenant constitutes a right and obligation both to God and between the promising debtors, namely, between the people and the king. What is at stake in this obligation is not only the public practice of orthodox religion and the honest worship of God, but also the second table of the Decalogue, of the correct and honest administration of justice. This is to say, both tables are involved.[29]

I concede to Barclay that in a case in which two debtors jointly promise to do something, if one fulfills what is promised, the other is released from it. Therefore, when either the king or the people has been afflicted with punishment by God because of their crime and transgression against the agreed compact, the other shall be released from it. But this rule—in which one debtor who fulfills an obligation releases the other debtor—permits an exception in the case in which a debtor fulfills not the entire obligation, but only his own part of it. Here one of the debtors who suffers the penalties of God cannot thereby discharge the entire obligation. . . .   §24

LET US NOW FOLLOW THROUGH with the two duties of ecclesiastical administration that we have mentioned. The first duty, which is the introduction of the doctrine and practice of orthodox religion in the realm, consists of the establishment of a sacred ministry and of schools.   §25

A sacred ministry is the public responsibility entrusted to chosen ministers for teaching the true knowledge of God and for conducting sincere worship of him. It is called by the Apostle Paul the ministry of reconciliation, the preaching of reconciliation, the ambassadorship of Christ, and the administration of the Word.[30]   §26

---

[27] *The Kingdom and the Regal Power*, IV, 8.

[28] Many testimonies exist concerning the compact of the people and king entered into with God: II Kings 11:17; 23:1–4; II Samuel 3:20; II Chronicles 15:12–15; 23:16. A formula for this compact together with a subscribing list of contractors is given in Nehemiah 10.

[29] This is evident from Deuteronomy 17:16 ff.; Joshua 1:8; I Samuel 12:15 ff.; Exodus 19 f.; 28–30.

[30] II Corinthians 5:18–20; Acts 6:4.

§27   In constituting this ministry, the first office of the supreme magistrate is to set forth by public edicts a system of penalties concerning the true acknowledgment and worship of God according to sacred scripture, and to promulgate, at whatever time seems best to him, penal decrees for violators of these edicts throughout the entire realm and the §28 provinces thereof, according to the example of pious kings. Secondly, the magistrate should legally validate orthodox canons of faith, or what are called the solemn confession and formula of true religion. These canons pertain to church doctrine and administration, that is, to the performance of ecclesiastical ceremonies and offices according to the norm of sacred §29 writings. . . . The third responsibility that falls to the magistrate is to constitute regular ecclesiastical jurisdictions, presbyteries, synods, and consistories, and to legislate through them concerning the call, examination, and ordination of bishops and pastors, and their direction, §30 judgment, and removal from office. . . . The fourth function of the magistrate is to provide that the individual ephors and provincial heads of the realm undertake the local responsibility for this ministry in their provinces. In each district of his province, the provincial head should constitute a presbytery by the election and consent of the church, and confirm it by his own authority. This presbytery is a senate drawn from the ministers of the church and from other pious, holy, upright, and prudent men elected by the people to guide the church, to conserve it, §31 and to build it up in Christ.[31] The fifth office of the magistrate is to see that the ministers of the church are legitimately—inwardly and outwardly—called, elected, and confirmed, and that those so called put forth, teach, and explain the doctrine of the law and the gospel. They should do this sincerely, truly, and fully from the Word of God, both in public and in private, in an orderly fashion, and in a manner that can be understood by the common people. In connection with this fifth office, he shall also provide that the ministers rightly administer and dispense the sacraments or tokens of faith; that in their presbytery they offer prayers, good counsel, and admonitions; that they direct its actions by proposing issues to be discussed, by gathering opinions on these issues, and by carrying through with matters of special importance; and that they, together with other presbyters, rightly exercise church discipline, and do anything else that has been assigned to the collegium of presbyters.

---

[31] Concerning the presbytery, see Chapter VIII above.

From these things it is apparent that the supreme magistrate   §32
has a responsibility to judge concerning the knowledge, discernment,
direction, definition, and promulgation of the doctrine of faith, that he
exercises this responsibility on the basis of sacred scripture, and that he
commands bishops in keeping with these scriptures. So Constantine
undertook to judge the Arian controversy. Whence it is evident that
clergymen have been subjected to the power of kings, except in those
matters that are proper to them. These matters are the preaching of the
Word and the administration of the sacraments, in which they are
subject to God and the church. But to the extent that they are citizens
they are subject, together with their families and goods, to the civil
power. . . .[32]

The establishment of schools is the means by which public   §33
schools and laboratories of piety and the liberal arts are set up and made
accessible in all provinces by the authority and command of the supreme magistrate of the realm. For the school is the laboratory of good
and pious citizens, and the seedbed of honorable arts and customs.
Indeed, it is the armory of the church and commonwealth. Arms of
every kind are produced in it not only for defending the true and sincere
worship of God against heretics, but also for defending and conserving
the welfare and soundness of the commonwealth. A school is indeed the
only means by which the pure and uncorrupted knowledge and worship of God is conserved and transmitted to posterity. For study opens
the eyes of the mind, and informs and sharpens the judgment. . . .

On the one hand, private, village, town, ordinary, and com-   §35
mon schools are to be established and made available. And, on the other
hand, so are public academies in which prizes for the learned and for
those fitted for the direction of church and commonwealth are determined and conferred. Each ephor establishes schools of the first kind in
the province entrusted to him. The supreme magistrate institutes
schools of the second kind, namely academies, and confirms them by
his own authority. . . .

THE OTHER DUTY of the supreme magistrate in ecclesiastical adminis-   §37
tration consists of the conservation and defense of the church, of public

---

[32] Romans 13; Matthew 17:27; Acts 26; Novel LXXXIII (pref.); LXXXVI, 1;
CXXIII, 20 f.; Marsilius of Padua, *The Defender of the Peace*, II, 4.

worship, and of schools. . . . This responsibility encompasses two parts. The first is the conservation of the church, of divine worship, and of schools. The other is their defense against enemies, persecutors, and disturbers.

§38   The conservation of religion and divine worship is the process by which the purity of heavenly doctrine and the orthodox consensus are maintained and transmitted to posterity. This is to be attended to by §39   the magistrate by two means. First, he will announce and hold ecclesiastical assemblies and visitations in every province of the realm, and if necessary in the realm itself. They are composed of faithful and pious ministers of the church of the realm. Through these assemblies and visitations the pastors and governors of the church are held to their duty, and any controversies concerning religion and defects in church management are recognized, corrected, and removed. Secondly, he will distribute suitable rewards to pious worshipers of God. . . .

§43   In these assemblies the clergy ought to examine and discern from the Word of God whether doctrine is sound and life corresponds to it, whether divine worship is uncorrupted and the sacraments rightly administered, whether ecclesiastical discipline prospers, whether schools are well constituted, whether church properties are correctly managed, whether false teachers and corrupters are dealt with, whether false doctrines circulate, whether the diaconate to the poor is rightly handled, and whether there is anything in the house of God that the magistrate should make his responsibility. These assemblies shall also provide that useful books on orthodox religion are produced, printed, published, and sold in the realm, and likewise that distinguished and excellent men useful to the church and commonwealth are attracted to the realm or province. The decrees of these assemblies are ordered by the supreme magistrate to be made effective in the entire realm and in the provinces thereof.

§44   Corresponding to these assemblies are visitations of the churches. Some of these visitations are special and domestic. They are conducted by the minister of the local church joined by the senior presbyter in the area. Others are general. These are conducted in church assemblies by an inspector[33] of the church joined by a local political

---

[33] [In Chapter VIII Althusius identified the inspector as one who presided over a diocese, or a bishop.]

official. Some general visitations are conducted in provincial synods by several designated inspectors and some political counselors of the magistrate. In these visitations the examination, inquiry, investigation, and exploration of doctrine and life occur. Doctrine is examined according to the articles of faith and the catechism, and life according to the established precepts of the Decalogue. An inquiry also occurs in these visitations concerning the state of the church and schools, the management of church properties, and the life and doctrine of the ministers of the church and of those for whom the ministers are responsible. The visitation also investigates the maintenance of church ministers and their families and the training of their children, lest the ministers be in want or constrained because of family privation to practice such a way of life that their ecclesiastical vocation is upset, impeded, or disrespected, or lest after their death their wives, children, and families are driven unavoidably to charity and live in humiliation.[34] Furthermore, the magistrate shall provide not only that these ecclesiastical ministers conducting the visitation perform their office well, but also that, if necessary, political ministers help them in it. For this reason, he shall order that ecclesiastical and political ministers extend mutual services to each other, and confer and communicate aid and counsel, as Moses and Aaron did.[35] But the magistrate should not permit political ministers to impede or disrupt ecclesiastical ministers. . . .

    Then the magistrate shall decree and promulgate laws concerning the preaching of sound doctrine; the right administration of the sacraments; the arrangement for adiaphorous matters according to decorum and good order; the announcement and convocation of catechetical

§45

§46

§48

---

[34] Examples of these pious visitations can be seen in I Samuel 7:3; II Kings 2:4, 6; I Kings 15:11; II Chronicles 31:4; 34:3, 8; 19:4–6; Acts 14:21; 15:36, 41; 18:23; and in many other places referred to by Wilhelm Zepper, *De politica ecclesiastica*, III, 11.

[35] Exodus 12:1; Leviticus 9:1; 11:1; 13:1; 15:1; Numbers 2:1; 4:1; 19:1; 20:23; 26:1; II Chronicles 17:7–9. Ecclesiastical ministers were employed by David (II Samuel 7:2; II Chronicles 29:25); Jehoash (II Kings 12:1 f., 10), and Josiah (II Chronicles 34:15, 20). For examples of aid provided and furnished by the magistrate in ecclesiastical affairs, *see* Joshua 5:2; 6:6; 8:30, 35; II Samuel 6:10; I Chronicles 23 ff.; I Kings 5:6–8; II Chronicles 15:8; 17; 24; 34 f.; Exodus 5:1; Numbers 1:17; 14 f.; 27:2; 32:2. See the examples of David (II Samuel 7:2; II Chronicles 29:25), Solomon (II Chronicles 29:15; I Kings 8:1), Jehoash (II Chronicles 34:5, 20), Zerubbabel (Ezra 3:2), and Hezekiah (II Chronicles 29).

classes, schools, and synods; the punishment or dismissal of mischievous or useless ministers of the church; discipline of the church; the calling of pastors; the diaconate to the poor; the management of church properties; and weddings and funerals. And if there are other things necessary for ecclesiastical administration that he decrees by his regulations, he should prescribe each and every one of them according to the sure reason and order of the Word of God. But the political magistrate should be very careful in this activity not to apply his own hands to these matters, but commit and entrust them to the clergy. He should concern himself only that the external actions of men conform to laws. And all men, even clergymen, are to comply obediently with these laws.

§49   The distribution of suitable rewards accomplishes much by engendering a love and zeal for religion in the people. When the pious worshipers of God are held in good repute, esteem, and honor, they are advanced to public offices and responsibilities for which they are equal and fitted. By this means the piety of the other life receives and enjoys the benediction and benefits of this life. . . .

We now turn to the defense and protection of orthodox religion and divine worship, of which there are two headings. The first is the reformation of the church, and the other is the removal and §50   abolition of any impediments. There is no doubt that the correction and reformation of the church from all error, heresy, idolatry, schism, and corruption pertains to the magistrate. . . .[36]

§51   The administrator ought to establish and permit only one §52   religion in his realm, and that the true one. He shall expel all atheists, and all impious and profane men who are obstinate and incurable. There is no doubt, however, that a magistrate can admit impious and profane men in whom there is hope of correction to sound and pure worship, or to those external means by which God wills to bring men to the true religion.[37] But he should by no means permit atheism, epicureanism, libertinism— that is, manifest impiety and profanity—in the realm.

§53   I also consider that a pious magistrate can in good conscience permit Jews to live in his dominion and territory, and to dwell and

---

[36] This is evident from the example of other pious kings. II Chronicles 17; 22; 31; 34; II Kings 18; 22 f.; Exodus 32; Joshua 22. *See* Socrates Scholasticus, *Ecclesiastical History*, V, 10.

[37] *See* the examples of Josiah, Jehoshaphat, and Hezekiah.

engage in business with the faithful.[38] But I do not think that magistrates should permit Jews to have synagogues. However, the theologians Peter Martyr and Jerome Zanchius conclude that even this can be done if the Jews are content to read the Bible and offer prayers in them, and not to blaspheme Christ or the church.[39] Their reason is that Christ and the §54 apostles are known to have gone into synagogues and to have conferred with the Jews. In the civil life of Jews with inhabitants, the most prudent and pious consider that the following precautions ought to be observed: (1) that the faithful not enter into wedlock with Jews, and (2) that they not share in their religion or their rites, cultivate too close friendship with them, or live familiarly with them. The Jews should have separate quarters, as is the case in Frankfurt, and bear insignia or marks by which they are easily recognized by all. . . .

The theologians determine how far it is permitted to have §55 private contact with infidels, atheists, impious men, or persons of different religions by distinguishing between the learned, the faithful, and uneducated, and the weak, and the purposes for which the contacts are to be held.[40]

The same can be said about papists born in the territory of the §56 magistrate or having homes there. The magistrate can in good conscience permit them to live within the boundaries of the realm if the pious do not partake of their superstitions, live familiarly with them, or contract marriages with them. Furthermore, the magistrate ought not to permit them temples for the practice of their idolatrous worship.

Distinctions should be made concerning heretics in a well-constituted imperium. For there are some heresies that tear up the foundation of faith, such as Arianism and the like. But there are others that, although they err in certain articles of faith, do not overthrow the foundation, such as the Novatian and similar heresies. Heretics of the §57 first sort should be severely attended to by the magistrate with exile,

---

[38] I maintain this by the example of the *Jus Civilis* (Code I, 9); Peter Martyr, *Commentarii* (Judges 1:36); Jerome Zanchius, *De redemptione,* I, 19, 5; George Sohn, *Commentarius* (Psalm 59); Lambert Daneau, *Politices christianae,* IV, 2; Socrates Scholasticus, *Ecclesiastical History,* III, 25; V, 2.

[39] [The pertinent references to Martyr and Zanchius are found in the preceding footnote.]

[40] *See* Peter Martyr, *Commentarii* (Judges 1:36). I have also discussed this in my *Civilis Conversationis Libri Duo.*

prison, or the sword. This is in order that they cannot have fellowship or intercourse with the faithful, impart their disease to others, or infect, ruin, or corrupt them. The magistrate should command men by public interdicts to abstain from fellowship with them.

§58

§59

Heretics of the second sort are to be excommunicated if, having been convicted of heresies and admonished by the church, they nevertheless persist in them. But those who uphold some error or doctrine that has not yet been condemned as manifest heresy are not for this reason to be driven from the church, nor the sacred services to be prohibited to them or social intercourse forbidden with them.[41] The magistrate can even order by published edicts that the orthodox are not to ridicule or heap abuse upon those whose error does not reach to the foundations of doctrine, and that instead of publicly judging them the orthodox are rather to cultivate friendship among them until the matter is legitimately discussed and decided in a free synod. . . .

§63

A magistrate in whose realm the true worship of God does not thrive should take care that he not claim imperium over faith and religion of men, which exist only in the soul and conscience. God alone has imperium in this area. To him alone the secrets and intimate recesses of the heart are known. And he administers his kingdom, which is not of this world, through his ministers of the Word. For this reason, faith is said to be a gift of God, not of Caesar. It is not subject to the will, nor can it be coerced. If in religion the soul has once been destroyed, nothing henceforth remains, as Lactantius says. We are not able to command religion because no one is required to believe against his will. Faith must be persuaded, not commanded, and taught, not ordered. Christ said to his disciples who were willing to destroy the Samaritans, "Are you ignorant of whose spirit you are sons?"[42] The emperor Constantine said that to inflict bodily punishments upon men whose minds have been captured is senseless and stupid to the extreme.[43]

§64

Those who err in religion are therefore to be ruled not by external force or by corporal arms, but by the sword of the spirit, that is,

---

[41] *See* the example of the Apostle Paul who did not turn away from the Corinthian church, corrupted as it was by many errors. I Corinthians 15. Nor did Christ reject his disciples even though they were involved in great errors, but he was patient with them and trained them to know better.

[42] Luke 9:55.

[43] Eusebius, *The Life of Constantine*, I, 38.

by the Word and spiritual arms through which God is able to lead them to himself. They are to be entrusted to ministers of the Word of God for care and instruction.[44] If they cannot be persuaded by the Word of God, how much less can they be coerced by the threats or punishments of the magistrate to think or believe what he or some other person believes. Therefore, the magistrate should leave this matter to God, attribute to him the things that are his—who alone impels, leads, and changes hearts—and reserve to himself what God has given him, namely, imperium over bodies. He is forbidden in his administration to impose a penalty over the thoughts of men. Heretics, so far as they are delinquent in external actions, are to be punished just as any other subjects, even the otherwise pious. But if the magistrate invades the imperium of God,   *§65* exceeds the limits of his jurisdiction, and arrogates to himself imperium over the consciences of men, he shall not do this evil with impunity. For because of this action, seditions and tumults, which persecution is want to cause, will arise in his realm. Thus, in the time of the Maccabees long wars and tumults arose because of persecutions. When the Scribes and Pharisees persecuted the doctrine of Christ, disorders were produced that had not existed before. When Paul was teaching at Ephesus, Demetrius stirred up sedition because of the persecution of Paul. Similarly, the Jews who persecuted Paul in the temple stirred up tumults. Today in France, Belgium, Hungary, Poland, and other realms persecution causes disorders, tumults, and seditions. But where there are no persecutions, there everything is peaceful, even though there are different religions. Consequently, we rightly say that the persecution of Christians has always been the cause of the greatest evils.

Whoever therefore wishes to have a peaceful realm should abstain from persecutions. He should not, however, permit the practice of a wicked religion lest what occurred to Solomon may happen to him.[45] But if he cannot prohibit it without hazard to the common-wealth, he is to suffer it to exist in order that he not bring ruin to the commonwealth.[46] So the emperor Constans, son of Constantine the

---

[44] "The arms of our soldiers are not of the flesh, but are made efficacious by heaven for the overthrow of the ramparts." II Corinthians 10:4. "The servant of God ought to be gentle toward all, fitted for teaching, and patient toward evil persons." II Timothy 2:24.

[45] I Kings 11:4 ff.

[46] Jean Bodin, *The Commonweale*, III, 7.

Great, permitted the religion and collegia of the Arians not for their benefit, but for the commonwealth's. And Theodosius tolerated this sect against his will.

Franz Burckhard therefore errs,[47] and the Jesuits with him, who think that the magistrate is not able to tolerate diverse religions. For it is not asked whether two or more religions may be possible, which we deny with them. Nor is it asked whether the magistrate is able to embrace two or more religions, which we deny. Nor is it asked whether the magistrate has the power of deciding against the Word of God about religion, which is denied. But it is asked, when certain cities or estates in a realm embrace different opinions in their creeds—for the defense of which each alleges the Word of God—whether the magistrate who embraces the opinion of one party may persecute the remaining dissenters by force of arms and the sword. We may say in this case that the magistrate who is not able, without peril to the commonwealth, to change or overcome the discrepancy in religion and creed ought to tolerate the dissenters for the sake of public peace and tranquillity, blinking his eyes and permitting them to exercise unapproved religion, lest the entire realm, and with it the household of the church, be overthrown. He shall therefore tolerate the practice of diverse religions as a skilled navigator bears with diverse and conflicting winds and clashing waves. Just as amidst these winds and waves the navigator brings his ship safely into the harbor, so the magistrate directs the commonwealth in a manner that keeps it free from ruin for the welfare of the church.

§66

§67   The second heading under the defense and protection of the church is the removal and abolition of all obstacles and impediments by which the welfare, development, and advancement of churches and

§68   schools are hindered. . . . The magistrate shall therefore publish interdicts that prohibit the importation or sale of heretical books in the

§69   province. He shall not permit heretics or atheists to be admitted to office in the church or schools, nor shall he tolerate conventicles and

§72   collegia for wicked religion to be secretly held. . . . The magistrate shall take care that in all matters in which he is able he does not fail to furnish whatever may be necessary for the true acknowledgment and reverence of God. . . .

---

[47] [*De autonomia.*]

XXIX–XXXVII

Secular Administration

XXIX W E HAVE COMPLETED our discussion of the ecclesi-   §1
astical administration of the magistrate, and turn
now to secular or civil administration. Secular administration is the
process by which the magistrate rightly and faithfully attends to the civil
functions of the second table of the Decalogue. These pertain to the
establishment and conservation of good order, proper discipline, and
self-sufficiency in the commonwealth, and to the extension of the
advantages and aids of this life and the avoidance of disadvantages. . . .

In this administration of justice the magistrate should always   §2
and regularly observe that moderation is exercised, and that the right of
each member of the commonwealth is conserved, neither diminished
nor increased to the detriment of another. The imperium of the king
ought not to be so enlarged that the liberty of the people is suppressed.
Nor should the orders and estates be so amplified that they treat the king
with contempt and violate the populace. Nor should popular license be
permitted to the extent that it reduces respect for the king or upsets the
affairs of the commonwealth.

The responsibility of the magistrate in this civil administration   §3
of the functions of the realm is twofold. It pertains, first, to the general
right (*jus generale*), and concerns the management of the necessary
means for conserving justice, peace, tranquillity, and discipline in the
commonwealth. It pertains, secondly, to the special right (*jus speciale*),
and concerns the management of the means necessary for procuring
advantages for the social life.[1] General right, in turn, involves (1) the

---

[1] [General right is discussed in Chapters XXIX–XXXI and special right in
Chapters XXXII–XXXVI. The latter refers to provisions for commerce, a

enactment and execution of useful laws, and the administration of justice, or νομοθεσία and δικαιοδοσία,[2] and (2) the endeavor to preserve concord. . . .[3]

§4   The enactment of law is the process by which the magistrate, with the consent of the optimates and estates of his imperium and realm, legislates what is fair, useful, and necessary to the commonwealth.[4] The magistrate shall especially see that the customs, temperament, and ancient rights of the nation are respected, and that new laws are accommodated to them. Moderation is thus to be exercised in writing new laws and edicts, and the wishes of those who must maintain these laws—that is, of the optimates and counselors of the realm—are to be ascertained. In the time of the monarchy, the Roman emperors enacted laws with the counsel of the senate, and in the time of the democracy laws were enacted through the classes and centurial divisions, a proposed law having been made public for seventeen days. So today general laws are produced in councils. It would be a sign of indiscretion and foolish arrogance for one man or a few to presume so much upon themselves that they considered themselves to be able to produce laws sufficiently suitable to a nation without its consent and the united judgments and counsels of many persons.[5]

§5   The magistrate should enact law that is equitable and useful. Equity makes law efficacious, august, and inviolable. Utility calls forth and retains an appreciation and respect for law. . . .

§9   The magistrate shall interpret the fundamental laws of the realm in keeping with the counsel of the ephors, and shall not abolish, annul, or reject something in them except with the expressed judgment, will, and command of the ephors. Much less shall he change, overthrow, or abolish laws concerning the legitimate worship of God once it has been intro-

---

monetary system, an official language, special duties and privileges, public security, councils of the realm, and military matters.]

[2] [the making of law and the administration of justice.]

[3] [Chapters XXIX–XXX and XXXI respectively.]

[4] In Psalm 108:9 Judah is called a legislator because of the power entrusted to it of making and administering laws for the realm. [The Tremellius–Junius translation of the Old Testament from the Hebrew into Latin (Frankfurt on the Main, 1579) renders the last line of Psalm 108:9 (108:8 in the R.S.V.) as "Judah is my legislator."]

[5] *See* Innocent Gentillet, *Against Nicholas Machiavell,* III, theor. 22; Junius Brutus, *Defence of Liberty Against Tyrants,* quest. 1 and 3.

duced into the realm. Rather shall he strengthen true religion and its practice, not according to the mandates of men, but the Word of God. Finally, he shall uphold and defend the fundamental laws of the realm by force and arms, if necessary, even if he shall thereby be pitted with one part of the realm against another, albeit a majority. . . .

Law should be accurately and precisely executed. For law *§14* without execution is like a bell without a clapper. It would be as if the magistrate were mute or dead. And commonwealths thrive only so long as good laws, which are the soul of a commonwealth, are respected in them. The magistrate has been constituted for the sake of executing law, and in this sense he is a living law. . . .

There are two species of the execution of law: the administra- *§15* tion of justice, and censorship.[6] The administration of justice consists in rendering to each his due according to corrective or distributive justice. Corrective justice presupposes equality or arithmetic proportion. Distributive justice, on the other hand, observes geometric proportion in its assignment of punishments and rewards. . . .[7] The magistrate shall *§18* apply punishments to evildoers who offend against the first or second table of the Decalogue in order that others who witness them may become apprehensive and be deterred from evildoing by the fear of punishment. Thus the desire and courage to sin are lessened in others. . . . He shall distribute rewards to the upright who properly deserve *§19* them in order that the love and desire for virtue may be stimulated, nourished, and retained among others. When honors and rewards are granted to the unworthy, renown is not esteemed and dies, and there is no stimulus to virtue. But reward is the food, nourishment, and incentive of virtue. The desire to do good and to receive renown is implanted by nature in man, for the sake of which he will attempt the most demanding things. And rivalry in virtue is nourished by the example of honor to another, so that rewards accomplish much more than punishments. . . .

The administration of justice is twofold. One part of it takes *§29* place between the magistrate and the subjects. The other occurs between one subject and another. The first part holds that the people

---

[6] [Althusius devotes the rest of Chapter XXIX to the administration of justice, and the whole of Chapter XXX to censorship.]

[7] [Aristotle, *Ethics,* 1130b30–1132b20.]

should give to the magistrate what they owe him, and on the other hand, that the magistrate should render to the people what he owes them. The subjects owe everything to the magistrate that is necessary for the administration of justice, for the defense of the subjects against violence and injury, for the removal of perils and disadvantages to the fatherland, and for the promotion of its benefits. The second part contains those things that pertain to the guardianship of subjects. By removing abuse, circumventing deceit, and punishing evildoers, con-

§30   flicts are resolved. The magistrate himself ought to judge conflicts and controversies between his subjects, and to appoint other pious and honest men as judges. As far as he is able, he should become acquainted in his own person with these conflicts, and judge them according to the

§39   properly acknowledged processes of law. . . . Other judges should be appointed by the supreme magistrate for less important cases in the administration of justice, and should be given the power and jurisdiction necessary for the fulfillment of their responsibilities. . . .

§49   It is useful to make court proceedings public because greater respect is thereby produced for their decisions, and those persons who are in similar situations become apprehensive when instructed by such examples and learn from them not to stir up controversy. Judges also are afraid to render corrupt decisions as long as they know public censure

§56   may be brought to bear. . . . The power of appealing freely to the superior magistrate from these intermediary and inferior judges ought to be granted persons who consider themselves to have been unfairly

§57   treated in a judgment against their right. The supreme magistrate should therefore establish a supreme tribunal and consistory for appellate cases. Cases that are said to be wrongly decided are accepted, examined, and ruled upon in this appellate tribunal by a number of judges from the various estates and orders of the realm. From this tribunal there is no power of appeal. This superior tribunal is said to belong not so much to the supreme magistrate as to the entire realm. For in it the king and ephors, or estates and orders of the entire realm, deliver judgments in the name of the realm, or learned and pious men judge in their name. . . .

§1   **XXX** CENSORSHIP IS THE INQUISITION into and chastisement of those morals and luxuries that are not prevented or punished by laws, but which corrupt the souls of subjects or squander their goods

unproductively.[8] Therefore, censorship corrects the things that are not §2
yet worthy of legal punishment, but when neglected or treated with
disdain furnish the cause of many and great evils. . . .

Among us today the censorship and inquisition of morals is §4
customarily entrusted to the sacred collegium, or the presbytery. Whoever does not obey it is forbidden by it to attend sacred services, so that
he becomes ashamed by this disgrace and exclusion.[9] If he is contemptuous of this exclusion and excommunication, he is accused of the
contemptuous offense by an officer of the court before the magistrate,
by whom he is deservedly punished.[10] Among the Jews it would seem
that the right of censorship, even over kings, was entrusted to the
prophets, as becomes apparent from the example of Samuel,[11] as well as
of Isaiah, Jeremiah, and others. . . .[12] The Romans are also observed to
have had censors of their morals. The Spartans had their ephors as
censors of kings. And to these ephors, optimates, and leaders of the
orders of the realm was given the right and power of censorship over the
supreme magistrate himself.

The form and practice of censorship consist of inquisition and
stigmatization. Inquisition occurs with respect to vices that do not §5
come into the courts because of the lack of an accuser or denouncer,
and yet offend the eyes of good and pious citizens. For the sake of
example, these vices receive a most serious rebuke and notation, even
though recourse is not had to legal punishment. Such vices are bad
morals and luxuries. I understand bad morals to include depraved §6
actions, lewdness, wantonness, drunkenness, brawls, errors, schisms,
heresies, perjury, and anything else that probity and modesty condemn

---

[8][Althusius draws heavily from the Bible in this discussion of censorship, and
then most often these contemporary writings: Jean Bodin, *The Commonweale*;
Petrus Gregorius, *De Republica*; Justus Lipsius, *Politicorum sive civilis doctrinae*;
Philip Camerarius, *Meditationes historicae*; Wilhelm Zepper, *De politica ecclesiastica;* and Benedict Aretius, *Problemata theologica*.]

[9] I Corinthians 5.

[10] Matthew 18.

[11] I Samuel 12–14.

[12] Jeremiah 1:10; 20; I Kings 17:1; II Kings 3:13. With a sharp censure Jeroboam
was rebuked by a prophet (I Kings 13), Asa by Hanani (II Chronicles 16), and
David by Nathan (II Samuel 12). So Jeremiah reprimanded the people and the
king (Jeremiah 17:20), Elijah rebuked Ahab (I Kings 18), and John the Baptist
rebuked Herod (Matthew 14), and Elisha rebuked the king of Israel (II Kings 3).

in every age and sex by which subjects are pauperized by the misuse of
§15   their goods or depraved and corrupted by vices. . . . Luxury, on the
authority of Lipsius, appears in respect to four things, namely, money,
housing, food, and clothes. . . .

§24   The stigmatization of censorship is the public declaration of
shame and disgrace, possibly with some kind of fine, administered by
the censor because of a less than decent life. . . .

§28   Chastisement and reproach by our censors, that is, by the
presbyters, consist in suspension from the use of the sacraments, and
prohibition and excommunication from the fellowship of the pious.
. . . These are the steps to be observed by censors; first admonition,
then corrective action or fines, and lastly, if these are disregarded,
excommunication. Such ecclesiastical discipline is rightly called the
teacher of virtue, the custodian of faith, the walls and bulwark of piety,
and the bond and sinew of the church. . . .

§29   Where there is no such censorship, the life of the prince, if it is
moral and pious, can be put forth and established in its place. For Pliny
rightly said that the life of the prince is the censure of citizens, which
when constant directs and transforms us.[13]

It is also important that not everything be corrected at once,
but gradually. For as Cicero says, none of us can be changed quickly.
Nor can one's life be altered or his character transformed suddenly.
Some evils the prince can remove more easily if he is patient with them.
Shame changes some men for the better, necessity others, and satiation
still others. For the souls of some men journey into evil, but do not
remain there. . . .[14]

§1   **XXXI** SO MUCH FOR THE ADMINISTRATION OF JUSTICE and for
censorship. We turn now to the endeavor to conserve concord
and tranquillity in public life. Concord and tranquillity consist in
consensus, peace, and good will among subjects and between subjects
and their magistrate, without mutual deceits or hatreds, for the purpose
§2   of preserving the public entity.[15] They are absolutely necessary in a

---

[13] [Pliny the Younger], *Panegyric on Trajan*.

[14] As Lipsius teaches from Seneca and others. *See also* Petrus Gregorius, *De republica*, IV, 12; Lambert Daneau, *Politices christianae*, VI, 4.

[15] *See* Novel IV; Digest I, 18, 13.

commonwealth. For nothing is better for a commonwealth than unity, and nothing worse than divisiveness. Therefore, concord is rightly called the unconquerable bulwark of the commonwealth. . . .

The care of this concord is entrusted to the magistrate. He §3 should conserve it by removing all causes of factions and seditions, and by entering into alliances with neighboring countries. For a city or commonwealth is like the physical body. Civil disturbances are its sicknesses, and the king or magistrate is its doctor. His first responsibility is to preserve it in good health, and his second is to restore it to good health if it has been weakened by illnesses. Consequently, the magistrate is called the custodian of the common society.

In every conflict between persons, in every faction and sedi- §4 tion, there are always two different parties. One defends the laws and rights of the commonwealth against those who act unjustly. The other §5 resorts to force without adequate reason. When a faction or sedition is confirmed by an oath, it is called a conjuration; when organized around a covenant, it is called a conspiracy.

A faction is a conspiracy or union of a few or of many in §6 dissension with other citizens. If the people divides into more than two §7 factions—into three, four, or five factions—friendship alliances will combine them into two; or else one united with another will subdue and overcome the others. Factions have their origin in the private and §8 public hatreds of different families, or in ambition, arguments, discord, animosities, jealousies, and sinister suspicions. In former times such factions existed between the Guelphs and the Ghibellines, the Samaritans and the Jews, and the Israelites and the Judeans. . . .

The magistrate overcomes factions when he destroys the seeds §10 that cause them—hatred, ambition, arguments, jealousies, strife—and reconciles the parties. He does this when he takes precautions that one party does not act abusively toward another, nor provoke it with words; when he does not permit intermediate magistrates and rulers to nourish hatreds and factions among themselves; when he anticipates and heads off by just means the envy that arises from virtue and renown; and when he defends good men from the calumny and injury of the envious. For a small spark when neglected has often started a great fire. Secondly, he should abolish the names and insignia of factions. Thirdly, he should not permit secret deliberations and meetings. . . .

§11   Sedition is the dissention of a united group against the magistrate, or the sudden and violent uprising against the magistrate. . . .

§13   There are various causes of sedition. The first is excessive and unusual
taxation by which the magistrate impoverishes his subjects, especially

§15   when imposed for unnecessary expenses. . . . The second cause of
sedition is the fear of those who have done harm and are afraid of

§16   punishment. . . . The third cause is excessive indulgence and laxity, or
the distress and indigence of the poor, as well as excessive riches. Great
riches produce luxury, sloth, a desire for political changes, and disorders. Poverty causes the same desire for political changes, a large
number of crimes, and many disgraceful things. . . .[16]

§25   The remedies by which sedition may be overcome are either

§26   general or special. Petrus Gregorius sets forth three general remedies. [17]
First is precaution, prevention, and foresight that seditions do not occur.
The second is appropriate corrective measures when they do arise. The
third is penalties and exemplary punishment of seditious persons. . . .

§70   There are two special remedies for overcoming sedition. The first is
negotiation and compromise, and the second is civil war. . . .

§75   The removal of factions and seditions is the first means of
conserving concord. The other, as I have said, is alliances. An alliance
with neighboring countries is entered into for the sake of peace,
tranquillity, and concord, or of aid against enemies. . . .

§1   **XXXII** THIS CONCLUDES THE DISCUSSION of the secular administration of the general right, that is, of the office of the
magistrate in administering the means for conserving justice, peace,
concord, and discipline among the subjects and inhabitants. We turn
now to the administration of the special right, that is, to the administration of the means for procuring advantages to the social life, or for
avoiding disadvantages to it. The administration of these special rights
involves the care and direction of (1) commercial activity, (2) money, (3)

---

[16] [Althusius presents seven more causes of sedition: unfairness in the administration of justice, ambition for office, conflict of religion, the admission of
foreigners with different customs to the social life, factions among the people,
idleness that comes from excessive abundance, and certain persons who would
overthrow imperium in the name of liberty.]

[17] *De republica*, XXXIII, 9. [The extensive discussion of these general reasons is
drawn largely from Gregorius, and is omitted in this translation except for the
initial listing of them.]

language, (4) duties and privileges, (5) public security, (6) councils of the realm, and (7) arms and war. . . .[18]

XXXIII   A UNIVERSAL COUNCIL is a meeting of each and all members   §1
       and estates of the realm called for the purpose of deliberating and making decisions about the condition and welfare of the common universal association, of averting troubles to it, and of attending to and improving its advantages. This council is called a universal meeting, a senate of the imperium or realm, an assembly of the realm, an epitome of the realm, *ein Reichstag, ein gemeine Reichsversamlung.*

The requisites of a legitimate council are (1) a purpose or   §2
matter to be acted upon in the council, (2) personnel, (3) a time and place, and (4) an order and form for holding the council. The purposes   §3
for which an assembly is held are those that concern the entire realm or associated body, one or more estates, or the subjects of the realm. Some of these purposes are grave and difficult. They relate to religion and divine worship, war, establishing peace and public tranquillity, taxes and collections, money, the ordering of political and ecclesiastical affairs, commerce, safe conduct and transit privileges, the supreme court of the realm, tyranny, public goods, and other rights of the realm. Some purposes are principally private in nature, such as the right of discussion, the possession of a castle, public violence, disagreements between estates, privileges, and the like.

The persons who hold an assembly and come together in   §4
council are twofold, namely, the supreme administrator or magistrate of the realm, and all the representatives of the realm. The supreme magis-   §5
trate presides over universal councils. Whence he has the right of directing and governing the whole proceeding: the right of calling a universal and ecumenical assembly, the right of proposing the things that are to be transacted, the right of gathering the members' opinions, the right of promulgating those things that have been decided by the assembly, and the right of adjourning it. The supreme magistrate, either

---

[18] [The first five are discussed in Chapter XXXII, the sixth in Chapter XXXIII, and the seventh in Chapters XXXIV–XXXVI. All seven have already been set forth in Chapters X–XVII on "Secular Communication." The present discussion of the last two contains new material that is of some importance in understanding the structure of Althusius' political thought, and is therefore partly included in this translation.]

in his own person or through others, carries out all those things in which the direction of the council consists.

§6   The right of calling an assembly and convoking the estates and orders is carried out by letters of announcement and summons sent to
§7   the individual estates of the realm. In these letters are contained the purpose of the assembly, and the time and place of it. Thereby those who are called can study the purpose and come instructed and informed, as well as know when and where they are to come.

§8   The proposition is the public declaration delivered vocally in the presence of all the orders that defines the purpose for which the
§9   assembly has been called together. The rogation is the collecting of the
§10   judgments of the deliberating and consulting estates. The promulgation of the things decided in the assembly is the reading aloud in the presence of all the orders of decisions confirmed by signed and sealed documents, and then their publication throughout the entire realm.

§11   The representatives of the realm called to the assembly are partly consultants, deliberants, and judges, partly petitioners, complainers, and defenders of their own interests in the matter at hand. The persons who consult and render opinions are all the members of the realm, or the estates and orders organized in their various collegia, or legates who have a mandate from these estates to perform this function.
§12   It is best that the collegia of the orders be of an uneven number in order that disagreement can be resolved between differing opinions of the orders by a majority vote, and that something definite can thereby be established. Or if the number is even, it is necessary that the supreme magistrate be granted a vote. By this means controversy is overcome and
§13   a definite decision is made. It is advisable that there be both ecclesiastical and secular persons in each collegium of the orders or estates, that each collegium have its own chamber, and that all the collegia combined
§14   have one common chamber. Those persons who have been called to the council and do not come lose their vote for this occasion. Those who are present reach their conclusions in their individual collegia either by unanimous consensus or by a majority of those voting.

§15   All the members of the realm are also expected to be petitioners and to make complaints. For it is permitted to all to complain freely in that estate in which they abide. And anyone who wishes to denounce things that need correction in the commonwealth is to be patiently heard. Thus the superior is informed about the state of the commonwealth and realm by such denunciations, and can discuss with the assembled orders the means by which the wants of the commonwealth can be relieved, its perils and disadvantages averted and removed, its advantages increased, and common support and aid made available. Those who defend their own interests are to be heard so that an injustice may not be committed against innocent persons.   §16

The place of the assembly is determined at the discretion of   §17
the person who calls it. Those who are called should be able to come to it conveniently and safely, and to find adequate lodging there. Or else it should be held where a remedy can best be found for some troubled part or estate of the commonwealth. Whence the place is to be decided according to discretion and the usual practice. The time of holding the assembly is also discretionary and according to custom.

The general order and form of holding this assembly is that,   §18
after prayers have been said, an address is made concerning the matter to be decided, or else both sides of the issue are set forth, argued, and considered. The voting is first within the orders meeting separately in their collegia, and then in a combined public session of the collegia. Opinions are asked for, listened to, compared, pondered, and examined. When all or a majority agree, a common judgment is established by which even a minority with another opinion is bound. . . . The opin-   §20
ion of the combined orders and estates prevails over the opinion of the presiding officer or the supreme magistrate. For greater is the authority and power in the many than in the one who has been constituted by the many and is less than they are. Many are also better able than one to see, understand, and judge. One is more likely than many to err and to be deceived, or to be carried away by feelings to make decisions that are not suitable. What is sought by many is more easily achieved, and what is decided by the authority of many is carried out and defended with greater concord, respect, and fidelity. Then too, if the opinion of the supreme magistrate, when contrary to the opinion of the orders and estates individually and collectively, were alone to be promulgated as the opinion of the universal council, then this council would be made useless. . . .

From all these things it is apparent that the use of assemblies   §29
was introduced because of the most just and necessary reasons. For the welfare of the people and the excellence of counsel depend upon a large number of prudent men, as Solomon says. Then it is an aspect of liberty   §30

that an enterprise should be administered with the counsel and authority of those who bear the danger of it, and supply the capabilities, support, goods, and spirit for it. Furthermore, the voices of individuals are less heeded than those of an entire province. Indeed, the voice of the realm is heeded most clearly, and its request is sufficiently powerful that the prince, even if he wishes, cannot fail to listen to it. Also, there are some public matters that cannot reasonably be handled by individuals. Rather they can best be investigated, deliberated, and settled by the whole to whom the matters at hand are better known than they would be to one or certain few. Moreover, the prince or the supreme magistrate retains the favor of his subjects by the use of assemblies because the subjects thereby see themselves as not excluded from the care and administration of the commonwealth, and they do not suspect evil counsel to be the cause when an activity perchance does not go well. But if none of the subjects is admitted to the counsels of the prince in difficult matters, the subjects would consider themselves to be despised, and would develop a hatred against the prince. Finally, those who have great influence with the king and hold major positions in the realm are held to their responsibilities by the fear of a council in which the demands of cities and others are heard. Whence the spirit of liberty is retained through this right of holding assemblies, and a remedy is thereby found for the machinations of the mighty, the flatterers, the unjust, and the greedy. Francis Hotman presents many examples of this. . . .[19]

§1   **XXXIV** THE CARE OF ARMS is the process by which the supreme magistrate keeps his forces always prepared and ready so that if an unexpected emergency should arise, or a hostile force should suddenly attack, he can defend the commonwealth and realm from harm and destruction.

§2   The care and handling of arms is twofold. One function of it is exercised in time of peace, and the other in time of war.[20] The care and handling of arms in time of peace is the program by which the citizens

[19] *De antiquo jure regni Gallici,* I, 14. [The remainder of Chapter XXXIII is devoted to long discussions of universal councils in ancient Israel, Greece, and Rome, and in contemporary Germany, France, England, Belgium and the Netherlands, Poland, and the free city of Venice.]

[20] [Chapters XXXIV and XXXV–XXXVI respectively.]

are trained in the arts of war at a time when there is no war, or by which the science of waging war is demonstrated to subjects and they are given practice in military exercises. . . .

XXXV WE TURN NOW to the care and handling of arms in time of §1 war. War is a hostile action legitimately undertaken and administered by the magistrate for the sake of preserving or seeking peace, and for deterring injury or defending the commonwealth against its enemies by force and arms. . . .[21] War is therefore a general §2 state of strife, and a proceeding in which two conflicting peoples who submit to no common magistrate settle their controversy by force and arms.[22]

The conduct of war contains two parts, namely, the undertak- §3 ing and the waging of war.[23] The undertaking of war is the process by §4 which the just principles and foundations of war are laid out and examined. Such are the just cause of war and the necessary preparation for war. A just cause of war is considered to be one that depends upon §5 both right and the authority of the supreme magistrate. The causes of war that rely upon right are (1) defense of liberty and of one's rights, and repulsion of a launched attack, (2) defense of the pure religion, (3) recovery of properties unjustly seized, (4) denial of justice, and (5) conspiracy with an enemy, and rebellion. . . .[24] But these causes can easily be reduced to two, the first of which is defense and the other vindication. The former repulses and the latter vindicates injury launched against God, the commonwealth, its subjects, or the church. I under- §6 stand defense to be either of your own nation or of another. . . . Vindication is a legitimate cause for war when a judgment and recovery of what has been seized has not yet taken place. . . .

---

[21] So George Obrecht defines it. [*De bello.*]

[22] So Lambert Daneau says. [*Politices christianae.*]

[23] [Chapters XXXV and XXXVI respectively.]

[24] *See* what I have said in Chapter XI [XVI in the 1614 edition, XIII in the 1603 edition]. Also *see* the following writers: Lambert Daneau, *Politices christianae,* VI, 3; Justus Lipsius, *Politicorum sive civilis doctrinae,* V, 4; Diego Covarruvias, *Regulae peccatum,* II, sect. 10; Henry Bocer, *De jure belli,* I, 5; Petrus Gregorius, *De republica,* XI, 1 and 2; Elias Reusner, *Stratagematographia,* I, 10; Peter Martyr Vermigli, *The Common Places,* IV, 16–18 and *Commentarii* (Judges 11). For examples of just wars *see* Genesis 14; I Kings 30; I Chronicles 10; Nehemiah 4; I Samuel 11; and throughout the books of Kings and Chronicles.

§7   The authority of the supreme magistrate in undertaking war, and the agreement of the orders of the realm, are so necessary for the waging of war that without them a war is said to be unjustly and §8   unlawfully undertaken. This authority to undertake war ought not to be employed by the magistrate unless all other remedies have failed, and there is no other way to repel an attack upon his subjects, to avoid and vindicate injustice to them, or to obtain peace and tranquillity in the realm. . . .

§9   There are two cases in which even an inferior magistrate without consulting his superior can undertake war. The first is when he is assaulted unjustly by another force and defends himself and his subjects against violent invasion. The second is when the superior magistrate does not do his duty, or exercises tyranny over his subjects.[25]

§10   But before undertaking war a magistrate should first check his own judgment and reasoning, and offer prayers to God to arouse and direct the spirit and mind of his subjects and himself to the well-being, utility, and necessity of the church and community, and to avoid all rashness and injustice. . . .

§17   The necessary preparation for war is the procurement of all that is required for the prosecution of war, together with a declaration of §18   war. Things and persons are required for prosecution of the war. Necessary things for war are money, arms, supplies, and the removal of §27   goods by which the enemy can be benefited. . . . The persons necessary for war are officers and soldiers. . . .

§1   **XXXVI** THE WAGING OF WAR is the execution by military actions of that which has been legitimately undertaken. It can be called §2   the conduct or administration of war. Military or warlike actions are those that are used to break the forces and strength of the enemy and to attain victory. These are the establishment of military discipline, and the inflicting of wartime losses upon the enemy and the avoidance of the §3   same to oneself. Military discipline is the training of the soldier to a hardy and brave life, as established by the leader of the war. . . . The §26   other action of war is the inflicting of losses by soldiers. These losses result from the pillaging of enemy lands, the siege of places and towns belonging to the enemy, combat, fire and demolition of villages and

---

[25] *See* Chapters XVIII and XXXVIII.

fortified places, deaths, captivities, and other similar war-inflicted disasters, miseries, and injuries. . . .

XXXVII THIS COMPLETES OUR DISCUSSION of the civil administra-   §1
tion of the public functions of the realm. We turn now to
the civil administration of public and private things of the realm. The
civil administration of public things—of which the ownership and
usufruct belong to the people—is the process by which the supreme
magistrate, serving as curator, guardian, and father, prudently employs and distributes these things in the service of the commonwealth
according as the need and utility of the realm require. He receives   §2
these things from the people, which remains their owner. Only the
management of them has been granted to him by the general mandate
of the people or realm. . . .

The necessity of disbursing public things of the realm or   §10
associated body is twofold. One is the maintenance of the magistrate.
The other is the administration of public functions requiring outlays
and expenses. Maintenance of the magistrate suitable to his person,   §11
office, dignity, and splendor requires expenses for food, fine and distinguished clothes, and for employment of servants and attendants. . . .
The administration of things of the realm is the other reason for making   §23
outlays. For expenses are required in the administration of the functions
of the realm and in paying salaries and stipends for food, housing, and
clothing of ministers, overseers, officers, princes, and others who are
necessary to maintain the government of the commonwealth. . . .

Although the rule is that the magistrate cannot alienate the   §47
goods of the realm by any manner or means, or dispose of them in his
will, nevertheless when public necessity and utility require he should be
able to alienate them for any of three principal reasons. The first occurs   §48
when he has children. For then he can make one of them his heir, and
give the remaining children other goods for their possession, but
without the latter holding the right of royal power or the right of
succession. . . . The second reason for the alienation of things is war or   §49
ransom for himself, or other causes such as dowries in the event of
matrimony. The third reason is the necessary defense of the common-   §50
wealth for which only the sale of property will avail. . . . For no other   §51
reasons, however, can the magistrate alienate the goods of the commonwealth, especially the cities, towns, and other places of the realm, which

he can least of all remove from his imperium and jurisdiction. Nor can he grant to any of them privileges freeing them from obedience. . . .

§98   Next is the care of the goods of private men that is entrusted to the magistrate with respect to their protection and defense against

§99   violence and injury. Private goods are of three sorts. The first are life and physical safety. The second are honor and reputation. And the third are outward goods. . . .

XXXVIII
Tyranny and Its Remedies

T HE NATURE OF JUST AND UPRIGHT administration
should be sufficiently clear from the things that we
have said. We will now throw light on the opposite of these things,
which is tyranny, and will add to this the remedies of tyranny by which
the commonwealth is liberated and preserved from so much evil.[1]
Tyranny is the contrary of just and upright administration. By it the
foundations and bonds of universal association are obstinately, persis-
tently, and insanely destroyed and overthrown by the supreme magistrate against his pledged word and declared oath. . . . A tyrant is
therefore one who, violating both word and oath, begins to shake the
foundations and unloosen the bonds of the associated body of the
commonwealth. A tyrant may be either a monarch or a polyarch that
through avarice, pride, or perfidy cruelly overthrows and destroys the
most important goods of the commonwealth, such as its peace, virtue,
order, law, and nobility. . . . [2]

§1

§3

When a ruler has failed only in some part of his office or
government, however, he is not immediately to be called a tyrant.
Regarding such a person one must consider that even the best at some
time or other are weak in the performance of their offices, and are not
for this reason to be thought of and treated as tyrants, provided the
foundations and bonds of the universal association remain safe and
unharmed, and are not shaken, assaulted, or upset by vices or faults of

§4

---

[1] [This chapter on tyranny was not part of the 1603 edition. On the other hand,
Althusius' *Dicaeologica* (1617) contains a chapter (I, 113) entitled "The Abuse of
Public Power" that is in part a discussion of tyranny and its punishment.]

[2] Thus Jacob Middendorf describes it. *Quaestiones politicae,* 16.

princes. Nor is one to be treated as a tyrant who, having already started on the road to tyranny, nevertheless does not obstinately and insanely persist on it.[3] For the wicked life of a magistrate does not invalidate his royal authority, just as a marriage is not dissolved by every misdeed committed by one mate against another—unless it is the misdeed of adultery, because this is directly contrary to the nature of marriage. So not every misdeed of a magistrate deprives him of his scepter, but only that in which he, having accepted and then neglected the just rule of administration, acts contrary to the fundamentals and essence of human association, and destroys civil and social life. . . . [4]

§5　　　　This tyranny, or tyrannical administration of a commonwealth, is twofold. One type of it is concerned with the overthrow and destruction of the fundamental laws of the realm. The other consists in the administration of functions and things of the associated body in a

§6　manner that is contrary to piety and justice. The first type of tyranny has two species. One specie occurs when the supreme magistrate violates, changes, or overthrows the fundamental laws of the realm, especially those that concern true religion. Such a tyrant was Athaliah.[5] Such also was Philip, king of Spain, who established an administration in Belgium by force and arms against the fundamental laws and hereditary ways of

§7　the commonwealth. . . . The other occurs when he does not maintain faith with the associated body, despises his oath, and breaks up the orders and estates, or impedes them in the performance of their offices.

§8　. . . The second type of tyranny is either general or special. General tyranny stands opposed to the universal association in all things, as when the supreme magistrate like an enemy plunders, perverts, and upsets the

§9　church and commonwealth. Likewise, general tyranny occurs when the supreme magistrate exercises absolute power, or the plenitude of power, in his administration, and violates the bonds and shatters the restraints

§10　by which human society has been maintained. . . . Special tyranny stands opposed to certain parts and aspects of just administration. This is

---

[3] *See* the arguments of II Samuel 11; 24; I Kings 11; John Calvin, *Institutes of the Christian Religion,* IV, 20, 24 ff.; Francis Zoannet, *De tripartitione defensionis,* III, num. 1–3; Jerome Gigas, *De crimine laesae majestatis,* I, quest. 56, 10.

[4] *See* Peter Ribadeneira, *Religion and the Virtues of the Prince,* II, 9; Petrus Gregorius, *De republica,* IX, 12; William Rose, *De justa reipublicae christianae auctoritate,* 1, 6.

[5] II Kings 11:2; II Chronicles 23.

to say, it is contrary to the just administration of the functions of the associated body, of its goods, or of the right of private persons. . . . [6]

Having become acquainted with the nature of tyranny, we are now to look for the remedy by which it may be opportunely removed. This consists in resistance to and deposition of the tyrant, which remedy has been entrusted to the optimates alone.[7] This resistance is the process by which the ephors impede the tyranny of the supreme magistrate by word and deed. And when he is incurable, or the rights (*jura*)[8] of the associated body cannot otherwise be kept sound, well protected, and in good condition, or the commonwealth free from evil, they depose him and cast him out of their midst. . . .

§28

§29

In order that the ephors may rightly exercise this right of resistance to a tyrant, it is necessary that they pay attention to the following matters: (1) what optimates or ephors can resist a tyrant and are responsible for doing so, (2) when, (3) in what manner, and (4) how long and how far?

§46

Concerning the first matter, the optimates of the realm[9] both collectively and individually can and should resist tyranny to the best of their ability. For since they have the right of creating the magistrate by the consent and command of the people, they also receive the power of judging and deposing him. . . . [10] Subjects and citizens who love their country and resist a tyrant, and want the commonwealth and its rights

§47

§48

---

[6] [The just administration of these public functions, public goods, and private rights has been described by Althusius in Chapters XXVIII–XXXVII on ecclesiastical and secular administration. Because special tyranny is simply the abuse of one or more of these three administrative areas, Althusius' detailed discussion of it is here omitted. One point only should be noted, namely, that Althusius does not consider a tyrant without title (*tyrannus absque titulo*) to be a tyrant at all, but only a private citizen who is an enemy of the realm. The reason is that such a person never rightfully became its supreme magistrate. Only a tyrant by practice (*tyrannus exercitio*) is a true tyrant.]

[7] As we have said in Chapter XVIII above.

[8] [laws.]

[9] [i.e., those optimates or ephors who have a responsibility for the whole realm as distinguished from special optimates and ephors whose responsibility is limited to that part or territory of the realm assigned to them.]

[10] Zachary Ursinus, *Dispositiones*, II, 44 and ult.; [Theodore Beza], *Concerning the Rights of Rulers*; Petrus Gregorius, *De republica*, XXVI, 5–7; Juan de Mariana, *The King and His Education,* I, 6 f.; Francis Zoannet, *De tripartitione defensionis,* III, num. 28; Lambert Daneau, *Politices christianae,* VI; Otto Cassman, *Doctrinae et vitae politicae,* 10; Code X, 53, 2; Institutes I, 25, 6; Digest L, 4, 11, 3.

§49

to be safe and sound, should join themselves to a resisting ephor or optimate. Those who refuse to help the resisting ephor with their strength, money, and counsel are considered enemies and deserters. Therefore, each and all ought to move quickly against a tyrant as against a common fire, and eagerly carry water, scale the walls, and confine the flame so that the entire commonwealth does not burn. Above all they ought to do this when a tyrant is engaged in the actual act of tyranny.[11]

§50
§51

Special ephors are obligated to defend only that part of the realm whose care and safety have been entrusted to them. But they certainly ought not to abandon the subjects and region over which they preside, unless they first have attempted all legitimate courses of action, and have given them up as hopeless. . . .

§53

What is to be done collectively by the estates or ephors of the realm is not permitted to one of them when the others do not consent. That is to say, one of the ephors may not take imperium away from the magistrate, declare him to be a private person, kill him, resist him beyond the boundaries of this ephor's own territory or of the region assigned to this ephor, or persecute him. For what concerns the whole cannot be exercised by individuals separately and by themselves when the rest or the largest part of them disagree. However, it shall be permitted one part of the realm, or individual ephors or estates of the realm, to withdraw from subjection to the tyranny of their magistrate and to defend themselves. . . .

§55

It should be observed, nevertheless, that even one ephor is required to drive from the entire realm the tyranny of an enemy and someone without title (*tyrannus absque titulo*) who wishes to force himself into the position of a legitimate magistrate when he is not one. A single ephor is expected to defend the associated body of which he is a member against force and injury. . . . So Holland, Zeeland, Frisia, Gelderland, and other confederates defended the remaining estates and orders of the Belgium provinces against the force and tyranny of Spain. But those writers are wrong who assign to the Roman pontiff the power of deposing kings and emperors.[12]

---

[11] Junius Brutus, *Defence of Liberty Against Tyrants,* quest. 3.

[12] *See* Petrus Gregorius, *De republica,* XXVI, 5–7; Marsilius of Padua, *The Defender of the Peace;* Lupold of Bebenberg, *De jure regni et imperii.* [Gregorius affirms, while Marsilius and Lupold deny, a papal power of deposing rulers.]

We turn now to the second matter, or when a tyrannical §56
magistrate may be resisted. This involves three aspects: when tyranny
proper—which pertains to a tyrant by practice (*tyrannus exercito*)—is to
be publicly acknowledged, when it is to be considered firmly entrenched, and what to do when other remedies are to no avail. . . . To §57
make such tyranny publicly acknowledged and recognized it is necessary that the optimates of the realm call a council and assemble a general
meeting of all orders of the people, and that they therein undertake to
examine and judge the activities and deeds of the tyrant. If there are no
ephors, then public defenders and deliverers should be constituted *ad
hoc* by the people itself. . . . Tyranny is said to be firmly entrenched §58
when the magistrate, having been admonished often by the optimates
without effect or correction in the performance of his office, still does
not cease from tyranny but instead persists in it, so that he can do
anything at all with impunity. Remedies other than deposition for §59
curbing and coercing tyranny should first be attempted time and again
until they prove to be without effect, in order that the remedy not
become more dangerous than the malady itself. For not only should the
permissible be explored, but also the expedient. On the other hand, §60
when there is danger in delay, when evil increases and gathers strength,
one may resist immediately and confront the tyrant courageously in
order that through delay the malady not become more difficult or even
impossible to cure.

Third, the manner of resisting one who has entered upon §61
tyranny is by defensive, not offensive means, namely, by action within
the boundaries of the territory assigned to the resisting ephor. The §62
tyrant is to be resisted, I say, by words and deeds: by words when he by
words only violates the worship of God and assaults the rights and
foundations of the commonwealth: by force and arms when by military
might and outward force he exercises tyranny, or has so progressed in it
that without armed force such tyranny cannot be restrained, confined,
or driven out. In the latter event, it is permitted to enlist an army from
among the inhabitants, confederates, friends, and others, just as against
an enemy of the fatherland and realm. . . . [13]

---

[13] *See* Valerius Maximus, *Memorable Deeds and Sayings,* VI, 3; Niccolò Machiavelli, *Discourses,* II, 20; Justus Lipsius, *Politicorum sive civilis doctrinae,* V, 9 f.;
Henrik Rantzau, *Commentarius bellicus,* I, 11.

§63   Fourth, he is to be resisted so long as tyranny endures, and so far as he assails or acts contrary to the declared covenant. He should be resisted until the commonwealth is restored to its original condition. And to this end the optimates can remove such a person from office, deprive him of his entrusted administration, and, if they cannot defend themselves against force by any other means, even kill him, and substitute another in his place.

§64   If an oppressed commonwealth, however, should solemnly consent to a change in its laws, and he who was a tyrant without title should receive the title, there should no longer be resistance to this legitimate magistrate. . . . [14]

§65   What, then, is to be decided about private subjects from among the people? For the position we have thus far taken about the ephors applies only to public persons. It plainly does not apply to private persons when the magistrate is a tyrant by practice because they do not have the use and right of the sword (*usus et jus gladii*), nor may they

§67   employ this right. . . . This is to be understood, however, in such a manner that these private persons are not forced to be servants of tyranny, or to do anything that is contrary to God. Under these circumstances they should flee to another place so that they avoid obedience not by resisting, but by fleeing.[15] Nevertheless, when manifest force is applied by the magistrate to private persons, then in case of the need to defend their lives resistance is permitted to them. For in this case private persons are armed against the magistrate who lays violent hands upon them by the natural law (*jus naturale*) and the arrangements constituting kings.

Accordingly, such private persons may do nothing by their private authority against their supreme magistrate, but rather shall await the command of one of the optimates before they come forth with

§68   support and arms to correct a tyrant by practice. But when a tyrant

---

[14] [Note the unannounced switches in the discussion from a tyrant by practice to a tyrant without title, and then back to a tyrant by practice in the next paragraph.]

[15] *See* Matthew 23; II Chronicles 2:13 f. So David fleeing from the tyranny of Saul is known to have withdrawn into the mountains. And Christ fled into Egypt because of Herod's tyranny. Petrus Gregorius, *De republica,* XXVI, 6 f.; John Calvin, *Institutes of the Christian Religion,* IV, 20, 23; Francis Zoannet, *De tripartitione defensionis,* III, 114 ff.; Junius Brutus, *Defence of Liberty Against Tyrants,* quest. 3.

without title invades the realm, each and every optimate and private person who loves his fatherland can and should resist, even by his private authority without awaiting the command of another. . . .

It is not to be thought that by attributing such power to the §71 ephors the right and power of the supreme magistrate is thereby diminished. Rather it is augmented and confirmed by the ephors' power. The reason is that he who might otherwise be undone by his own fault and negligence is upheld by a strength not his own and thereby delivered from ruin. For it pertains to the power and duty of §72 ephors to see that the imperium and administration of the supreme magistrate is established according to justice and the norm of laws, and that he does not depart from what is called true and legitimate administration. Were he to do so his administration would be nothing other than a plundering, or the conspiracy of a band of robbers and evil men.[16] Even God is not thought to be less powerful because he is intrinsically unable to sin. Nor do we think someone is less healthy because he is attended by medical doctors who dissuade him from intemperance, forbid him from eating harmful foods, and even purge his body from time to time when it needs cleansing. Whom should we consider to be his true friends: these medical doctors who care for his health, or those flatterers who obtrude everything harmful and unhealthy upon him?

One of the estates,[17] or one part of the realm, can abandon the §76 remaining body to which it belonged and choose for itself a separate ruler or a new form of commonwealth when the public and manifest welfare of this entire part altogether requires it, or when fundamental laws of the country are not observed by the magistrate but are obstinately and outrageously violated, or when the true worship and disclosed command of God clearly require and demand that this be done. And then this part of the realm can defend by force and arms its new form and status against the other parts of the realm from which it withdrew. Thus the Israelites broke loose from the house and imperium of David and founded their own realm. . . . [18] Thus also subjects can withdraw their support from a magistrate who does not defend them

---

[16] Augustine, *The City of God*, IV, 4.

[17] [*optimates*. This word has generally been rendered as "optimates" in this translation, but "estates" would seem to be closer to Althusius' meaning in this particular instance.]

[18] I Kings 12.

when he should, and can justly have recourse to another prince[19] and submit themselves to him.[20] Or if a magistrate refuses to administer justice, they can resist him and refuse to pay taxes.[21]

§77   ALBERICO GENTILI HAS RECENTLY disapproved of this position concerning the power of the ephors against a tyrannical magistrate,[22] as William Barclay[23] and Giovanni Beccaria[24] also do. But they have been persuaded by the most trivial reasons, indeed I would even say no reasons. It should also be noted that Henning Arnisaeus has a different viewpoint from mine concerning the marks of tyranny.[25] The chief reason that Gentili employs is this. The paternal right and imperium are not to be taken away from a father, much less is force to be inflicted upon him. And therefore not upon the prince either. But I say that there are cases in which this is permitted,[26] especially when some precept of

§78   the first table of the Decalogue requires it. For the precepts of the second table are inferior to the precepts of the first table, as examples indicate.[27] And as Christ says, "whoever loves father or mother more than me is not worthy of me."[28] The prince is called by analogy the father of his country because he ought to embrace his subjects with equal affection. However, analogy proves nothing but only illustrates, as the logicians teach. Whence an argument entered upon from analogy is said to be defective. Whoever is a father is such by nature. A magistrate is

---

[19] Alberico Gentili, *De jure belli*, I, 23.

[20] Tiberius Decianus, *Tractatus criminalis*, VII, 49, 29.

[21] Lucas de Penna, *Super tres libros codicis* (Code I, 10); Andrea Alciati, *Commentaria* (Code I, 2, 5); Tiberius Decianus, *Tractatus criminalis,* VII, 49, 27 f.

[22] *De absoluta regis potestate.*

[23] *The Kingdom and the Regal Power*, III, 6. [The lengthy answers Althusius gives later in this chapter to Barclay's arguments against ephors will be omitted in this translation because they duplicate extensive material already included in chapter XVIII.]

[24] *Refutatio cujusdam libelli sine autore, cui titulus est De jure magistratuum in subditos.* [The anonymous book Beccaria attempted to refute was actually by Theodore Beza, and is referred to elsewhere in this translation.]

[25] [*De jure majestatis.* Althusius neither elaborates upon nor responds to Arnisaeus' viewpoint.]

[26] *See* Digest XI, 7, 35; Exodus 23.

[27] Luke 9:3, 24 f., 59 ff.; I Kings 21:10 ff.; Mark 9:42 ff.; Matthew 5:18, 29; 9:13; 10:37; 13:5, 11; Acts 5:29; I Samuel 19:17 f.; Hosea 6:6.

[28] Matthew 10:37.

not a father by nature, but only by election and inauguration. A father supports his children. A prince does not support his subjects, but is supported by them. And he collects treasures not for his subjects, but for himself.

And we do not say that a tyrannical prince is immediately to be killed, but that resistance is to be made against his force and injury. In one instance only can he justly be killed, namely, when his tyranny has been publicly acknowledged and is incurable: when he madly scorns all laws, brings about the ruin and destruction of the realm, overthrows civil society among men so far as he is able, and rages violently: and when there are no other remedies available. When a mad and foolish parent cannot manage his own responsibilities properly, his son can be assigned as trustee.[29] And a parent who abuses his paternal power can be rightfully deprived of it.[30] Whence Andreas Gail[31] and Fernando Vásquez[32] assert the same thing about an intermediate magistrate who abuses his jurisdiction. Subjects abandoned by their prince who does not defend them when he should can have recourse to another prince. . . . [33]

The Jesuit Beccaria proceeds further and denies that there are any orders or optimates.[34] I think we have sufficiently refuted this opinion already by rational arguments and by sacred and profane examples. . . . [35] But the philosopher and theologian Bartholomaeus Keckermann acknowledges optimates and ephors, or estates, only in the more imperfect principality, and does not recognize them in the more perfect and distinguished principality.[36] But in my judgment this is wrong because of previously stated reasons and examples of the best polities, especially of the Jewish polity constituted as it was by God. For we should not fashion a Platonic commonwealth and polity, or the

§112

§123

---

[29] Digest XXVII, 10, 1 f.

[30] Code VIII, 51; Digest I, 6, 2; *Institutes* I, 8.

[31] *Practicarum observationum*, I, obs. 17.

[32] *Illustrium controversiarum*, I, 8.

[33] Alberico Gentili, *De jure belli*, I, 23; Tiberius Decianus, *Tractatus criminalis*, VII, 49, 28 f.; Lucas de Penna, *Super tres libros codicis* (Code I, 10, 1).

[34] [*Refutatio cujusdam libelli sine autore, cui titulus est De jure magistratuum in subditos.*]

[35] Chapter XVIII above. [Althusius' restatement here of some of the arguments contained in that chapter are omitted from this translation.]

[36] [*Systema disciplinae politicae.*]

Utopia that Sir Thomas More invents,[37] but only a commonwealth as in this ocean of human affairs can be adapted to the weakness of our nature.

Furthermore, who permitted the fullest power of ruling, which is called absolute, to be conceded to the king in such a more perfect state? We have said that absolute power is tyrannical.[38] It would follow from this that no power would be left to the associated political body, and that the power of doing and managing those things that we have attributed to the ephors would be taken away from it. But if we nevertheless declare that power has been left to the associated body, then it is necessary that we also grant to it the exercise and capability of acting. Why give authority (*jus*) to someone to whom the use of it is denied? Clearly, whoever wishes law to be superior to the king, and the king to be subjected to law, or as we have plainly said, whoever considers justice and God himself to be the supreme lord, must also grant to the associated body those things that we have attributed to the ephors. . . .

---

[37] *Utopia.*

[38] We have support from Diego Covarruvias, *Variarum resolutionum,* III, 6, 8; Arius Pinellus, *De rescindenda venditione,* I, 2, 25 f.; Friedrich Pruckmann, *De regalibus,* 3.

XXXIX

Types of Supreme Magistrate

W E HAVE COMPLETED our discussion of the consti-   §1
tuting of the supreme magistrate, and of his
administration and office. We turn now to the types of supreme magistrate. One is monarchic, and the other is polyarchic. . . . The nature of   §6
monarchy is that the command and power of one person administers the
commonwealth. This power, which does not depend upon the will of
another, is the supreme power in the strict sense. By it one person has the
right of ruling the rest both corporately and individually. Other rulers,
who under him guide the particular parts of the commonwealth assigned to them, depend upon him and are, as it were, his officials
through whom he as the monarch carries out his mandates.

There are some who maintain that the monarch can decide   §7
about weightier matters, such as war, peace, and other arduous business,
without consulting the counselors, ephors, and optimates of the realm.[1]
Others deny this, and are of the opinion that the optimates are to be
consulted in such matters, without whose consent nothing pertaining to
these activities is to be decided, established, and promulgated.[2] I prefer
this latter opinion, as is evident from the things I have said above. . . .[3]

But, you may ask, how can a government be called a monarchy   §8
when the power of the monarch is not absolute and free, when it is
understood to be confined within certain prescribed limits and to be

---

[1] William Barclay, *The Kingdom and the Regal Power,* III, 4.
[2] Fernando Vásquez, *Illustrium controversiarum,* I, 23; Friedrich Pruckmann, *De regalibus,* 4, 7; 18, 64; 33, 20; Digest XXVIII, 4, 3; Code I, 2, 5; I, 14, 8; IV, 13, 5; VI, 37, 10.
[3] Chapters XVIII, XXVII, and XXXII.

able to do nothing against the laws and the will of ephors and universal councils of the realm? Obviously liberty, as the jurists say, is to be defined as the natural faculty by which each person is permitted to do what he wishes unless something is prohibited by force or law. Even the emperor acknowledges himself to be bound by laws.[4] For this reason our authority depends upon the authority of law. And indeed it is better for imperium to submit its dominion to laws. Thus, for an emperor to be unable and forbidden to do wicked and prohibited things does not take away from his power or his liberty, but defines the ends and deeds in which his true power and liberty consist. For it is not the property of imperium that it is able to rule in any manner whatever, nor is it the property of power that it can do anything whatever, but only what agrees with nature and right reason. So God is not able to lie, as the Apostle Paul said,[5] nor can he make two different things, such as light and darkness, exist at the same time in the same place. He is not for this reason less omnipotent. Nor is the king said to be impotent because he cannot ascend into the heavens, touch the skies with his hand, move mountains, or empty the ocean. Therefore, the supreme power of the monarch will consist in what is circumscribed by justice, laws, and right reason (*jus, leges, et recta ratio*), not in unrestrained and unbridled action against nature and reason.[6] It is therefore appropriate to reason and nature that the covenants and laws of the realm to which the king has sworn be upheld, and that the consent of counselors and optimates be obtained in ardous matters. . . .

§9   The types of commonwealth are to be determined by the more pre-eminent, prevalent, and predominate part, just as in the constitutions and temperaments of man. For although those who are either sanguine or phlegmatic or choleric or melancholy can be lacking in none of the four temperaments (*humores*) without risk of life, it nevertheless happens that each man is characterized by one of these temperaments more than by the others. Whence from the predominat-

---

[4] Code I, 14, 4.

[5] [Does Althusius have Hebrews 6:18, which is non-Pauline, in mind?]

[6] *See* Fernando Vásquez, *Illustrium controversiarum,* I, 15; I, 26, 22; I, 45; Diego Covarruvias, *Variarum resolutionum,* III, 6, 8; Arius Pinellus, *De rescindenda venditione,* I, 2, 25 f.; Bartolus, *Commentarii* (Digest IV, 4, 38), where he says "Great is Caesar, but greater is reason and truth"; Friedrich Pruckmann, *De regalibus,* 3.

ing and more powerful temperament a man is called sanguine, phlegmatic, choleric, or melancholy.[7] In a similar way the commonwealth can also be compared to the human body so far as the types of its administration are concerned. For what administration of a commonwealth can exist or endure that lacks either intermediate magistrates or estates or counselors or a definite head? Moreover, the estates, as I have said, represent the aristocratic element, the councils the democratic, and the head—whether it be one person or many in the place of one— the monarchic. This is similar to the human body in which the head has the likeness of the ruling king, the heart with its five external senses has the likeness of the estates, and the remaining members of the body together have the likeness of the entire people or populace. These intermediate magistrates frequently depend immediately upon the people when it predominates, in which case the people prescribes the principles of their administration, and constitutes and dismisses them. In this event the government is called a democracy. Sometimes they are dependent immediately upon one person who predominates. Whence it is called a monarchy. At other times they are dependent upon one, two, three, or four who predominate, and for this reason the government is called an aristocracy. . . . *§10* *§11*

    If you further ask what is the democratic element in monarchy and aristocracy, I respond that in both it is the assemblies of the realm in which the people has reserved to itself the right to vote (*jus suffragii*). On the other hand, if you ask what is the aristocratic element in democracy and monarchy, I respond that it is the estates of the realm and the intermediate magistrates. Monarchy is represented in aristocracy and democracy by the concord and consensus of those who rule in which many voices are accounted as one voice and will. Without this common will aristocracy and democracy cannot endure; they immediately disappear and are transformed into other types of administration. Since these things are so, as we affirm, every type of commonwealth is mixed, just as the constitution of man, as we have said, is combined from four temperaments. For what is monarchic in a commonwealth conserves and restrains in office what is aristocratic and democratic; and *§13* *§14* *§15*

---

[7] [This is an allusion to an old physiology in which four fluids (*humores*)—blood, phlegm, choler (yellow bile), and melancholy (black bile)—were understood to enter the body and determine by their relative proportions therein the health and disposition (*humor*, pl. *humores*) of the person.]

what is aristocratic and democratic checks and restrains in office what is monarchic. This arrangement is best, and is more likely to endure. §16   Remedies are thus brought forth for various faults and vices to which single types of commonwealths in themselves are subject. This happens no less than in the human body where a choleric disposition is mitigated by a phlegmatic one, and a sanguine disposition is restrained by a melancholy one. Thus one bodily disposition may be the preservation of another, and vices arising from excess and from deficiency may correct each other. It is evident that a polity is to be judged best that combines the qualities of kingship, aristocracy, and democracy.

Vincent Cabot, however, asserts that a state is called mixed when the king has one kind of supreme power, the senate another, and the people still another.[8] Indeed, he calls it mixed when they have the same power, but not over the same things, as when the people has responsibility over the citizens and the senate over aliens. It will also be a mixed state, he says, if the king, senate, and people have the same power over the same things. Likewise it is mixed when the laws are made by the decision of the king, senate, and people; when the king, senate, and people rule at the same time; or when the senate or people alone can do nothing without the king. But I do not approve of these mixtures. Nor does use and practice admit them, except so far as the people in electing a king or supreme magistrate have reserved certain power to themselves. §18   . . .[9] For it is the nature of the rights of sovereignty that whoever has one of them is considered to have the others necessarily, for he cannot have the use of one of them unless the others are also granted to him. For they are connected and unitary. It is therefore necessary that their exercise belong to one and not to many at the same time, except that the many by mutual consent and concord can act as if they were one in the administration of these rights. For one realm cannot have two kings, as one earth cannot have two suns. And two supreme powers or imperia cannot exist at the same time. . . .

§23   Bartholomaeus Keckermann has a somewhat different view from mine on the mixed constitution and order of the common-

---

[8] *Variarum juris*, II, 4.

[9] *See* Chapter XIX above for the mixture that I have considered to be the best. This kind is thought to have existed in the Spartan commonwealth. *See* Niels Krag, *De republica Lacedaemoniorum,* 4; Caspar Contarini, *De republica Venetorum,* I; Laelius Zecchus, *De principe,* I, 4; Hermann Kirchner, *Respublica,* disp. 3, 7.

wealth.[10] He does not rightly understand what he calls my opinion of the mixed state. For it is evident from the preceding things and from my entire political teaching that there is no type of magistrate that is immune from mixture. I do not recognize in this political association any pure and simple state. Because of the weakness of human nature such a state could not endure for long or be well suited for social life. Therefore, as water without some mixture of earth would be tasteless and devoid of nourishment, so such simple and imaginary states as the Platonic and Utopian polities would be useless for social life. Nor has my opinion ever been different: what is the optimum, and what is the measure of everything else, ought to be the beginning of the discussion. I have attempted to advance from the things that are more general and better known, by which everything that follows receives illumination, to less well known particulars, and finally to the most special matters of all, which so depend upon the things that have gone before that without them they cannot be understood. For the law of method requires this procedure. . . .

Monarchy is thought by many persons to be better and more useful than the other kinds of magistrate.[11] The reasons they give are principally the following: (1) Authority in one man is more conspicuous, and at the same time engenders more respect and love, than in a multitude. (2) Monarchy is more agreeable to nature in that one creature always dominates and rules the others of its kind, just as one soul rules the body, and one God the world. (3) This government is more readily adapted both for acquiring advice and for carrying it out without divulging secrets. (4) This state is not as readily subject by its nature to change and confusion. Whence history indicates that republics have not endured as long as monarchies. (5) Monarchy is older, for it dates from the beginning of the human race.[12] (6) God used this form in the government of his people. [13] (7) One man can better and more easily turn the rudder on a boat than can many. (8) Monarchy follows

§30

---

[10] *Systema disciplinae politicae*, II, 4.

[11] Petrus Gregorius, *De republica*, V, 3 f.; Jean Bodin, *The Commonweale*, VI, 4; Melchior Junius, *Politicarum quaestionum,* I, quest. 4; Jacob Simanca, *De republica,* III, 2 f.; Sir Thomas More, *Utopia*, I, 2; Justus Lipsius, *Politicorum sive civilis doctrinae*, II, 2; Aristotle, *Politics*, 1310ᵃ 39–1313ᵃ 17.

[12] Genesis, 11 f.

[13] Numbers 11; 16; Exodus 18; 24; Joshua 1; Deuteronomy 17.

the example of wise peoples. (9) There are many disadvantages of other forms of commonwealth, and to the extent that they possess real advantages they have the likeness of a monarchy, or else approach closely to it. For no one, as Christ testifies, can serve two masters, much less

§31 many masters. Nor can anyone easily satisfy the judgment and will of many. Nevertheless, this monarchical form of the commonwealth is greatly infested by plots and snares that are very often planned and carried out by subjects against their monarch.[14]

§32 A polyarchic supreme magistrate is one in which those who are furnished by the subjects with equal or the same supreme imperium rule and administer the rights of sovereignty. That is to say, the succession of administration is communicated among a number of

§45 persons. . . . This polyarchic magistracy can be either aristocratic or

§46 democratic. It is aristocratic when to a few noble or wealthy optimates, or to certain others, are given jointly and indivisibly the supreme imperium over the remaining subjects both individually and

§47 corporately, as well as the use of the rights of sovereignty. The nature of aristocracy requires that the power and right of ruling belong jointly, indivisibly, and continuously to a number of partners equally, and that this form of government be protected by special laws against monarchy and democracy. . . .

§57 The state or magistrate is democratic when certain persons elected alternately and successively from the people for definite periods of time rule all the others both individually and corporately in the name of the associated body of the realm, or of all the inhabitants thereof. Thus they exercise the rights of sovereignty and supreme power according to the votes of the entire people gathered by centurial divisions, by tribes, or

§61 by curia. . . . The nature of democracy requires that there be liberty and equality of honors, which consist in these things: that the citizens alternately rule and obey, that there be equal rights for all, and that there be an alternation of private and public life so that all rule in particular

§62 matters and individuals obey in all matters. . . . It is also necessary that democracy by its nature enjoy special and pre-eminent arrangements by which it is protected against monarchy and aristocracy. . . .

---

[14] Aristotle, *Politics*, 1310ᵃ 39–1313ᵃ 17; Melchior Junius, *Politicarum quaestionum,* I, quest. 4; Philip Beroald, *De optimo statu;* Francesco Patrizi, *De regno,* I, tit. 3; Jean Bodin, *The Commonweale,* II, 2; Vincent Castellani, *De officio regis,* I, 1; Matthew Scholasticus, *De vero et christiano principe,* I, 5.

And these are the things about political art (*ars*)[15] that I have   *§83*
thought ought to be discussed. I cannot be persuaded to treat separately,
as other political scientists do, the causes that lead to the destruction of
the association or the overthrow of the commonwealth. For as a straight
line shows up a crooked one, and virtue casts light on vice, so also an
association rightly and legitimately constituted is an indicator of vice,
corruption, and evil. Nevertheless, I do not judge it to be alien to
political art that vices contrary to each type of association be explained
and subjoined as inferences thereto, and that precepts are illustrated by
them, as I have done in appropriate places. But to propose precepts
about the vices, defects, and faults of association, or about symbiotic
evil, is altogether alien to that political art we profess. Were this not so,
political art would be twofold, one part pertaining to symbiotic good
and the other to symbiotic evil. And these two parts would have two
ends each contrary to each other. The logicians and methodists discuss
this matter more fully.

Nor can I here approve the opinion of Bartholomaeus Keck-   *§84*
ermann[16] and Philip Hoenonius, [17] who think that in politics the types
of supreme magistrate are first to be taught, then the mixed state
constituted from the three types that we have discussed, and only then
the provinces and cities. This conflicts with the law of method. For it
cannot be denied that provinces are constituted from villages and cities,
and commonwealths and realms from provinces. Therefore, just as the
cause by its nature precedes the effect and is more perceptible, and just as
the simple or primary precedes in order what has been composed or
derived from it, so also villages, cities, and provinces precede realms and
are prior to them. For this is the order and progression of nature, that the
conjugal relationship, or the domestic association of man and wife, is
called the beginning and foundation of human society. From it are then
produced the associations of various blood relations and in-laws. From
them in turn come the sodalities and collegia, out of the union of which
arises the composite body that we call a village, town, or city. And these
symbiotic associations as the first to develop can subsist by themselves
even without a province or realm. However, as long as they are not

---

[15] [science.]

[16] [*Systema disciplinae politicae.*]

[17] [*Disputationum politicarum.*]

united in the associated and symbiotic universal body of a province, commonwealth, or realm, they are deprived of many of the advantages and necessary supports of life. It is necessary, therefore, that the doctrine of the symbiotic life of families, kinship associations, collegia, cities, and provinces precede the doctrine of the realm or universal symbiotic association that arises from the former associations and is composed of them. In practice, however, all these associations are to be joined together for the common welfare of the symbiotes both individually and corporately. For the public association cannot exist without the private and domestic association. Both are necessary and useful in order that we may live advantageously. . . .

§85   I do not think that special doctrine is necessary for the particular political state, although other modern writers disagree. For although political art is general, it always and everywhere agrees with and can be accommodated to every particular and special place, time, and people. This is so even though various and separate realms often use laws of their own differing from those of others in some matters. What else are the dukedom, principate, lordship, dynasty, county, landgraviate, mark, and the like, or what else can they be, except provinces, members, orders, and estates of the realm to which they belong? Even if they sometimes use laws that are peculiar to them and differ legitimately from those of the rest of the realm, they are still provinces of the realm.[18]

§86   Nor have I wanted to define the political types so far as their establishment, increase, extension, and conservation are concerned. The same principles apply to the establishment, increase, extension, and conservation of polities. For the commonwealth is conserved and extended by the same arts by which it is constituted, as our definition of politics sufficiently explains.[19]

---

[18] As we have said above in Chapter VIII.
[19] Chapter I.

Collation of This Translation
with the 1614 Edition

Latin titles are chapter headings of the 1614 edition. Roman numerals refer to chapters, arabic numerals to the numbered sections into which Althusius divided his chapters. Three dots indicate untranslated material within the numbered section they precede and/or follow. However, deletions by the translator of mere references to other writings are not so designated. A section number sometimes will be repeated to indicate additional translated material following a deletion within that numbered section (e.g., §46 ...; §46 ... in The Family in the collation below). Semicolons indicate the end of segments of the Latin text that have been selected for translation according to the objectives set forth in the Translator's Introduction, namely, "to retain in Althusius' own words the complete basic structure of his political thought as it finds expression in the *Politica*, and furthermore to include the chief arguments by which he clarified his position in relation to those of his contemporaries" (page xxix above).

I
The General Elements of Politics
I *De generalibus affectionibus Politicae*: §§1–39.

II–III
The Family
II *De privata domesticae et naturalis consociationis communicatione, ejusque specie priore, niminum de consociatione conjugali*: §§1–6; §12 ...; §§13–16; §§37–38; §§40–42 ...; §43 ...; §44 ...; §45 ...; §46 ...; §46 .... III *De consociatione propinquorum*: §§1–2; ... §16 ...; §18; §§20–21 ...; §§23–24 ...; §§27–28 ...; §34 ...; §35 ...; §36 ...; §37 ...; §42

IV
The Collegium

IV *De consociatione collegarum*: §§1–7 ...; §§8–10; §§12–18; §20; §§22–24; §30 ...

V–VI
The City

V *De consociatione universitatis, ejusque causis*: §§1–11; §§22–24 ...; §§25–30 ...; ... §§34–36; §38 ...; §§38–41; §§48–50 ...; §§51–56; §§58–62; §64. VI *De civitatis speciebus et civium communicatione*: §§1–6 ...; §§15–17 ...; §28 ...; §§29–31 ...; §§32–35 ...; §§39–43 ...; §§44–45 ...; §§46–48 ...; §§49–52 ...

VII–VIII
The Province

VII *De juris provincialis communione*: §§1–2 ...; §3 ...; §§4–12 ... . VIII *De juris provincialis administratione*: §§1–3 ...; §§3–6 ...; §6 ...; §§7–8 ...; §§9–10; §§12–16 ...; §§18–24 ...; §24 ...; §§27–28; §31 ...; §§32–38 ...; §40–41 ...; §45 ...; §47 ...; §48; §50 ...; §50...; §51 ...; §§51–52 ...; §§53–55 ...; §56 ...; §61 ...; §§63–65 ...; §§66–70 ...; §88 ...; §§91–92

IX
Political Sovereignty and Ecclesiastical Communication

IX *De jure majestatis ecclesiastico*: §§1–4 ...; §5; §9 ...; §9 ...; §§10–13 ...; §15 ...; §§16–22 ...; §§23–24 ...; §25; §§27–32 ...; §§33–34 ...; §§35–36 ...; §§37–39 ...; §39; §41 ...; §41 ...; §42 ...; §§42–45 ...; §45

X–XVII
Secular Communication

X *De lege atque ejus exsecutione*:§§1–3 ...; §§4–10 ...; §11 ...; §11 ...; §12. XI *De majestatis jure speciali*: §§1–5; §7; §13 ...; §14 ...; §16 ...; §§17–18 ...; §20 ...; §23 .... XII *De collatione regni ordinaria*: §§1–2. XIII *De collatione extraordinaria*: §1 ... XIV *De muneribus regni personalibus*: §1; ... §§2–3. XV *De privilegiis quorundam regnicolarum*: §§1–4; §13 ...; §14. XVI *De protectione universalis consociationis*: §§1–2; §4; §17. XVII *De cura bonorum corporis consociati*: §§2–3 ...; §14; §15 ...; §§24–25 ...; §§26–27 ...; §§30–31 ...; §54 ...; §54 ...; §§55–58; §60

XVIII
The Ephors and Their Duties

XVIII *De ephoris , eorumque officio*: §§1–7 ...; §8; §§10–15; §§18–22 ...; §§25–32; §40 ...; §41 ...; §42 ...; §§43–44 ...; §§47–52 ...; §§53–57; §59 ...; §§59–61 ...; §§62–66; §§68–75; §§83–84 ...; §85 ...; §86 ...; §§86–87 ...; §§88–89 ...; §§90–91 ...; §§92–96 ...; §§98–107 ...; §§108–110 ...; §§111–112 ...; §113; §§123–124

XIX–XX
The Constituting of the Supreme Magistrate

XIX *De regni, sive universalis imperii, commissione*: §§1–2; §4 ...; §§5–8 ...; §§9–11 ...; §§14–18; §§23–24 ...; §§25 ...; §27 ...; §29 ...; §30 ...; §33; §§35–37; §39; §49; §§70–75 ...; §§75–77 ...; §77 ...; §78 ...; §§80–81 ...; §83; §85 ...; §85 ...; §87; §90 ...; §90 ...; §§92–93 ...; §98 ...; §101. XX *De promissione obsequiorum et homagio*: §1; §§5–6 ...; §7 ...; §§10–11 ...; §12 ...; §13 ...; §§19–21 ...

XXI–XXVII
Political Prudence in the Administration of the Commonwealth

XXI *De lege, ad quam suscepta Reipublicae administratio est instituenda*: §1 ...; §2 ...; §§5–6 ...; §§8–9 ...; §10 ...; §§11–12 ...; §13 ...; §§14–17 ...; §18 ...; §18 ...; §§19–20 ...; §§20–23 ...; §§24–27 ...; §§27–28; §29 ...; §§30–35 ...; §37 ...; §40 ...; §41. XXII *Lex propria Judaeorum, an utilis Reipublicae Christianorum et quatenus abolita*: §§3–4 .... XXIII *De natura et affectione populi*: §§1–11; §14 ...; §15 ...; §16 ...; §17 ...; §19 ...; §20 .... XXIV *De natura et affectione imperii duplici* §§1–2 ...; §§3–4 ...; §6 ...; §8; §14 ...; §15; §17 ...; §§17–19 ...; §26 ...; §27 ...; §31 ...; §32 ...; §§32–34. XXV *De auctoritate summi magistratus*: §1; §3; §§15–16; §§24–25 .... XXVI *De usu, experientia, et delectu magistratus*: §1; §§3–4; §5 ...; §6 ...; §8 .... XXVII *De consiliariis magistratus*: §1 ...; §2 ...; §3; §§6–7 ...; §9 ...; §27 ...; §30 ...; §§40–42 ...; §43 ...

XXVIII
Ecclesiastical Administration

XXVIII *De administratione ecclesiastica*: §§1–5 ...; §§5–7 ...; §7 ...; §8 ...; §9 ...; §10 ...; §§13–17 ...; §18 ...; §19 ...; §§23–24 ...; §§25–28 ...; §29 §§30–32 ...; §33; §35 ...; §37 ...; §§37–39; §§43–46 ...; §§48–49 ...; §§49–50 ...; §§51–54 ...; §§55–59 ...; §§63–67 ...; §§68–69 ...; §72 ...

XXIX–XXXVII
Secular Administration

XXIX *De sanctione legum et administratione justitiae*: §1 ...; §2–3 ...; §§4–5 ...; §9 ...; §14 ...; §15 ...; §18 ...; §19 ...; §§29–30 ...; §39 ...; §49; §§56–57. XXX *De censura*: §§1–2 ...; §4 ...; §§4–6; §15; §24 ...; §28 ...; §28 ...;§29. XXXI *De studio concordiae conservandae*: §§1–2 ...; §§3–8 ...; §10 ...; §11 ...; §13 ...; §15 ...; §16 ...; §§25–26; §70; §75 .... XXXII *De administratione civili mediorum ad vitae socialis commoditates necessariorum*: §1 .... XXXIII *De conciliis universalibus consociationis universalis*: §§1–18 ...; §20 ...; §§29–30 ... . XXXIV *De cura et tractione armorum tempore pacis*: §§1–2. XXXV *De cura et administratione armorum tempore belli, et primum de belli susceptione*: §1 ...; §§2–5 ...; §§5–6 ...; §6 ...; §§7–8 ...; §§9–10 ...; §§17–18 ...; §27 .... XXXVI *De gestione et administratione belli*: §§1–3 ...; §26. XXXVII *De administratione civili rerum publicarum et privatarum*: §§1–2 ...; §§10–11; §23; §§47–48 ...; §§49–50 ...; §51 ...; §§98–99 ...

XXXVIII
Tyranny and Its Remedies

XXXIX
Types of Supreme Magistrate

The Writings of Johannes Althusius

Jurisprudentia Romana

Juris Romani Libri duo: Ad Leges Methodi Rameae conformati: Et Tabulâ illustrati. Basle: Waldkirch's, 1586.

> [*Two volumes on Roman law:* Corresponding to the laws of the Ramean method: Illustrated by a table.]

Jurisprudentia Romana, vel potius, Juris Romani ars; Duobus Libris comprehensa, et ad Leges Methodi Rameae conformata, Studio Johannis Althusii. Editio altera, aucta et correcta. Herborn: From the press of Christophorus Corvinus, 1588.

> [*Roman Jurisprudence, or the art of Roman Law;* comprehended in two volumes, and corresponding to the laws of the Ramean method. By Johannes Althusius. Second edition, augmented and corrected.]

Jurisprudentiae Romanae Libri Duo. Ad Leges Methodi Rameae conformati; Et Tabulis illustrati. Editio altera, aucta et correcta. Accessit *Cynosura Reidiniana Juris Civilis:* Quâ Tum prima totius Juris Principia, Titulorum propria; generaliora, notabiliora, necessariora: tum frequentiora rariora, obsoletiora, perpetuis numeris monstrantur. Basle: From the press of Conrad Valdkirch, 1589.

> [*Two volumes on Roman Jurisprudence.* Corresponding to the laws of the Ramean method; and illustrated by tables. Second edition, augmented and corrected. Reidanus' *Guide to Civil Law* has been added: in which the first principles of the whole law, the particular, the more general, more remarkable, and more necessary points of the headings: then the more frequent, more rare, and more obsolete points are shown in continuous numbers.]

Jurisprudentiae Romanae methodice digestae Libri Duo. Editio altera correcta et epitome ac brevi anacephalaeosi Dicaeologicae aucta. Herborn: From the press of Christophorus Corvinus, 1592.

> [*Two volumes on Roman Jurisprudence methodically set forth*. Second edition, corrected and augmented by an extract and a short summary of the main points of a Theory of Justice.]

Jurisprudentiae Romanae methodice digestae Libri Duo. Editio tertia correcta et epitome ac brevi anacephalaeosi Dicaeologicae aucta. Accessit *Cynosura Reidiniana Juris Civilis:* qua tum prima Juris Principia, Titulorum propria, generaliora, notabiliora, necessariora: tum frequentiora, rariora, obsoletiora, perpetuis numeris monstrantur. Herborn in Nassovia: At the press of Christophorus Corvinus, 1599.

> [*Two volumes on Roman Jurisprudence, methodically set forth*. Third edition, corrected and augmented by an extract and short summary of the main points of a Theory of Justice. Reidanus' *Guide to Civil Law* has been added: in which the first principles of law, the particular, the more general, more remarkable, and more necessary points of the headings; the more frequent, more rare, and more obsolete points are shown in continuous numbers.]

Jurisprudentiae Romanae methodice digestae Libri Duo. Editio quarta, correcta et epitome ac brevi anacephalaeosi Dicaeologicae aucta. Herborn: From the press of Christophorus Corvinus, 1607.

> [*Two volumes on Roman Jurisprudence, methodically set forth*. Fourth edition, corrected and agumented by an extract and a short summary of the main points of a Theory of Justice.]

Editio quinta, correcta et epitome ac brevi anacephalaeosi Dicaeologicae aucta. Herborn: From the press of the heirs of Christophorus Corvinus, 1623.

> [Fifth edition, corrected and augmented by an extract and a short summary of the main points of a Theory of Justice.]

Civilis Conversationis Libri Duo

Civilis conversationis Libri Duo: Methodicé digesti et exemplis sacris et profanis passim illustrati. Editi á Philippo Althusio. Hanau in Hesse: From the press of Guilielmus Antonius, 1601.

> [*Two volumes on civil intercourse:* Methodically set forth and illustrated throughout by sacred and profane examples. Edited by Philippus Althusius.]

Civilis conversationis Libri Duo recogniti, et aucti. Methodicé digesti et exemplis sacris et profanis passim illustrati. Editi á Philippo Althusio. Hanau in Hesse: From the press of the heirs of Guilielmus Antonius, 1611.

> [*Two volumes on civil intercourse,* revised and augmented. Methodically set forth and illustrated throughout by sacred and profane examples. Edited by Philippus Althusius.]

Ethicus Althusianus, Hoc est Libri Duo De Conversatione Civili, Methodicè digesti exemplisque tam sacris quam profanis locupletissimè illustrati à Philippo Althusio. Amsterdam: From the press of Johannes Janssonius, 1650.

> [*Althusian Ethics, or Two volumes on civil intercourse,* methodically set forth and copiously illustrated by sacred as well as profane examples by Philippus Althusius.]

Politica

Latin Editions

Politica Methodice digesta et exemplis sacris et profanis illustrata: Cui in fine adjuncta est Oratio panegyrica de utilitate, necessitate et antiquitate scholarum. Herborn in Nassovia: From the press of Christophorus Corvinus, 1603.

> [*Politics methodically set forth and illustrated by sacred and profane examples:* At the end is added the Panegyric on the utility, necessity and antiquity of the schools.]

Politica Methodicè digesta atque exemplis sacris et profanis illustrata; Editio nova priore auctior, et cum Indice amplissimo. Cui in fine adjuncta est, Oratio panegyrica De necessitate et antiquitate scholarum. Arnheim: From the press of Johannes Janssonius, 1610.

> [*Politics methodically set forth and illustrated by sacred and profane examples;* new edition, with more additional material than in the earlier ones, and with a very voluminous index. At the end is added the Panegyric on the necessity and antiquity of the schools.]

Politica Methodicè digesta atque exemplis sacris et profanis illustrata; Cui in fine adjuncta est Oratio panegyrica, De necessitate et antiquitate scholarum. Groningen: From the press of Johannes Radaeus, 1610.

> [*Politics methodically set forth and illustrated by sacred and profane examples.* At the end is added the Panegyric on the necessity and antiquity of the schools.]

Politica Methodicè digesta atque exemplis sacris et profanis illustrata; Cui in fine adjuncta est Oratio panegyrica, De necessitate, utilitate et antiquitate scholarum. Editio tertia, duabus prioribus multo auctior. Herborn in Nassovia: (Corvinus), 1614.

> [*Politics methodically set forth and illustrated by sacred and profane examples;* at the end is added the Panegyric on the necessity, utility and antiquity of the schools. Third edition, with far more additional material than in the two former ones.]

Politica Methodice digesta atque exemplis sacris et profanis illustrata; Editio tertia priore auctior, et cum Indice amplissimo. Cui in fine adjuncta est Oratio panegyrica, De necessitate et antiquitate scholarum. Arnheim: From the press of Johannes Jansonnius, 1617.

> [*Politics methodically set forth and illustrated by sacred and profane examples.*
> Third edition, with more additional material than the earlier ones,
> and with a very voluminous index. At the end is added the Panegyric
> on the necessity and antiquity of the schools.]

Politica Methodicè digesta atque exemplis sacris et profanis illustrata; Cui in fine adjuncta est Oratio panegyrica. De necessitate, utilitate et antiquitate scholarum. Editio quarta. Herborn: From the press of Corvinus, with the costs paid by Johannes Georgius Muderspachius and Georgius Corvinus, 1625.

> [*Politics methodically set forth and illustrated by sacred and profane examples.*
> At the end is added the Panegyric on the necessity, utility and
> antiquity of the schools. Fourth edition.]

Editio quinta. Herborn in Nassovia, 1654.

> [Fifth edition.]

Politica Methodice digesta of Johannes Althusius (Althaus). Reprinted [with minor abridgements] from the Third Edition of 1614. Augmented by the Preface of the First Edition of 1603 and by 21 hitherto Unpublished Letters of the Author. With an Introduction by Carl Joachim Friedrich. Harvard Political Classics, Vol. 2. Cambridge: Harvard University Press, 1932.

> [*Politics methodically set forth,* by Johannes Althusius.]

Politica Methodicè digesta atque exemplis sacris et profanis illustrata; Cui in fine adjuncta est Oratio panegyrica, De necessitate, utilitate et antiquitate scholarum. Editio tertia, duabus prioribus multo auctior. 2nd reprint of the 3rd edition printed in Herborn in 1614. Aalen: Scientia Publisher, 1981.

> [*Politics methodically set forth and illustrated by sacred and profane examples.*
> At the end is added the Panegyric on the necessity and antiquity of
> the schools. Third edition, with far more additional material than in
> the two earlier ones.]

English Translations

The Politics of Johannes Althusius. An abridged translation of the Third Edition (1614) of *Politica Methodice digesta atque exemplis sacris et profanis illustrata.* And including the Preface to the First and Third Editions. Translated, with an introduction by Frederick S. Carney. Preface by Carl J. Friedrich. Beacon Series in the Sociology of Politics and Religion. Boston: Beacon Press, 1964; London: Eyre & Spottiswoode, 1965.

German Translations

Grundbegriffe der Politik. Selections from the 1603 editon of *Politica methodice digesta.* Edited by Erik Wolf. Deutsches Rechtsdenken, no. 8. Frankfurt am Main: Vittorio Klostermann, 1943.

> [Includes the preface to the 1603 edition of *Politica* as well as extracts from Chapters I, II, IV, V, IX, and XVIII.]

2nd Edition. Edited by Erik Wolf. Deutsches Rechtsdenken, no. 3. Frankfurt am Main: Vittorio Klostermann, 1948.

In *Quellenbuch zur Geschichte der deutschen Rechtswissenschaft.* Edited by Erik Wolf. Frankfurt am Main: Vittorio Klostermann, 1950.

"Politik als Einigung der natürlichen Lebensgemeinschaften." In *Die Politische Wissenschaft,* edited by Carl Joachim Friedrich. Orbis Academicus Sec. I, Vol. 8. Freiburg and Munich: Karl Alber, 1961. [Selections following the partial translation by Erik Wolf (see his 1st edition, *Grundbegriffe der Politik,* above).]

Dicaeologica

Dicaeologicae Libri Tres, Totum et universum Jus, quo utimur, methodicè complectentes: Cum parallelis hujus et Judaici Juris, tabulisque insertis, atque Indice triplici; uno, auctorum; altero, capitum singulorum; et tertio, rerum et verborum locupletissimo et accuratissimo. Opus tam theoriae quàm praxeos aliarumqué Facultatum studiosis utilissimum. Herborn in Nassovia: From the press of Christophorus Corvinus, 1617.

> [*Three volumes of a Theory of Justice,* embracing in a methodical fashion the whole and universal law that we make use of: With parallel references from Roman and Jewish law, with inserted tables and three indexes, listing, respectively, authors, the various chapters, and very copiously and precisely things and words. A work very useful in theory and practice for scholars of subjects other than law.]

Cum gratia et privilegia Caesaris Majestatis. On sale at the press of Christophorus Corvinus, 1618.

> [With the gratitude and privileges of His Imperial Majesty.]

Editio secunda priori correctior. On sale in Frankfurt at the press of the Heirs of Christophorus Corvinus, 1649.

> [Second edition, more accurate than the former one.]

Reprint of the edition printed in Frankfurt am Main in 1649. Aalen: Scientia Publisher, 1967.

Documentary Collections Edited by Althusius

Recess und accord buch / Das ist/ Zusamen verfassung aller ordnung/ decreten / resolution/ recessen/ accorden und verträgen/ So zwischen weilandt den wolgebornen Graffen und Herren/ Herrn Edzardten und Herrn Johan löblichen andenckens/ Herrn und Graffen zu Ostfriesslandt/ etc. Und jetzigem regierendem Graffen und Herrn/ Herrn Enno Graffen uñ Herrn zu Ostfriesslandt Herrn zu Esens/ Stedessdorff und Wittmundt / etc. unserm gnedigen Herrn/ Und den dreyen Stenden/ als Ritterschaft/ Stetten uñ Haussmansstande/ uñ in specie der Stadt Embden/ der Grafschafft Oistfriesslandt/ zu underschiedlichen zeiten uffgericht und publiciret worden. Printed in Emden by Helvicus Kallenbach, official printer, 1612.

> [*Book of ordinances and contracts* / that is/ a compilation of all regulations, decrees, resolutions, ordinances, contracts and treaties/ between the former high-born counts and masters/ master Edzardten and in master Johan's memory, master and count at East Frisia. And between the presently ruling Count and master, Master Enno, Count and master at East Frisia and Esens, Stedessdorff and Wittmundt, etc. our gracious Lord and three orders/ that is the knighthood, cities and citizens, especially of the city of Emden/ of the county of East Frisia/, which have been at various times enacted and published.]

Printed in Emden by Joachim Mennen, official printer, 1656.

Statuta Und Ordnungen / Eines Erbaren Raths der Stadt Embden/ Wornach sich die Partheyen so wohl/ alss die Verordnete Commissarii, Secretarii, Notarii, Procuratores, Stadtdiener/ und jedermenniglich/ in Gerichts- und Rechtssachen/ wie auch ihren respective Amptern und Diensten etc. hinführo verhalten sollen. Printed in Emden by Helwich Kallenbach, official printer, 1625.

> [*Statutes and regulations* / of an honourable counsellor of the city of Emden / according to which the parties as well as the delegated commissioners, the secretaries, notaries, procurators, city servants and everyone in matters of court and law and in the various offices and services should behave henceforth.]

Select Bibliography

Heinz Werner Antholz. *Die politische Wirksamkeit des Johannes Althusius in Emden.* Abhandlungen und Vorträge zur Geschichte Ostfrieslands, no. 32. Aurich, 1955.

Frédéric Atger. *Essai sur l'Histoire des Doctrines de Contrat Social.* Paris, 1906.

Michael Behnen. "Herrscherbild und Herrschaftstechnik in der *Politica* des Johannes Althusius." *Zeitschrift für Historische Forschung* 11 (1984): 417–72.

Joseph Bischof. *Die Volkssouveränitätslehre bei Johannes Althusius und Franz Suarez.* Vienna, 1944.

Wilfried Buchholz. *Rousseau und Althusius.* Breslau, 1922.

R. W. and A. J. Carlyle. *A History of Medieval Political Theory in the West.* Vol. 6. Edinburgh, 1936.

Frederick S. Carney. "The Associational Theory of Johannes Althusius." Ph.D. diss., University of Chicago, 1960.

———. "Associational Thought in Early Calvinism." In *Voluntary Associations: A Study of Groups in Free Societies.* Edited by D. B. Robertson. Richmond, Virginia, 1966.

Won-hong Cho. "The Theory of State and Law of Johannes Althusius" (in Korean; summary in German). Ph.D. diss., National University of Seoul, 1992.

Karl-Wilhelm Dahm, Werner Krawietz, and Dieter Wyduckel, eds. *Politische Theorie des Johannes Althusius.* Beiträge des internationalen Symposiums vom 12–16 Juni 1984 in Herborn aus Anlass des 400-jährigen Bestehens der Hohen Schule zu Herborn. *Rechtstheorie*, Supplementary vol. 7. Berlin, 1987.

William A. Dunning. *A History of Political Theories from Luther to Montesquieu.* New York, 1931.

Hendrik Jan van Eikema Hommes. "Die Bedeutung der Staats- und Gesellschaftslehre des Johannes Althusius für unsere Zeit." In *Recht und Staat im sozialen Wandel.* Festschrift für Hans Ulrich Scupin zum 80. Geburtstag. Edited by Norbert Achterberg, Werner Krawietz, and Dieter Wyduckel. Berlin, 1983.

Daniel J. Elazar. *Exploring Federalism.* Tuscaloosa, Alabama, 1987.

A.P. d'Entrèves. "Giovanni Althusio e il problema methodologico nella storia della filosofia politica e giuridica." *Rivista internazionale di folosofia del dritto.* XIV (1934).

Francesco Ercole. *Da Bartolo all' Althusio.* Florence, 1932.

John Neville Figgis. *Political Thought from Gerson to Grotius.* Cambridge, England, 1956.

―――. "Political Thought in the Sixteenth Century." *Cambridge Modern History.* Vol. 3. New York, 1905.

Carl Joachim Friedrich. *The Age of the Baroque.* New York, 1952.

―――. "Introduction" to the *Politica methodice digesta of Johannes Althusius.* Cambridge, Massachusetts, 1932.

―――. "Johannes Althusius," *Encyclopedia of the Social Sciences.* Vol. 2. New York, 1930.

―――. *Johannes Althusius und sein Werk im Rahmen der Entwicklung der Theorie von der Politik.* Berlin, 1975.

Pieter Sjverds Gerbrandy. *National and International Stability: Althusius: Grotius: van Vollenhoven.* Oxford, 1944.

Otto von Gierke. *The Development of Political Theory.* Translated by Bernard Freyd. New York, 1939. Also available as *Johannes Althusius und die Entwicklung der naturrechtlichen Staatstheorien. Zugleich ein Beitrag zur Geschichte der Rechtssystematik.* 7th unaltered edition with a preface by Julius von Gierke. Aalen, 1981. (The first edition appeared in 1880 as no. 7 of *Untersuchungen zur Deutschen Staatsund Rechtsgeschichte.*)

―――. *Natural Law and the Theory of Society 1500 to 1800.* Translated by Ernest Barker. Five subsections of Vol. 4 of *Das deutsche Genossenschaftsrecht* (Berlin, 1913). Cambridge, England, 1934; reprint, Cambridge, England, 1950.

G. P. Gooch. *English Democratic Ideas in the Seventeenth Century.* New York, 1959.

J. W. Gough. *The Social Contract.* 2nd edition. Oxford, 1957.

Thomas O. Hueglin. "Have We Studied the Wrong Authors? On the Relevance of Johannes Althusius." *Studies in Political Thought* 1, no. 1 (Winter, 1992): 75–93.

————. "Johannes Althusius: Medieval Constitutionalist or Modern Federalist?" *Publius* 9, no. 4 (1979): 9–41.

————. *Sozietaler Foederalismus: Die politische Theorie des Johannes Althusius.* European University Institute Series 13. Berlin and New York, 1991.

Charles S. McCoy and J. Wayne Baker. *Fountainhead of Federalism: Heinrich Bullinger and the Covenantal Tradition.* Louisville, Kentucky, 1991.

Pierre Mesnard. *L'Essor de la Philosophie Politique de XVIe Siècle.* Paris, 1952.

Stanley Parry. "The Politics of Johannes Althusius." Ph.D. diss., Yale University, 1954.

Ernst Reibstein. *Johannes Althusius als Fortsetzer der Schule von Salamanca.* Freiburger Rechts- und Staatswissenschaftliche Abhandlungen. Vol. 5. Karlsruhe, 1955.

Patrick Riley. "Three Seventeenth-Century German Theorists of Federalism: Althusius, Hugo and Leibniz." *Publius* 6, no. 3 (1976): 7–41.

George H. Sabine. *A History of Political Theory.* London, 1951.

J. H. M. Salmon. *The French Religious Wars in English Political Thought.* Oxford, 1959.

Hans Ulrich Scupin. "Der Begriff der Souveränität bei Johannes Althusius und bei Jean Bodin." *Der Staat* 4 (1965): 1–26.

————. "Demokratische Elemente in Theorie und Praxis des Johannes Althusius." In *A Desirable World.* Essays in honor of Professor Bart Landheer. Edited by A. M. C. H. Reigersman et al. The Hague, 1974.

————. "Untrennbarkeit von Staat und Gesellschaft in der Frühneuzeit. Althusius und Bodin." In *Recht und Gesellschaft.* Festschrift für Helmut Schelsky zum 65. Geburtstag. Edited by Friedrich Kaulbach and Werner Krawietz. Berlin, 1978.

Peter Jochen Winters. *Die "Politik" des Johannes Althusius und ihre zeitgenössischen Quellen. Zur Grundlegung der politischen Wissenschaft im 16. und im beginnenden 17. Jahrhundert.* Freiburger Studien zur Politik und Soziologie. Edited by Arnold Bergstraesser. Freiburg and Breisgau, 1963.

Erik Wolf. *Das Problem der Naturrechtslehre.* Karlsruhe, 1964.

————. *Grosse Rechtsdenker der Deutschen Geistesgeschichte.* Tübingen, 1951, 1963 (4th ed.).

Kurt Wolzendorff. *Staatsrecht und Naturrecht in der Lehre vom Widerstandsrecht des Volkes gegen rechtswidridge Ausübung der Staatsgewalt.* Breslau, 1916.

Dieter Wyduckel. *Althusius-Bibliographie:* Bibliographie zur politischen Ideengeschichte und Staatslehre, zum Staatsrecht und zur Verfassungsgeschichte des 16. bis 18. Jahrhunderts. Edited by Hans Ulrich Scupin and Ulrich Scheuner. Berlin, 1973. 2 vols. (See especially Vol. 1, Part 2B:

"Lebensabrisse und Würdigungen von Leben und Werk des Althusius" [No. 218 *ff*, p. 19 *ff*] as well as Part C5: "Herborn und seine Hohe Schule" [No. 855a *ff*, p. 60 *ff*].)

———. "Johannes Althusius." In *Die Deutsche Literatur. Biographisches und bibliographisches Lexikon*. Series II: Die Deutsche Literatur zwischen 1450 und 1620. Edited by Hans-Gert Roloff. Vol. 1. Bern, 1991. (This article lists Althusius' works written in Latin and identifies libraries in which the texts can be found.)

Index

223